D0078006

Houses and Homes
Housing for Canadians

John Sewell

James Lorimer & Company, Publishers
Toronto, 1994

©1994 by John Sewell

All rights reserved. No part of this book may be reproduced or transmitted in any form or by any means, electronic or mechanical, including photocopying, or by any information storage or retrieval system, without permission in writing from the publisher.

James Lorimer & Company Ltd. acknowledges with thanks the support of the Canada Council, the Ontario Arts Council and the Ontario Publishing Centre in the development of writing and publishing in Canada.

Cover art is *Cottingham School with Yellow Flag* (detail) by Christiane Pflug. Oil on canvas. 1971.

Canadian Cataloguing in Publication Data

Sewell, John, 1940-
  Houses and Homes

Includes bibliographical references and index.
ISBN 1-55028-437-1 (bound) ISBN 1-55028-436-3 (pbk.)

1. Housing - Canada. 2. Housing policy - Canada.
I. Title.

HD7305.A3S4 1994   363.5'0971   C94-930431-X

James Lorimer & Company Ltd., Publishers
35 Britain Street
Toronto, Ontario M5A 1R7

Printed and bound in Canada

To Vivian, Loraine, and Marion
for our lives together
and our houses and homes

Contents

Chapter 1

An Introduction to the Issues

Not a year goes by without someone making the claim that Canada is in a housing crisis. Indeed, that seems to have been the country's fate for the past half-century. "In Canada we have hardly begun to attack the real hard core of our housing problem," said housing reformer and planner Humphrey Carver in 1948 (Carver 1948, p. xiii). "The truth is," wrote the distinguished social analyst and activist Albert Rose in 1980, "that throughout the twentieth century Canada has been in the midst of a continuous housing crisis" (Rose 1980, p. iii).

Fifty years ago the crisis appeared to be mostly a problem of poor-quality housing and lack of toilets and running water. Since the 1960s, the concern has focused on questions of affordability and how Canadians generally are spending a larger percentage of their income on housing than they did ten or twenty or thirty years earlier. This has brought the debate around to how best to address these affordability issues. One would be wrong to say that this has always been an important housing policy issue, however: only since the 1970s has affordability attracted broad interest.

There are those who take the position that there is no crisis in housing in Canada; the crisis lies elsewhere. Hans Blumenfeld, one of the most astute planners in Canada from the 1950s until his death in 1990, held that view, although given his provocative approach he may have done so more to engender thoughtful debate than to create the basis for policy. He noted that while households have decreased in size, the size of dwelling units has increased. The average number of rooms per dwelling unit increased from 5.4 to 5.7 from 1971 to 1981. Blumenfeld concluded in the late 1980s that an average of more than two (2.07) rooms was available for every man, woman and child in Canada, and even if kitchens were not counted, the average was at least a comfortable 1.63 rooms. Blumenfeld con-

2 Houses and Homes

cluded, in his own wry way, "It appears that there is no overall housing shortage in Canada." (Blumenfeld 1991, p. 199-201).

Blumenfeld acknowledges a number of problems that do need addressing. The problem of affordability or inadequate income "calls for more income rather than for more housing." He sees no easy answer to the mismatch between the size of a household and size of its dwelling, particularly since occupying an excessively large housing unit may be more an expression of conspicuous consumption than of need.

Blumenfeld's approach throws light on the difficulty of separating matters that are purely questions of housing from those more closely related to other social concerns. Should housing be viewed as a utility — as basic and important as sewage treatment, for instance — or as a welfare good? However housing is categorized, the problems remain to be addressed. As a study of the housing situation in Halifax in the 1930s put it:

> It is not a question whether we shall pay or shall not pay. It is a question whether we shall pay for better housing or for the damage done by that which is worse. Let us make no mistake about it. It is only a question whether we should house them in hospitals, mental institutions, reformatories and jails; or whether we shall house them in [clean], light and sanitary surroundings where both body and soul will have a chance. Which shall it be? (Citizens Committee 1932, cited in Bruce 1934, p. 34)

There are some who argue about housing on the basis of "rights," as in an individual having a "right to housing." This claim is based on various documents and treaties, such as the Universal Declaration of Human Rights and the Canadian Charter of Rights and Freedoms. Article 25(1) of the former document states:

> Everyone has the right to a standard of living adequate for the health and well-being of himself and his family, including food, clothing, housing and medical care and necessary social services, and the right to security in the event of unemployment, sickness, disability, widowhood, old age or other lack of livelihood in circumstances beyond his control.

This declaration is secured by the International Covenant on Economic, Social and Cultural Rights, and thus can be the basis of a legal action against a signatory, such as Canada. As well, it can be argued that this statement is shored up by the sections of the Charter of Rights and Freedoms proscribing cruel and unusual punishment (of those driven from the shelters onto the streets) or requiring equal treatment under the law. (See Parkdale 1988.) David Hulchanski takes the argument a step further by suggesting the problem might lie in an overly narrow and exclusionary definition of property rights (Hulchanski 1993b, p. 74). What remains unresolved in this definitional approach is whether a declaration by the courts supporting the "right to housing" would mean much in terms of Canadian housing policy. Would such a declaration result in more housing being made available to lower income households, and if so, how?

The need for good housing policies
Given the wide acknowledgement of housing problems, the need for reasonable housing policies is obvious. Further, the economic impact of housing is astoundingly large. In 1985, for instance, $4 billion was invested in new Canadian issues of corporate bonds, in comparison with $30 billion loaned by the private sector in new residential mortgages. Debt outstanding on corporate bonds was $34 billion, while debt outstanding on residential mortgages was $115 billion (Poapst 1993, p. 94). In 1992, some $11 billion in equity financing was raised on Canadian stock markets, while $88 billion, or nearly eight times as much, was loaned by the private sector on new residential mortgages (*Report on Business,* January 1, 1994, p. 1; Canadian Housing Statistics 1992, p. 48). If dollar value is the measure, it makes more sense for the evening television news to run charts about housing, not about the stock market. Housing services occupy about 11 per cent of the Gross National Product (Fallis 1993, p. 77).

What has passed for national and provincial housing programs during the past half-century has been a hodge-podge of initiatives, some of which have made a bad situation worse, many of which have provided support to those who least need it. Some programs have been well thought out and successful, but too often, housing programs have represented public money spent badly to accomplish questionable results.

Worse, there has often been insufficient analysis of the effect of programs, making it very difficult to learn from mistakes. In beginning his study of housing policies during the 1970s, George Fallis notes that data on housing programs were not systematically gathered to see who participated and who benefited. He observes that the measure of benefit was usually the government's cash outlay, with no attempt to evaluate the generous terms on which government mortgages were made, for instance, or to measure the value of the subsides from the participants' viewpoint. He concludes,

> In such an environment it is not surprising to find that housing policy zigzagged as it did during the 1970s ... Moreover, the development of our housing policy never seemed to reflect an integrated, coherent view of all programs; the equity of the total package was not examined. A something-for-everyone approach was adopted, with new initiatives mounted for high-income households before even a small fraction of the problems of poorer households had been dealt with. (Fallis 1980, pp. 140-41)

Housing is such a bedrock of society — Canada is not a country to be lived in without shelter — that its influences permeate all aspects of social and economic life. Is an allowance for housing part of a housing policy or part of an income maintenance strategy? Is housing construction intended primarily to create jobs or to create affordable places to live? If one can only accomplish one of these aims, which should it be?

"The housing market is a complex web of interrelated sectors," writes J.B. Cullingworth. "Policies in one place affect policies in others."

> Housing cannot be treated in isolation: it is inextricably interrelated with broader issues of inflation, incomes policy, income maintenance, inner city decline, and a perplexing range of difficult social and economic trends. (Cullingworth 1979, p. xix)

Some sorting of the roles played by housing will help throw various policy options in contrast. For some, housing is a consumer good, providing shelter. For others, it also is an investment — indeed the only major investment of many families. For those working in the construction industry, it provides jobs and incomes (Shaffner 1975, cited in Rose, 1980, p. 11) Should government attempt to enable every household to own a house so that every household has one major investment, or does that go beyond the proper concern of

Photo: Charlotte Sykes

Although wealthy families lived in large stand-alone homes, most urban Canadians in the nineteenth century lived in row houses. Houses were often occupied by more than one family since buildings were easily subdivided into rooms and flats.

housing policies? To what extent should government be concerned about the ability of families to afford housing? When should government use housing initiatives as a tool for serious job creation?

Concentrating policy energy just on the provision of new housing will do a disservice to the existing housing stock. Unlike automobiles which need to be replaced every five or ten years, houses and apartments last for a century or more. New construction adds only a small percentage to the total stock each year, which implies that housing policy should be primarily concerned with issues surrounding the existing stock, although that would never be obvious by looking at government actions over the past decades (Cullingworth 1979, p. xv). Thus housing policies must deal with new and existing units; they are bound as well to touch on other aspects of social and economic life.

Roles and responsibilities for housing

Housing responsibilities in Canada are not assigned to any one level of government by the Constitution Act, 1867. Municipalities are responsible for land use planning — that is, giving permission to build and maintain specific kinds of housing to be built in particular places. The lead on housing policy has often been taken by cities: the City of Toronto undertook the country's first public housing project in 1947 with its own money, requesting support from the Toronto electorate for the expenditure; municipalities have been the driving force behind many non-profit housing schemes since 1973. But given its sizable tax and expenditure base, the federal government has played the largest role in housing policy, through the National Housing Act and its various amendments. All provinces have been important actors too, particularly in ensuring an adequate servicing base for new development, but also in helping to implement (and sharing in the funding of) federal programs.

In the early 1990s, under Brian Mulroney's leadership, the federal government tried to withdraw from any role in housing and treat housing as the exclusive jurisdiction of the provinces, claiming that it was a sector "more properly the responsibility of the provinces whether or not ... specifically assigned in the Constitution" (Canada's Future 1991, p. 36). This arrangement was endorsed by all provinces and national political parties in the Charlottetown Agreement, but was never carried forward because the agreement was rejected by national plebiscite in October 1992. Numerous arguments were advanced in opposition to the Charlottetown Agreement, of which two advanced by the Co-operative Housing Federation of Canada are of particular relevance. They state:

- Housing is a complex public service industry, in which all levels of government are involved, of necessity, if not by choice. The federal government, through its fiscal policy and economic powers, would continue to exert a strong influence on housing markets even if it granted exclusive jurisdiction to the provinces. It therefore must remain a partner at the table with other levels of government, the private and voluntary sectors, and the citizens themselves as we address our country's future housing needs.
- Exclusive provincial jurisdiction will add nothing to our collective ability to house Canadians well: the provinces

already have jurisdiction over housing. What is actually proposed is to take something away: the possibility of future federal participation. Historically, the federal role in housing has been pre-eminent, and while needs change ... the federal government must not shut itself out of the field permanently. It must preserve the ability to use national institutions to address problems that are national in scope or common to different parts of the country. (CHFC 1991, p. 2)

The federal government decided, regardless of the rejection of the Charlottetown Agreement, to substantially reduce its involvement in housing programs and to remove itself from any further participation in social housing programs, effective in 1994. The election of a new government under the leadership of Jean Chrétien may change this emphasis, although no housing commitments were made by the Liberal Party in the election campaign they won in October 1993.

Although federal participation in housing programs since the 1940s has been crucial to the supply of housing in Canada, including housing for lower-income households, the amount actually spent by the federal government (currently just under $2.0 billion a year) is a very small part of the total federal budget, and much less than the annual subsidy paid to wheat farmers. During the eighties, federal housing expenditures amounted to $14.5 billion out of a total government expenditure of $971 billion — 1.49 per cent of the total. (This figure does not include "tax expenditures" — that is, government programs that relieve individuals and companies from paying taxes that would otherwise be due.) This percentage was not constant during the decade: the average of federal expenditures on housing during the first half of the decade was 1.68 per cent, and during the last half, 1.37 per cent (Hulchanski 1991). Most of this money was spent paying the federal share of subsidies on 500,000 units of public housing, non-profit and non-profit co-operative housing, and rent supplements. From this we can calculate that the annual expenditure was not much more than $2,500 (or $200 per month) for every unit of social housing.

One reason for this relatively low level of expenditure is the federal policy on housing set at the end of the Second World War and followed by almost all subsequent federal governments. It was announced by C.D. Howe, the federal Treasurer, in the House of Commons in 1946: "It is the policy [of this government] to ensure that as large a portion as possible of housing be built by the private

Photo: City of Calgary Archive

Suburbia. The compact neighbourhoods of the nineteenth century were abandoned after World War II for the vast open spaces of the suburbs, well caught here in a 1969 photo of Ogden Road in Calgary.

sector" (House of Commons Debates 1946, p. 3753, cited in Carver 1948, p. 15).

David Mansur, appointed in 1946 as first president of Central Mortgage and Housing Corporation (CMHC), the federal government's housing arm, echoed Howe, saying that the "first duty" of CMHC was "finding ways and means for private enterprise to look after needs in the economic (housing) field" (McKellar 1993, p. 137).

This approach was at great variance with that followed in many European countries. There, governments took a public utility approach to housing rather than a "semi-welfare approach" that concerned itself with just the poor. Thus, after the war 60 per cent of the housing built in Sweden was non-profit, as was 70 per cent in the Netherlands and the United Kingdom, one-half in Denmark, one-third in West Germany. Even under Margaret Thatcher, 24 per cent of all housing in the United Kingdom was non-market. In Europe, the federal (or national) government role was to provide financing and subsidies; local governments administered programs and housing (OAHA 1964, p. 13 ff.).

Canada has generally adopted the "semi-welfare approach," aided by a policy of filtering down housing to those with low incomes based on the assumption that when expensive housing is built, someone moves out of less expensive housing and makes it available to a family with a lower income. Only in the 1970s with the introduction of the non-profit housing programs was there a hint of full-scale housing activism.

The roles of the three levels of government in housing provision have already been touched on: the federal government as the main policy maker and, where required, funder; the provinces as supporters (and sometimes administrators) of federal programs, and in some cases as the innovators in local programs; municipalities as controllers of land use approvals, and occasionally sponsors of housing initiatives.

The federal government established Central Mortgage and Housing Corporation in 1946 to administer housing programs at the federal level, under the direction of the minister responsible for housing. In the 1970s the name was changed to Canada Mortgage and Housing Corporation. The federal government has been loath to establish a separate ministry for housing and has usually made the Minister of Public Works responsible for this area and for CMHC. Most provincial governments have also taken the position that housing can fit into other portfolios.

Governments have established agencies to build and manage government housing. Most provinces have specific agencies that manage public housing projects, many of which were built following legislation passed in 1964. Some cities have established non-profit housing companies, following 1973 National Housing Act (NHA) amendments. Provinces with rent control have set up various agencies to administer the relevant legislation.

A number of private sector interests are intimately involved in housing policy and provision. Companies involved in land development bring new land onto the market for housing development. Most land developers are not house builders: instead, they supply land to house builders, which are often relatively small companies building scores of houses a year. Few house builders construct 300 or more houses a year. In 1984, for example, only sixty-three of these firms across the country had annual revenues of more than $10 million, representing 250 houses at $40,000 apiece (McKellar 1993, p. 139).

Most developers and home builders specialize in what they do. They learn about a market in one city, or one part of a city, and work there almost exclusively. The nature of local politics requires personal knowledge of local councillors; this probably accounts for the limited geographic reach of most developers and builders. Further, a builder who knows the suburban house market will rarely be found constructing apartment buildings or condominiums downtown. Someone who builds apartments over stores might try an infill project, but probably wouldn't venture out into the suburbs. Again, the detailed nature of the municipal approvals system means that developers and builders learn about one kind of product and stick to it. This specialization sometimes makes innovation difficult.

Since the passage in 1973 of NHA amendments supporting non-profit housing and non-profit co-operatives, a whole host of non-profit groups have arisen to propose, build and manage this kind of housing. Social and religious groups form non-profit companies for housing purposes, often to achieve just one project. Some non-profit groups become more established, acquire a staff to look for development opportunities in their community, and build projects regularly. There are national and provincial organizations for non-profit housing companies, and there are consultants who specialize in advising them in development proposals, building, and management.

The non-profit co-operative sector has emerged with strong organizations to help establish new housing co-ops and to support existing co-ops. It too has national and local organizations.

Critical to housing is the money needed to build and buy it. Most comes from the private sector. Those providing the financing play an important role, perhaps even comparable at some times to the government's policy-setting role. If lenders see no advantage in participating in the creation of rental stock, then rental housing will probably not be built. If interest rates are high, construction will probably fall off since buyers will find prices too steep.

Financiers can also set the terms of how money is borrowed. The instrument developed for housing in the late 1940s was the equal payment mortgage. Its term was generally thirty-five years, and the amount paid each month for the life of the mortgage was enough to ensure that the last payment fully discharged the debt. This mortgage instrument made sense when one family member (usually the father) was expected to work at the same job until retirement: the house would be fully paid for just as the family went on pension, and the rate of inflation was high enough to ensure that fixed payments (and thus ownership) became easier and easier to afford. In the 1990s, when few can expect to work in any one job until retirement, it is almost impossible to find a mortgage for anything more than five

Photo: CMHC

Redeveloping the city. Suburbia surrounded cities in the latter half of the twentieth century, but cities themselves changed as office jobs replaced industrial and manufacturing jobs. The new community of False Creek, sponsored by the City of Vancouver in the early 1970s, was located on derelict industrial land and is shown here in the foreground with Vancouver's downtown in the background.

years. Further, mortgage instruments have been devised that allow interest rates to vary, and indeed monthly payments to vary.

But this is not to say that there is great flexibility in the financing of new housing. Lenders have learned to be conservative in their policies and often the tried and true solution gets built instead of something more innovative and affordable. Municipalities, too, must bear their fair share of blame for not allowing more affordable housing and more supportive communities. Few banks want to lend $10,000 to renovate a house and build a second unit when that unit will be contrary to zoning laws.

The role that consumer groups play in setting or changing housing policy is small. Some tenant organizations have managed to press provincial governments on rent control issues, and some community groups have pushed municipal governments to keep certain types of housing out of their communities. But no national tenants' organization whose objective is to set national housing policy exists in Canada, as in some European countries, nor are there provincial or national organizations of homeowners or first-time home-buyers. The housing policies and programs that do get adopted are worked out informally among the public and private sector players, generally free from direct influence by Canada's many housing consumers.

Housing policies and urban change

Canada has changed immensely in the last fifty years. In 1941 the population was less than 12 million; by 1991 it stood at more than 26 million. In 1941 only 30 per cent of the population lived in cities of more than 100,000 inhabitants, and almost the same proportion lived on farms. Now, over half the country's population live in these large cities, and only 6 per cent on farms.

In 1941 there were 2.5 million occupied dwellings, or 2,240 for every 10,000 population; fifty years later there are more than 9.5 million dwellings, or 3,500 for every 10,000 people. The average number of people per dwelling has fallen from 4.5 to 2.9, an indication of how our families have shrunk (Miron 1993b, p. 26; Skaburskis 1993, p. 157; Hulchanski 1988, pp. 2-3).

C.D. Howe might well look back with satisfaction on the results of his 1946 policy statement. Discounting the war years at the beginning of this period, almost 6 million dwellings were constructed in thirty-five years, almost all by the private sector. The previous thirty-five years had seen little more than 1 million dwelling units built, so the change was quite remarkable. The number of units constructed in any one year depended on the state of the economy and on government proposals to increase housing starts. When the economy bounced around in the 1970s and early 1980s, housing starts rose and fell with depressing regularity; nevertheless, with only a few exceptions, Canada has been able to count on 200,000 or more new housing units being built every year since 1970.

The boom years were the 1970s and the late 1980s, although the whole period is one of phenomenal growth. Before the mid-1960s, about three-quarters of new housing was in the form of single-family suburban houses. After the mid-1960s, one-third of the supply was high-rise apartments, the proportion of single-family suburban houses falling to one-half.

Public mortgage insurance introduced in 1954 under the National Housing Act was one very influential program. Administered by CMHC, it protected mortgage lenders from the purchaser's default on new suburban houses and made loans virtually risk-free (Hulchanski 1988, p. 23). This program did much from the 1950s through the 1970s to encourage the growth of suburbs by stimulating private sector funding for residential construction. The strict conditions on interest rates set in the early years by CMHC were dropped in 1969.

The financing of new residential construction and existing residential properties has increased enormously, from $6 billion in 1974, to $22 billion in 1984, to $60 billion in 1989 and more than $80 billion in 1992 (CMHC statistics). Housing critic John Miron suggests that perhaps too much has been invested in housing (Miron 1993, p. 363).

What is clear is the enormous growth of residential lending in Canada during the past forty years, particularly during the later 1980s. In that decade prices rose to such a frenzy that the debt created in real estate later led to the collapse of some substantial real estate companies and considerable write-offs for others. For many Canadians, the unchecked venture into real estate inflation in the 1980s simply led to even higher housing costs.

The growth that began in the 1950s occurred almost entirely in cities as Canada changed from a largely rural economy before the Second World War to one that was largely urban. This growth signified a change in the way cities looked, felt and functioned. The traditional older-city shop-lined roads ("shopping strips") around the corner from houses on narrow lots were quickly surrounded by low-density tracts of houses on large lots, interrupted every few miles by a shopping centre. People got to work not by public transit, but by car. Today, almost two-thirds of the Canadian population lives in suburbia (Bourne 1993, p. 274). One American writer made these comments about suburban growth:

> It devours vast amounts of rural land, including some of the best farmland ... It squanders energy ... It wastes people's time, condemning them to solitary imprisonment in their cars for hours each day ... It is by nature homogenizing and intolerant of diversity, both economic and social, failing to provide "odd little corners for people with odd little lives" ... It fails to provide decent public places that bring people into casual face-to-face contact. (Kunstler 1993, p. 260)

While suburbia was being built, older parts of the city were demolished and replaced with high-rise towers surrounded by unused grass. The growth was so sudden and had such force that few were able to raise their voices and question whether the changes being worked upon Canadian cities were desirable.

The explosion in housing stock was not accompanied by a reduction in housing prices. In fact, just the opposite occurred: prices increased relative to income. These increases were not a problem for those who already owned a property — they were almost always a benefit — but they did affect those trying to enter the market. Many families spent larger and larger proportions of their income on housing. Tenants particularly were faced with problems of affordability. C.D. Howe would not have been as proud of this outcome of his policy statement.

In the 1940s Humphrey Carver and others assumed that the average family should spend no more than 20 per cent of its income on housing costs; by the 1980s the assumption was that families should spend 30 per cent, while in reality at least a quarter of all renter households in Canada spent more than 30 per cent. The change in quantity and type of housing stock actually made the housing situation for most Canadians worse, not better.

George Fallis argues that Canada has seen three distinct periods of housing policy: from 1954 to 1963, characterized by stabilization and growth; from 1964 to 1977, a period of equity and affordability; and after 1978, characterized by stagflation and restraint. The middle period saw the greatest number of initiatives to address the housing problems of low-income Canadians, particularly by Pierre Trudeau's government: programs to assist the construction of private rental housing; programs to create non-profit housing and non-profit co-operatives; and in 1975, following on federally imposed wage and price controls, rent controls in all provinces. Assisted and social housing programs began to wind down in the mid-1980s as the Mulroney government, elected in 1984, withdrew from the promotion of equity, and more generally from national programs.

Yet it was just as the federal government was withdrawing that housing problems for some became most acute. Homelessness became a serious issue in the 1980s. As a result of gentrification, lower priced housing disappeared, and without vibrant social housing programs, many found there was literally nowhere to live but in the street. Their numbers were augmented by those unable to function in a society where mental hospitals were shut down, unemployment continued to grow, and social nets that had been in place for decades were quietly being withdrawn.

In 1947, the Canadian Welfare Council, worried about the housing problems of the time, concluded that "these special problems can no longer be regarded as temporary features of the post-war period which will correct themselves spontaneously" (Carver 1947). Like the Council, we might assume that these problems — the same kind of problems the Council worried about in 1947 — will not be resolved by themselves. They need attention, study, and action, the very initiatives in which this book hopes to play a helpful role.

Chapter 2

Family Income and Housing Need

All housing comes with a price attached, and that price is critical for decisions about who lives there. The relationship of housing cost to family income is a key issue, since a housing unit isn't accessible to a family that can't afford to pay the rent.

Equally important is ensuring that the right kind of housing is available when it is needed. New housing can't be produced overnight: it takes five years, more often ten, from the original idea of investing in new housing to being able to step across the threshold. To ensure that an adequate supply of housing is available in communities, it is necessary to understand the factors that result in housing demand, and to predict the kind and size of housing that will be required to meet that demand.

An accurate estimate of housing needs is important for a number of reasons: it enables government to determine capital needs, anticipate servicing requirements with sewers and other facilities, and set economic targets; it also allows the private sector to direct investment opportunities.

Housing needs can be met in different ways. Do families want high-rise or low-rise accommodation? Ownership or rental? Is the demand for new subdivisions or for redevelopment of existing neighbourhoods and infill development? What if the demand is for sprawl when the municipality wants compact development? How much demand will be taken up by families renting out part of their homes? How will the infrastructure for new housing — sewers, water, roads, schools — be financed and paid for? Answers to these questions begin to sort out how needs will be implemented. This chapter also explores these questions.

A third issue is the difficulty of assessing the costs and benefits of government action. As we shall see, one cannot be confident in assigning clear effects to any policy in the housing field.

This chapter looks at these three issues — affordability, need and the difficulty of assessing costs and benefits — which are important for understanding what lies behind the planning of housing programs and how supply can be influenced.

Affordability and need

When is housing affordable? If a family willingly pays half its income to meet mortgage payments, can one conclude that its house is affordable? If a family grudgingly pays a quarter of its income to meet its rent, can one conclude that its rental unit is not affordable?

Obviously, affordability should not be determined by simply reviewing the willingness of a household to pay. Less personal and emotive criteria are needed to permit reasonable comparisons. There are a number of different ways to define affordability, none without shortcomings. As one commentator notes, "the concept of affordability is slippery: it can be defined precisely only by measurement, and current measures are inadequate for various reasons" (Marks 1986, p. 102).

When affordability is discussed, it usually pertains to problems faced by renters because their difficulties are much more significant than those of owners. But the term can be applied to owners as well. One writer, for instance, notes that in 1961, 75 per cent of all families in Ontario could afford to carry the costs of a mortgage and of owning an average house. In 1975, that number had slipped to 39 per cent — indicating a massive change in the affordability of ownership within fourteen years (Fallis 1980, p. 36).

The number of households with problems of affordability is usually the barometer used to measure the need for new housing programs. If few households have these problems, then little government intervention is required: if many find it difficult to afford housing, more needs to be done. Thus the definition of affordability is a key political issue with a direct impact on what governments feel they need to spend and do on housing.

The following are common measures of affordability:

Rent-to-income ratio: The most common way to measure affordability is to use a rent-to-income ratio. But settling on a reasonable rent-to-income ratio is not easy. On average, Canadian households spend less than 20 per cent of income on housing. That figure, however, is an average, and includes the two-thirds of households who own rather than rent, among whom are a number who have already paid off their mortgages (Hulchanski 1988, p. 7). It would be more relevant to measure the number who rent or have not fully paid for their home.

Fifty years ago, a rent-to-income ratio of 20 per cent was considered fair. Humphrey Carver observed that "a commonly accepted rule-of-thumb [is that] a family can afford to pay one-fifth of its income for housing accommodation" (Carver 1948, p. 73). Carver found that in the mid-1940s many tenant households paid much more than 20 per cent of income for rent: the 12 per cent of families in Toronto who had incomes of less than $1,000 a year paid 40 per cent or more of their income for rent (p. 75).

Twenty-five years ago, housing was considered affordable if a household paid no more than 25 per cent of its income in rent. Thus, when the public housing program was established in the mid-1960s, it was assumed that tenants should be required to pay 25 per cent of income to rent.

More recently, a 30 per cent ratio has come into vogue and is widely used by CMHC and by British Columbia, Alberta, Ontario and other provinces, apparently on the assumption that 30 per cent better reflects the public's perception of what is really affordable. Since this ratio is used to determine the rent that is paid by public housing tenants, there may be a more cynical explanation: the ratio may have been changed to increase rental income from tenants in public housing in order to reduce required subsidies from government. Or, it might have been altered to minimize the housing problems that exist, a tactic similar to that of some Conservatives at the federal level who in 1993 tried to propose a new definition of poverty that would have resulted in many fewer Canadians living below the poverty line.

But even if 30 per cent is agreed to be a reasonable ratio of income that households should pay for housing, there are many renters who pay much more. In 1976, 23 per cent of all renters in Canada paid more than 30 per cent of income in rent. By 1986 that proportion had risen to 27 per cent, suggesting that affordability problems were getting worse (Hulchanski 1988, p. 9). According to other data, in 1981 24.4 per cent of renters were paying more than 35 per cent of income in rent, which makes the problem look very serious indeed (Ontario 1987, p. 38). These figures force us to look at the Canadian

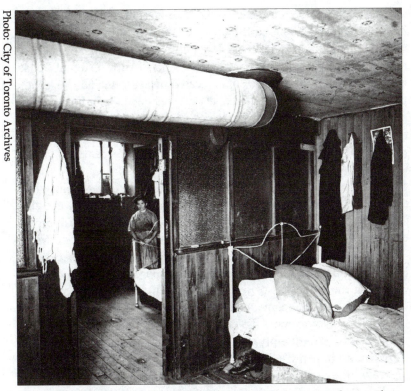

Photo: City of Toronto Archives

Housing conditions at the beginning of the twentieth century frequently left much to be desired. This shows the interior of a Toronto house just after the turn of the century.

average of less than 20 per cent of income spent on housing with less complacency.

Thus one criticism of the rent-to-income measure is that there is no firm basis for deciding what ratio is best. A more challenging criticism is the observation that for low-income households paying 25 or 30 per cent of income for accommodation is much more difficult than paying 25 or 30 per cent of a larger income. The 25 or 30 per cent ratio may make sense for a middle-income family, but where income is much tighter, a lower figure — say 10 or 15 per cent — might be a much more reasonable measure of real-life affordability.

A related criticism is the income base on which the ratio is calculated. Most often gross income, before deductions, is used. Some have argued that the ratio should be calculated on net income, interpreted loosely as take-home pay, since that represents disposable income. The objection made to the take-home pay base is that different people take home different amounts, depending on union dues, pension deductions, charitable deductions and so forth, so that take-home pay represents different levels of benefit for different households. Others think a more sophisticated measure such as household disposable income — income after taxes, and including transfer income from government programs — is more appropriate (Fallis 1980, p. 27). Applying the ratio on any basis other than gross income has the effect of increasing the percentage of income paid for housing.

Real-life affordability: A second way to measure affordability is to determine costs from real-life situations in specific cities, and then compare the costs with available household income. This approach has been popularized by the Social Planning Council of Metro Toronto, which for some years did real-life shopping for necessities — food, toiletries, clothing, housing, transportation and so on — to establish the real costs of living in a city like Toronto. Costs were then compared to income available. Those who didn't have enough money left over to meet the costs of housing were deemed to have problems of affordability. (Of course, what those with this kind of problem do in real life is skimp on other necessities or share limited space with others, to ensure that they are somehow housed.)

This method of measurement provides specific information on particular places, but it requires a considerable amount of work to assemble the detailed information. Few social agencies are willing or able to undertake this work; therefore, this method is not now used as a country-wide measure of housing affordability.

Core need: This measurement tries to take into account the adequacy of the housing as well as the amount paid, based on a 30 per cent rent-to-income ratio. Thus, not only will a family be considered to be in core need if it is paying more than 30 per cent of its income for housing, but it will also be considered in core need if it pays less than 30 per cent but the housing is physically inadequate or crowded.

This measure has been used by CMHC for its housing programs since the late 1980s. In 1988, a total of 906,000 households in Canada, or over 2 million people, were determined to be in core need (Engeland 1990-91). Of those renter households in core need, 803,000 were paying more than 30 per cent of income for housing. By 1991, the situation had worsened considerably; 1,164,000 households, or 12.2 per cent of the total, were in core need.

The breakdown by province is shown in Table 2.1.

Table 2.1		
Renters in core need, by household		
	1988	*1991*
British Columbia	130,000	164,000
Alberta	79,000	94,000
Saskatchewan	28,000	37,000
Manitoba	44,000	41,000
Ontario	268,000	387,000
Quebec	295,000	341,000
New Brunswick	21,000	28,000
Nova Scotia	26,000	45,000
Prince Edward Is	3,000	7,000
Newfoundland	11,000	20,000
Totals	906,000	1,164,000
Source: Canadian Housing Statistics 1991.		

Core need problems mostly occur in cities — only 5 per cent of renters in core need live in rural areas. In 1988 households in core need were broken down as follows:

Table 2.2	
Couple families	166,000
Lone parents	152,000
Seniors	249,000
Non-elderly, unattached	329,000
Source: Engeland 1990-91, pp. 8-9.	

On average, it was found that in 1988 renters in core need generally spent 46 per cent of their income on housing. These ratios generally continued to apply in the 1990s.

As already noted, the 30 per cent rent-to-income ratio is the most restrictive measure of affordability used in Canada, although the 30 per cent is simply an arbitrary measure, so the core need calculation suffers from the same criticism already noted for ratio-to-income measures. It also requires detailed information on housing and crowding conditions, which may be difficult to capture.

By way of international comparison, a 1981 study found that in 1974, 17 per cent of Canadian households were in core need, while 22 per cent of American households were in core need (CMHC/HUD 1981). If this ratio still holds, then problems of affordability in the United States are considerably greater than in Canada.

Cost-to-income-to-inflation: Fallis suggests that the comparison of housing cost to income might be a useful measure of affordability when seen in the light of the movement of all other prices as well. Has the cost of housing risen more quickly than other prices? He compares changes in the Consumer Price Index (CPI) for all items and for housing during three decades, starting each decade at the same measure:

Table 2.3
Indexes for all consumer prices and the rent component of those prices

Year	All items	Rent component
1961	100	100
1966	111	104
1971	133	123
1971	100	100
1976	161	120
1981	237	157
1981	100	100
1986	132	133
1988	148	146

Source: Fallis and Murray 1990, p. 53.

Fallis concludes, "Rents rose slightly less than other prices in the 1960s, far less than other prices in the 1970s, and the same as other prices in the 1980s (Fallis and Murray 1990, p. 53). Fallis agrees that the rent component of the Consumer Price Index may understate actual rents, and thus the picture in this chart may be somewhat more positive than in reality. However, even with this adjustment, it is fair to say that the relative price of rental housing declined between 1960 and 1988.

This comparison with the CPI, of course, is not the whole story. The critical question is not so much the price of things in general, since some things that are too expensive are simply not purchased. Housing, however, is a necessity, and everyone must have it. The comparison must be made between actual incomes of real people and the actual costs of real housing, and the issue is the amount of a particular renter's income required to meet the rent — which leads back to a measure something like rent-to-income and core need.

The force of Fallis's analysis, as he makes clear, is that "the problem of homelessness has not emerged over a period when rental housing has become significantly less affordable ... Of course, for certain individual households, and in certain specific neighbour-hoods, the relative price of rental housing has risen significantly. But these are exceptions rather than the overall situation" (p. 53). This analysis helps provide an understanding of why more people have problems affording housing when for many in the middle class "it doesn't feel like that." Quite simply, the problem isn't generally experienced throughout the population; it isn't shared by the popu-lation at large. The inequities in society have become more pro-nounced but not more broadly spread.

Other measures: CMHC has recently developed an "affordability indicator" to define the number of renters who can afford to buy a home. The indicator is intended to apply to young households that are first-time home buyers — that is, tenant households between ages 20 and 44. The indicator is based on a 10 per cent down payment; monthly payments for mortgage, property tax and heating not ex-ceeding 32 per cent of the household budget; and current mortgage rates for a three-year term, amortized over twenty-five years. Apply-ing these factors, CMHC concluded what percentage of family rent-ers (that is, households with children) could afford to purchase a home in the first half of 1991. (See Table 2.4.) Figures were some-what lower for households without children.

It may be more interesting to interpret these data in reverse; that is, to use the data to determine what percentage cannot afford to buy. If the goal is to ensure that families with children can afford to purchase a home, then why is it that in Vancouver and Toronto

Table 2.4

Renter families with children who can afford to purchase a home

City	Percentage
Vancouver	29.5
Calgary	40.0
Winnipeg	49.9
Toronto	29.9
Ottawa	39.0
Montreal	42.0
Halifax	48.0

Source: Canadian Housing Statistics 1991.

two-thirds of young families find home ownership beyond their means?

One might also conclude that there is little value in talking about home ownership as a factor in affordability, since homeowners are so well off compared to renters. The average net worth of homeowners in Canada is about eight times that of renters — in 1971 figures, $71,000 compared to slightly under $9,000 (Steele 1993, p. 54). This difference leads one to assume that the important affordability problems to address are those of renters, not those of owners.

One simple method often used to measure the need for housing is to look at the length of waiting lists for public and other social housing providers. It is assumed that if the waiting lists are growing, the need for affordable housing must be growing.

Public housing waiting lists are assumed to be particularly good indicators: public housing is considered so undesirable that the people who apply for it must be in desperate situations, showing the general extent of housing problems in society. Of course, these assumptions might not be true. In addition, there is often some overlap between waiting lists, where one family applies to more than one housing provider. This measure needs to be recognized for its looseness and informality.

Various other ways of measuring affordability have been proposed and sometimes used. Some have related the rent-to-income ratio to family size, on the assumption that large families spend less on housing and more on other necessities. One critic has suggested that a scheme should be developed that compares changes in rent to changes in income, so that the measure includes some of the dynamic found in the real world and captures the problem experienced by families with low incomes when rent increases more than income (Marks 1986).

As should be clear from the above discussion, there are a number of different approaches to measuring affordability. Many of them conclude that the problem of affordability is significant.

Income distribution

All measures of affordability reflect to some extent how income is distributed in Canada. Income distribution is usually measured by dividing the population into groups of equal numbers, arranged by income. One common procedure is to divide Canadian families into five groups (or quintiles) of equal size (each group would have about two million families in it), with the first group having the lowest incomes and the fifth group, the highest incomes. This allows the percentage of total Canadian family income available to each group to be measured.

In 1991, the share of family income by quintiles in Canada was as follows:

Table 2.5				
Shares of total income of families, by quintile, 1991				
Pre-tax distribution:				
Bottom	Second	Third	Fourth	Top
6.4	12.2	17.6	23.9	40.0
Post-tax distribution:				
7.7	13.3	18.1	23.6	37.3
Source: "Income Share and Average Income by Quintiles" (Ottawa: Statistics Canada, 13-210), p. 31.				

It is clear that the income available to the top one-fifth of Canadian families is six times greater than that available to the bottom one-fifth of Canadian families. The top two-fifths of Canadian families garner almost two-thirds of all incomes, while the bottom three-fifths receive just over one-third of total family income.

The after-tax situation, which accounts for loss of income through taxes, and income gains through redistributive programs such as welfare, pensions and unemployment insurance, shows a small change in favour of those with lower income; however, the inequities are largely undisturbed. Those with lower incomes have gained slightly because of government programs, but those programs do little to create a more equitable society. It should be noted that 1991 is a typical year for income distribution in Canada in the second half of the twentieth century: if anything, it shows more fairness in income distribution that the 1960s and 1970s, when the pre-tax family income of the top quintile was almost ten times that of the bottom quintile. Quintile shares move up or down a percentage point every few years, but generally one can say that in Canada those in the top quintile have six or seven times more income than those in the bottom quintile.

The extent of poverty, like that of housing affordability, depends on the definition used, but as a general statement most people would agree that many of those in the bottom quintile are considered to be living in poverty.

Of course, it is the general distribution of income in Canada that underlies questions of housing affordability. Those facing problems of affordability are found in the bottom two quintiles, and they are not just tenants. In 1986, it was estimated that 7.3 per cent of Canadian families and unattached individuals who owned their own homes were considered to be living below the poverty line; 25.6 per cent of renters were considered poor (Hulchanski 1988, p. 34).

One of the key questions about housing policy is the extent to which various programs and policies help alleviate problems of affordability. It is next to impossible for any housing program to reasonably address and fully resolve widespread inequities in the way income is distributed: at best, such policies can make a small dent.

Defining housing needs

As a 1964 study noted, "an acknowledgment of housing need lays the foundation and defines the scope of a housing policy. Generally however, the term 'housing need' refers to the number of dwellings required for the satisfactory accommodation of the population and the calculation is usually related to such physical need over a specific period of years" (OAHA 1964, p. 57). Then, citing the 1957 Royal Commission on Canada's Economic Prospects, it came to almost the same conclusion as was already noted about affordability: need is "a notoriously slippery customer" (p. 57). This section will attempt to explain some of the complexities and the resulting slipperiness.

An understanding of housing needs is what leads to public and private decisions about new housing supply. Governments must determine which programs should be put in place to discourage some actions and encourage others, depending on which needs they think have priority and which can be funded through the public purse. Private companies must make decisions about where to invest money to create new housing and about what kind of housing should be created. If there is an unmet need, the private sector may be able to fill that need and make a profit on investment.

Problems result if future housing needs are not addressed. For instance, there was a severe housing shortage following the First World War. The result was overcrowding as households doubled up. Many were concerned about neighbourhood decay — a set of conditions that only worsened in the following depression. The Second World War saw a continuing housing crisis, partly because of a shortage of materials for new housing, and after the war a great surge in new households. A 1944 study estimated that Canada would need 731,000 new dwellings in the next decade, and if the problem of families doubling up during the war was to be addressed, 480,000 units in the ensuing five years. This was an enormous number of new dwellings for Canada, since during the 1930s only about 25,000 were built each year. The 1944 estimates of housing need called for a quadrupling of new housing starts (Carver 1948, p. 4).

Humphrey Carver's assumption was that housing need could be addressed through a vigourous housing policy. While during the 1920s and 1930s only 50,000 new dwellings were built for every one million of Canada's population, in the United States 75,000 units were built for every million of population, and in Great Britain 83,000 units for every million. Carver believed that the problem for Canada was simply settling on an appropriate policy, and then getting the country to perform as well as others (Carver 1948, p. 4).

During the 1950s a significant amount of new housing was built to respond to strong demand, although problems of affordability continued for many households (OAHA 1964, pp. 57-58). If housing need had been more directly addressed during these periods, better steps could have been taken to prevent the resulting housing crises.

As the century wore on, housing needs changed. The issue was no longer meeting the raw numbers of new units, but instead ensuring that the units provided met specific needs, particularly those of families that had difficulty affording housing. Thus, estimates of housing need became more particular as did the types of program attempted in meeting it. (See, for instance, Miron 1988, and Clayton 1987.)

One should note that governments rarely devise housing programs simply to satisfy housing needs: those programs are more often proclaimed to create jobs. New housing is a significant employment generator. Residential construction has accounted for about 5 per cent of Gross Domestic Product since mid-century, and it has significant economic spin-offs: every new housing unit requires a stove and refrigerator, and often involves purchases of carpets, furniture, entertainment equipment and so forth (Hulchanski 1988, p. 12). Once governments understand need, they can create programs that encourage the private sector to meet it while simultaneously creating jobs. Much of the need, however, cannot be met in this way.

In addition to assessing need at the macro level, it must also be determined on a micro or local level to permit municipalities to plan for growth and change. To absorb new housing successfully, municipalities must do considerable planning and incur significant capital expenditures. New housing requires sewage and water treatment plants, roads, schools, community centres, hospitals and other public facilities. The extent and type of public facilities depend on who is being housed — obviously senior citizens have different needs than families with small children.

A further question that must be addressed is the time frame for the projections of housing need. The cost of infrastructure to serve a growing community is significant, and the better the picture one has of future population change the better the investment decisions can be. Over the longer term, small errors in projection are magnified considerably; thus the more distant the projection, the more likely the chance of error.

The following matters must be taken into account:

Population change: Population can grow naturally, through births outnumbering deaths. Fertility rates have changed considerably in this century, climbing after the Second World War (the baby boom) and falling since 1960, so that by 1980 the number of births in Canada no longer offset the number of deaths. At the same time, life expectancy has increased, both because of a reduction in child mortality and because adults now live longer lives. The assumptions underlying fertility and mortality rates can often change quickly, without warning.

Population can also grow through immigration. The rate of immigration can be quite volatile. For instance, although Canada has always encouraged considerable immigration, the actual number permitted into the country each year has fluctuated depending on political opinion. Canada has seen three waves of immigration in the past fifty years: that associated with European resettlement after the Second World War; immigration from Asia and the Caribbean from the mid-1960s to mid-1970s; and a third burst since the mid-1980s. Since policies change, it is difficult to estimate the rate of immigration over the next ten years (Miron 1993b, p. 24).

Migration also occurs within Canada's borders. For some decades, residents have moved from the Atlantic provinces and the Prairies into Ontario and British Columbia. Job opportunities are often at the root of these movements.

Estimating the change in population within a municipality is subject to a number of unforeseen variables not related to fertility, mortality or immigration. In 1971, it was estimated that by 1990 the Town of Markham, on the outskirts of Toronto, would have a population of 20,000. However, in 1974 it was decided to offer Markham substantial sewage capacity, which had not been contemplated in the 1971 estimate; by 1985, Markham's population exceeded 100,000 (Sewell 1993, p. 212).

Conversely, the town of Elliot Lake in Northern Ontario had a population of about 20,000 in 1980, and the community seemed to have a bright and growing future. Within the next decade the market for uranium collapsed, the uranium mines around Elliot Lake were closed, and the population fell precipitously, reaching about 13,500 in 1990.

Macro projections about national immigration figures must be applied with care at the micro level. Experience has shown, for instance, that although immigrants to Canada are allocated to centres across the country, about half of all immigrants end up in the Toronto area, whether for linguistic, cultural or employment reasons. It is not reasonable to assume that immigration will be spread evenly among cities: knowing past local experience is as helpful as knowing future national projections.

Household size and income: Knowing the expected population is useful, but it is necessary to know who is to make up that population in order to settle on the kind of housing that will be needed.

The housing needs of older people are clearly different than the needs of families with children. Families with children need larger units than single people or couples without children — and, some would say, different kinds of units, perhaps with direct access to a front or back yard.

Further, knowing the size of age groups as well as the ratio of sexes will help forecast expected family or household formation patterns. Older age groups are less likely to form new households than younger age groups. As well, patterns of ownership and renting change with age: middle- and older-aged households are more likely to own than to rent. (See Foot 1986, p. 14. Chapter 1 of Foot's study is useful for an understanding of demographics.)

Different age groups also have different demands and expectations. In the 1980s, David Foot was able to use demographic projections to predict an explosion in demand for country homes and cottages by noticing the bulge in families who were entering their late forties and early fifties, years when "recreational" homes are most desired and most affordable.

Cultural and behavioural change: As cultural ideas change, so do housing needs. In the nineteenth century, the extended family was assumed to be the norm: large houses accommodated all kinds of family members, including children of relatives, close relatives who were mentally and physically ill, and unrelated persons who acted as servants. Today, except for certain cultural groups, extended families are now unusual. Those same nineteenth-century houses might now be occupied by an older couple or divided into several units and occupied by separate households.

Before the First World War, it was assumed that housing had to be close to public transit and shops. Thus, lots were small and shopping strips were the norm. With changing ideas of how cities should be built, and the accessibility offered by the private automobile, vast tracts of suburban housing could be built and marketed without regard to proximity to transit, main streets or shops.

In mid-century, it was assumed that many younger single adults would live at home or move into rooming or boarding houses: by the late 1960s notions of personal privacy and sexual activity had changed and it was assumed that younger single adults would have their own apartments. Living in a rooming house was a sign of failure.

*Houses built for one housing purpose have often been changed to serve
other needs. This large house, built in the last two decades of the
nineteenth century in Toronto's Rosedale, has recently been converted to
four units. (Note the too-obvious hydro boxes on the building's wall.) In
the 1970s Rosedale residents pressured City Hall to amend the zoning
bylaw to permit the conversion of an existing house to three units,
preferring conversion to obsolescence or demolition.*

In the 1970s, many apartment buildings were built for senior
citizens, and those living alone were given what was called a "bachelor" unit consisting of one large room with a small kitchen and a
bathroom. Today such units are seen as undesirable: tenants prefer
units with a separate bedroom, and in some cities it is very difficult
to find occupants to rent bachelor units for any price.

Other cultural changes have to be factored into the assessment of
housing need: ideas of self-reliance; changing attitudes to divorce,
remarriage and cohabitation; changing ideas of food, cooking and
eating; and opportunities to work at home rather than in an office
(which might require a larger unit with an extra room).

Economic matters: Periods of affluence will result in fundamentally
different housing needs and demands than periods of decline. If
incomes are rising relative to housing costs, households will want to

move to larger or better accommodation. Rising incomes might also result in more households being formed as the young strike boldly out on their own, or more households being maintained as the old find they can afford to live for a longer period in their own home.

Periods of decline usually see housing demand contract significantly: the unemployed have to move in with a friend or family member; fewer people wish to buy a new home; rents stabilize and landlords find waiting lists for units running dry.

There is always the question of how widely affluence is spread. The latter half of the 1980s has often been interpreted as a period of significant affluence in Canada, yet it was during that decade that food banks were established in all Canadian cities and problems of homelessness became widespread. The prosperity was not generally shared, and as noted in Chapter 11, those who had more money at their disposal purchased housing that had been occupied by those with lower incomes, forcing many of the original inhabitants onto the street. The cost of the affluence to those at the bottom of the bottom income quintile was substantial. It actually increased the problems of housing affordability experienced by some households with lower incomes.

Public policies: What should not be overlooked in the factors contributing to housing need is the effect of public policy. Policies that support home ownership might very well create a demand for more ownership units if they allow more households to think that they can afford ownership. Policies that discourage rental units might drive up rents as vacancy rates decline because new rental units are not being constructed. Tight-interest policies might decrease housing supply and increase housing need — potential purchasers find they can't afford high interest rates, or investors think that they can obtain adequate returns without having to build and own rental properties. Thus, assessments of housing need must take into account the "feedback" effect of government programs designed to respond to perceived need.

Vacancy rates

The need for rental housing is often measured by vacancy rates; that is, the number of rental units that are vacant.

Because of difficulties in data collection, vacancy rates are usually measured only for buildings with six or more units. This limitation misses some rental units, such as houses, second units within houses, and duplexes. Thus, the traditional measure often distorts real vacancy rates.

Low vacancy rates imply that renters have limited choice and enable landlords to charge higher rents. There is no firm agreement about the most "desirable" vacancy rate — landlords would clearly like it as low as possible, whereas renters would like it quite high, with lots of choice. However, there seems to be some consensus that a vacancy rate of less than 3 per cent, or 30 of every 1,000 rental units, indicates that renters do not have an adequate choice.

Surveys of rental prices usually include units then rented, and are not an accurate reflection of the asking prices for vacant units. In fact, vacant units will almost always cost more than occupied units, since it is fair to assume that renters occupy the least expensive units first. For instance, if the average cost of a two-bedroom unit is $800, one might find that for the 25 or 30 two-bedroom units that are vacant out of every 1,000, the asking price is $900 or more. This difference in price may be minimized if rent controls are in place, but no system of controls will ever be entirely successful in making all rental rates comparable. Indeed, there is some evidence that even with controls, vacant units are offered at prices 40 per cent higher than average occupied rental rates (Fallis and Murray 1990, p. 54).

Low vacancy rates are associated with other problems as well:

When vacancy rates are low, the matching of people and dwellings is more difficult, causing some problems for those who would like to move, but far greater problems for new arrivals or new households. All newcomers and all new households must bear extra search costs, and certain households fare worse than others. When vacancy rates are low, landlords can discriminate against certain types of tenants. When a single parent with a child or a visible-minority person applies for an apartment, the landlord can turn them away knowing full well another tenant can be found quickly. Thus, in tight rental markets possible "problem" tenants — for example, families with children, especially single-parent families, those with psychological disabilities, or those without long job histories — will suffer ... Landlords can more readily exercise their racial, religious, or other prejudices. (Fallis and Murray 1990, pp. 54-55)

Table 2.6

Average vacancy rates in Canadian metropolitan areas

Year	Percentage
1966	3.2
1971	5.0
1976	1.3
1981	1.2
1986	1.6
1988	2.6

Source: CMHC, cited in Fallis and Murray 1990, p. 53. The rates apply to private buildings of six or more units.

Average vacancy rates have fallen during the last twenty years, creating what Hulchanski calls a "growing urban housing crisis," although rates rose toward the end of the 1980s.

Marion Steele quarrels with the interpretation that vacancy rates have generally declined. (See Steele 1991.) Studying Ontario, Steele concludes that many illegal second units have been created in private homes in recent years, and that most condominium units — which would not be included in vacancy rate surveys since they are treated as privately owned — are rented out. Together, these sources account for a significant number of rental units not reflected in vacancy rate calculations. Steele reviews newspaper advertisements in Toronto for 1971 and 1989, showing a 69 per cent decrease in the ads for rental units in large complexes and a fivefold increase for rental units in small complexes. An increase in ads for small complexes is also apparent in Ottawa over the same period (p. 24).

Steele concludes that CMHC's survey showing 0.3 per cent vacancy for units in buildings of six or more units in Toronto in October 1989 (that's only 3 of every 1,000 rental units vacant) does not capture the whole story: the advertisements show many more vacancies in the small buildings that were not measured. "On reasonable assumptions, the overall vacancy rate in 1989 was several times the vacancy rate in rental buildings of 6 or more units" (p. 29).

Thus the CMHC vacancy rate survey of buildings with six or more units may not be reliable either as an indicator of the number of vacant units actually available or as a measure of housing need. Further, as Steele notes, even a higher vacancy rate does not mean that the extra units available are affordable (p. 30). Second units in homes may generally be cheaper than traditional units, but new condominium units are often rented out at the high end of the market.

Meeting housing needs

Needs can be determined, but can they be met? The housing market is not homogeneous. It is segmented into a number of different and in many cases unrelated markets. Housing needs for single individuals will be satisfied in different ways and different places than for families with children. What works for high-income families is not what is needed by low-income families. If, as argued in Chapter 4, neighbourhoods and communities should be a mix of income and household sizes, then different housing needs must be satisfied in each community, and different housing markets must be appealed to.

Developers often try to find a special market niche in the community they know best and then exploit it to the exclusion of the other markets that also exist there. The developer who knows about small-scale rental buildings probably doesn't know much about the market for luxury homes.

One of the complications in meeting need is gauging the kind and location of housing desired in a particular locale. Successful developers are those who are prescient about need — as, for instance, were those developers in the early 1980s who built small and inexpensive condominium units in the downtowns of many Canadian cities and found a ready market for that product. In the mid 1990s some developers are predicting a rise in demand for small, compact units in two- and three-storey buildings in the suburbs — almost a repetition of the nineteenth-century idea of the neighbourhood containing shops and offices within easy walking distance. These developers use a much different marketing approach than do those who offer single-family homes on fifty-foot lots.

Government policy can lead rather than follow these changes, and shape tastes as well as respond to them. Cities that permit high-density condominiums are much more likely to see them built than those reluctant to grant the needed rezoning and plan-amendment applications. As governments struggled with financial problems in the early 1990s, many cities began to look favourably at the merits of new units being built within existing urban areas where new infrastructure would not be needed but where new property tax revenue could be generated. This signalled a major shift in how housing need might be met: after forty years of expansion and greenfield development, some cities were talking of pushing for "brownfield" redevelopment. Needless to say, developers who had assumed that supply would continue to be provided on greenfields found the new policies as bewildering as when city councils across Canada in the 1970s began to oppose the rezonings that permitted high-rise apartment buildings to destroy neighbourhoods.

Some initiatives to meet housing need lie not in government action, but in what property owners do. In spite of strong zoning rules to the contrary, many communities find that demand for housing is met by homeowners illegally renting out a basement apartment, thus managing to provide housing while generating income to pay the mortgage. As already noted, there may be a large number of rental units provided through such conversions.

This kind of "uncounted" accommodation can also be found in large apartment complexes. In the mid-1980s, it was thought that the real population of the 110 public housing projects managed by the Metro Toronto Housing Authority was not 100,000, as shown on the Authority's records, but closer to 125,000, as tenants provided space for friends and relatives who otherwise would have difficulty finding accommodation.

Thus housing need is not always met by government or the development industry: ordinary people often create their own informal solutions. Those solutions are not always fully reflected in studies.

The difficulty of drawing conclusions

The discussion of affordability, need and vacancy rates makes apparent the complexity and difficulty of drawing firm conclusions. With some issues, such as vacancy rates, the question arises of whether conclusions can be drawn based on the available information. With others, such as gentrification, the question is what the information actually means. With still others, the difficulty is determining the effect of a particular program or government or public action, as in assessing the effects of rent control or Multiple Urban Residential Buildings (MURBs), a subsidy scheme for apartment buildings in the 1970s. Who, for instance, benefited from the MURBs program, and what was the extent of that benefit? The answers to these questions will indicate whether the program should be re-introduced.

Thoughtful critics try to reach conclusions firm enough to be the basis for predictions about the future. This can be done by analyzing the factors impinging on a situation, but trying to sort out how much a particular factor weighs often involves assigning values that are not widely shared or understood. The clearest way that this can be done is through a mathematical equation where all the elements can be factored in, or in its visual expression, a graph. These equations and graphs are often daunting, given the complexity of the problem at hand. Fallis (Fallis and Murray 1990, p. 74) proposes the following equation to calculate the difference between market rent and rent actually charged under a rental housing program:

$$r - R = (m - M)[[1 - (1 + r) * - 30]/[1 - (1 + r) * - 50]],$$
where
r   is annual market rent
R   is annual rent paid
m   is annual market mortgage payment
M   is annual mortgage payment
r   is discount rate at which the government obtained the mortgage
* means the next figure is a factor

and the mortgage is amortized over thirty years on a building with a life of fifty years.

If correct, the equation helps to provide an understanding of the public housing program. This example has been selected because of its *simplicity*. Many economic equations pertaining to housing programs are much more complex.

One should not underestimate the difficulty involved in sorting out these issues. Since housing is a necessity; since it has such influence on our economic and social life; since it is so intertwined with taxation policies; since it affects different households in different ways; and since it often is a matter of contentious and important political values there is little that can be done to simplify them. These complexities and difficulties can be used as an excuse for poor or inappropriate programs and actions, but such excuses should not be allowed to stand: instead, the difficulties and complexities should be admitted, and the best decisions made in their light. One decision should not be considered acceptable simply because all the other decisions looked difficult.

Conclusion

There are various ways of determining housing affordability, but whatever method is used, problems of affordability loom large in

Canada, affecting at least 10 per cent of households. Projections of housing need are complicated and fraught with dubious assumptions and leaps into the unknown, but they must be done in order to plan ahead as best as possible in the hope that the population may be well housed. Not every good projection will result in a solution: programs based on good projections may prove politically unpopular, and unpopular programs or policies are simply disregarded — the case with second units in homes.

Affordability and housing need are the two bases of almost all housing policy and decision-making in Canada, in both the public and private sectors. It is with an understanding of these matters that the key questions of housing policy options and their impacts can be addressed.

Chapter 3

Building Good Homes

Fifty years ago, worries about "good housing" focused on housing conditions: plumbing and the availability of water; the state of repair; questions of overcrowding (Hannley 1993). Today, worries about good places to live focus on design and the appropriateness of the structure for those living in it.

This change in emphasis follows rising standards of living that have brought reasonable housing conditions to most Canadians — save for indigenous peoples and some families living in remote rural locations. The fact that so much housing has been built since the end of the Second World War — 80 per cent of the stock fits in this category — means that much of the housing is too new to have fallen into serious disrepair, although problems are beginning to become apparent. Other positive influences on housing repair have been the introduction by many municipalities of tough building codes governing new existing units, and programs supporting repair and renovation.

Varieties in housing forms

The twentieth century has seen a considerable rethinking of housing structures. The growth of the middle class meant greatly increased demand for private homes; with this demand came many experiments departing from the traditional styles of the "family seat" or the row house. American architect Frank Lloyd Wright designed low-lying ranch houses in the earlier years of the century. In 1910 Adolph Loos designed the Steiner House in Vienna — an elegant plain building of straight lines, flat roof and rectangular windows, with flat, undecorated stucco — a building so far before its time that it could have been built last year (Pevsner 1936, especially Chapter 7).

Housing in nineteenth-century urban Canada was a mixture of large free-standing structures and elegant (or, less frequently, plain) row housing. Where needed, parts of both kinds of structures were rented out as rooms or flats. Buildings were almost never constructed to function as apartment structures.

A strong argument can be made that Canada's contribution to housing typologies is the semi-detached house built in most Canadian cities during the first forty years of this century. It is some twenty feet wide and three or three and a half storeys high, with a hallway running along the common wall. It is immensely adaptable and can easily be broken into separate units (one per floor, or one unit on the top two floors, the other on the ground floor and basement) and then easily transformed back into a single unit. As well, the ground floor can be used for non-residential purposes, such as a retail store, office or repair shop. These useful qualities have not endeared it to builders in the last five decades, and it is now rarely built. (For American house typologies of this century, see Rowe 1991, especially Chapter 3, and Rowe 1993.)

These houses gave way to the modest bungalow shortly after the Second World War, then the larger, more spacious and stylish suburban ranch-style home, based loosely on Frank Lloyd Wright's design (McKellar 1993). The common theme for post-war houses was land and more land. James Murray and Henry Fleiss remark that there was a shared image "of a vast country of 'boundless open spaces' amply extensive to support an individual house as the ideal shelter for each and every family" and that "underlying all is the faint implication that anything other than the detached house is somehow a second class solution" (Murray and Fleiss 1970, p. 2).

Macklin Hancock, the designer of Canada's most influential suburban development, Don Mills, explained why he proposed houses on large lots:

For single family houses, lots are designed wider and less deep than is usual in most subdivisions. In the opinion of the designer, elbow room is a desirable characteristic and allows for increased spatial interests and an ability to site houses both broadside to the street and with the narrow dimension to the street. In many subdivisions, too, the rear portion of the lots is poorly maintained and a burden to the home owner. The more square lot gives insulation between houses ... Because the houses are small, open planning has been encouraged in order to increase the visual space within the units. Individual lot widths have been made an average of 60 feet in order that more space will be provided between the housing units. With more

land immediately surrounding the houses, design sitings were
directed toward a better use of this land and a closer contact
with the land. (Cited in Sewell 1993, p. 88)

Thus "elbow room" and "closer contact with the land" became important elements underlying the planning of many new houses built
in Canada in the second half of this century. Added to these elements
was the need to accommodate the automobile. Since the early 1970s,
many houses have been overwhelmed by two- and three-car garages
that hide the residential portion of the house from the street.

A major change in technology resulted in a whole new style of
housing — the high-rise apartment tower. Since the First World War,
a small number of modest walk-up apartment buildings could be
found in most Canadian cities. Then, with the availability of elevators
at the end of the Second World War, the invention of fast and
efficient high-rise construction techniques was exploited by a culture
that argued that independent apartment living was both liberating and
good. In the mid 1960s, apartments became very popular for young
baby-boomers first leaving the parental home. Since that time, high-
rise apartments have become increasingly popular places. More than
one million Canadian households now call them home (Bourne 1993,
p. 280).

Now, in the mid-1990s, a renewed interest is being shown in more
compact housing forms, particularly row housing. One example of
this interest is the GROW home, designed by faculty at the Architecture School of McGill University. It is based on the simple concept that young families rarely have enough money to afford a large,
fully finished house, and that what they need is a simple shell that
can be finished through do-it-yourself improvements as the family
finds the money for changes. While a typical semi-detached house
is about 1,400 square feet, the GROW home is 14 feet wide, has two
storeys with basement and about 1,100 square feet of floor space,
and consists of high-quality basics: walls, floors, roof, water, electricity; but no interior finishes. It provides basic good housing at a
most economical construction price (about $60,000 in 1992 dollars
plus, of course, land costs), and allows for the family to make the
house into a home when they have the time and resources. After five
decades of the market being supplied with expensive finished housing, the GROW home seems like an appropriate invention (Friedman
and Cammalleri, 1992).

Photo: Avi Friedman

Surprisingly, the idea of a modest house less than twenty feet wide lay dormant for almost fifty years, until revived by the GROW Home concept of McGill University's Affordable Homes Program. The GROW homes in this photo are in Phase I of Point-aux-Trembles, an eighty-seven unit project in the Montreal area. The houses were constructed in the late 1980s and sold for under $80,000 apiece.

Varieties of housing tenure

In the latter half of the twentieth century, variety in housing form was accompanied by variety in housing tenure. Traditionally the choices in Canada were between fee simple ownership and rental. There had been a few experiments with co-operative ownership, where owners were obligated to share the expenses of some common elements yet retained their right to sell the co-op share on the open market. Co-operative ownership, however, never became widespread. Then, in the 1970s several other varieties of tenure became available. Non-profit housing became a federal government program in 1973, ushering in two new forms of tenure: tenancy in a non-profit project, which gave no particular new rights although it implied a more responsive form of management; and membership in a non-profit co-operative, which transferred no marketable asset (non-profit co-op members had nothing to buy or sell), but which provided a direct say in management because of membership.

An entirely different form of tenure that came into force in the 1970s was condominium ownership. It permitted unfettered ownership of a unit and shared ownership of common elements in the structure, with the obligation to share in the upkeep and maintenance of common elements, often through payment of a monthly sum to the condominium corporation. In many cases condominium units were rented out, and while one management company ran the whole building, the units in fact were owned by different individuals. Such condos became the preferred option for investors in Multiple Unit Resident Buildings (MURBs), discussed in Chapter 7.

These new options in tenure permitted much more resident involvement in management policy, sometimes with distressing results. Some condo owners found they were prevented by a majority of other condo owners (or at least by a majority of those who voted) from pursuing recognized ownership ideas such as keeping pets or raising children in the condo. Court cases were brought to challenge these kinds of decisions, which invariably were interpreted as signs of the tyranny of the majority: local decision-making was seen to be sometimes small-minded.

Densities and housing form

Many people assume that "high-density" and "high-rise" are synonymous, but that is not the case. As Oscar Newman notes, "There is ... a danger in labeling density, per se, as the culprit, because many different building types and configurations can be built at the same density" (1972, p. 195).

Density is a way of measuring housing intensity on a piece of land, not housing form. It can be measured in two ways. One measure compares the number of units of housing to each acre of land: units per acre or *upa*. One acre contains about 43,000 square feet, and is roughly 200 feet by 220 feet in size. One house on one acre of land would have a density of 1 upa. The current average Canadian suburban density of seven houses on one acre of land — each house would have a lot of 60 feet by 100 feet, or 6,000 square feet — would be 7 upa. (American suburban densities are half that.) A building containing 100 apartment units on the same acre would have a density of 100 upa. Most suburban apartment buildings stand on lots that are mostly open space, and no matter how high they are their densities are rarely more than 60 upa.

The second measure of density compares the number of square feet of floor space in the buildings to the number of square feet of land in the development: coverage, or floor space index *(fsi)*. A one-storey building that goes to all edges of the lot on which it sits has a density, or coverage, or fsi, of 1x. A two-storey building that covers only half the lot also has a coverage of 1x, as does a four-storey building on one-quarter of its lot. A four-storey building that covers the entire lot is fsi 4x.

Residential density is usually measured in upa; office and commercial density in fsi. When permissible residential density is stated in fsi, it is in the developer's interest to put as many residential units in the space as possible, which is achieved by making those units as small as possible. Thus the fsi measure for housing often encourages smaller units to be built. If the measure is upa, then there is no limiting factor on the size of the apartments, and the developer can make units as commodious as the market will support. Some cities have found that in the downtown core it is advisable to impose restrictions using both measures: restricting upa alone might encourage developers to build exceptionally large luxury units, resulting in buildings much larger than originally contemplated by the planners. To control this, the upa density is often given an fsi cap.

Knowing the density tells nothing of the building form. Some architects think that municipalities would be much better off if they set design guidelines — such as height limits — and forgot about density as a planning control. Design controls are much easier to understand than the more abstract concept of density, and thus provide residents much more predictability about what actually could get built within zoning.

Moderately dense communities can easily be built in three- or four-storey structures, without resorting to a high-rise form. Houses with a lot size of 20 feet by 100 feet can be built at about 20 upa, and narrower houses could have a density even higher. In the Fairview Slopes neighbourhood of Vancouver, the density permitted is 1.5 fsi, permitting 60 or 70 units per acre, with height limits on new structures between 25 and 35 feet. The resulting housing is compact, attractive and apparently financially successful.

Habitat, designed by Moshe Safdie and built in Montreal in 1967, is often cited as a wonderful example of a medium-density housing project, but others quarrel with this judgement of success, and of course the very high cost of construction has prevented repetition of this experiment. Oscar Newman notes: "The primary criterion that

Photo: CMHC

Habitat, designed by Moshe Safdie, was built in Montreal for Expo 1967.
It is a dramatic form, but the density of twenty units per acre is no greater,
and probably lower, than that of the townhouses shown in Chapter 1,
although Habitat was considerably more expensive to build and operate.

this housing was made to satisfy by its architect was visual excite-
ment. Built at a density of twenty units to the acre, the equivalent of
row housing, it cost over ten times as much to build" (Newman 1981,
p. 306).

Municipal and other non-profit companies have provided excellent examples of high-density low-rise, usually in the form of six-
and seven-storey structures. Many alternatives to the high-rise tower
are available.

It is clear that many choices of housing form exist, without requiring that high-rise buildings be constructed. In many cases, the high-
rise is a choice of style, not a choice of economics.

There is no such thing as a general optimum residential density,
as planner Kevin Lynch points out. "At any level of density there are
dull and meaningless places as well as intriguing and meaningful
ones" (Lynch 1984, p. 263).

What is good housing?

The design of housing is critical to its ability to house people well. Architecture critic Ada Louise Huxtable notes, "A great deal of irreparable damage can be done to the complex human psyche, and to patterns of human behavior, by bad building" (cited in SITE 1982, p. 39).

But what is good housing? So many people assume that single-family housing is the optimum housing for families with children that it is difficult to persuade them even to consider other options. However, given that many families are not able to afford single-family houses, what should be provided for them?

Architect James Murray proposed the following starting point for answering questions about good housing form:

> Multi-storey buildings are not a good environment for raising a young family, so we must aim at finding "walk-up" designs at densities close to those achieved by vertical buildings ... The design principles for livability at high density appear to be:
>
> * expression of the identity of each family unit
> * retention of human scale in the environment of large scale housing
> * provision of some private outdoor space for each family. (Murray and Fleiss 1970, p. 3)

To these elements one might wish to add other important characteristics: affordability; appropriate light and adequate air, particularly where the climate is warm; visual and acoustic privacy; ease of access between the home and other destinations such as work and shopping; good neighbours. One might also wish to include the ability to work at home — both the space to do so and the necessary equipment. We quickly enter into a whole host of issues that go beyond the physical confines of a particular place to live.

Is a single-family house an appropriate place to live if a family member relies on a wheelchair to get around? Wouldn't an apartment building with elevators and no barriers posed by stairs be more appropriate? Is a community where households are all the same kind and age — a retirement home or a senior citizen building fits this definition — a good place to live, whatever the physical form of its housing? Is an isolated house with poor transit connections a better home than a small apartment with good transit opportunities? Is a small dwelling better for family cohesion than a large one?

Housing should be designed so that it is safe — that is, so one can move in and around it without fear of attack from others. As noted in Chapter 8, many housing projects built during the past fifty years fail this basic test. Designing housing that enhances social intercourse and permits neighbourly relations between individuals, whether they know each other or not, is a matter of considerable importance, and should not be taken for granted.

Given the great variety of factors that must be taken into account in assessing the appropriateness of housing, perhaps the best conclusion one can come to is that bad housing is housing that a family thinks is inappropriate for its needs. Good housing is housing that a family feels comfortable in, given all the factors at play. Thus the key to good housing is choice: enough choice should be available for families to suit their own needs, and if their housing is inappropriate, then to be able to find something better. Bad housing is housing that families are forced to live in because, for whatever reason, they are unable to leave. Bad housing is the housing that is vacant when everyone has choices.

Governments wishing to provide good housing for all families should ensure that a reasonable variety of choices is available for all families.

High-rise apartment towers

With the choice between traditional house forms and high-rise buildings comes the question: is one better than the other to live in? James Murray asked that question in 1962, just as the high-rise boom took off:

> What are the relevant advantages and disadvantages for individual and family life inherent in different forms of housing, for example between high-rise buildings which release ground space, and horizontal multiple units which cover more of the site but provide private gardens for a majority of units? What is the nature of privacy and does the concept of privacy vary between various social and economic groups? This privacy might be visual, acoustic, proprietary or psychological in derivation. What is the threshold of tolerance for individual interference in the interest of community objectives? Is there a density of families upon a site at which physical and social

deterioration sets in — if so, is this density a constant for all conditions? (Murray 1962, pp. 9-10)

The answers have proven to be contentious.

The invention of the elevator toward the end of the nineteenth century led quickly to the development of high buildings where office work was done (Huxtable 1984). But it was not until after the First World War that architects began to think of high-rise buildings as places to live. In the 1920s Walter Gropius in Germany and Le Corbusier in Paris both imagined high-rise residences, the latter suggesting cities of several hundred thousand living in a single structure sitting on stilts in a field (Sewell 1993). The repetitious nature of apartment units in towers fit well with Le Corbusier's vision of housing, which he referred to as "machines for living."

Both men were extremely influential in the architectural community, and through his Bauhaus School, Gropius trained the architects who in the 1950s designed the largest buildings in New York and other American cities. Tom Wolfe refers to Gropius as the Silver Prince and denigrates and castigates both his product and style.

Sometimes the towers are of steel, concrete, and glass; sometimes of glass, steel, and small glazed white or beige bricks. Always the ceilings are low, often under eight feet, the hallways are narrow, the rooms are narrow, even when they're long, the bedrooms are small (Le Corbusier was always in favour of that), the walls are thin, the doorways and windows have no casings, the joints have no moldings, the walls have no baseboards, and the windows don't open, although small vents or jalousies may be provided. The construction is invariably cheap in the pejorative as well as the literal sense. That builders could present these boxes in the 1950s, without a twitch of the nostril, as luxury, and that well-educated men and women could accept them, without a blink, as luxury — here is the objective testimony, from those too dim for irony, to the aesthetic sway of the compound aesthetic, of the Silver Prince and his colonial legions, in America following the Second World War. (Wolfe 1981, pp. 70-71)

What astounded Wolfe was the easy manner in which these structures found acceptance among a wide public, particularly when they satisfied none of his basic preconditions for good housing.

So what if you were living in a building that looked like a factory and felt like a factory, and paying top dollar for it? Every modern building of quality looked like a factory. That was *the look of today*. (p. 72, italics in the original)

High-rises became the style, and they were built everywhere. Between 1957 and 1984, most of the new housing constructed in the older parts of Canadian cities was in the high-rise form. By 1990, for example, more than 600 high-rise apartment towers had been built in the City of Toronto alone, providing one-third of the total residential units in the city (Toronto 1986). And Toronto wasn't alone: there is no sizable city in Canada where the number of high-rise residential towers is small enough to count easily. Apartment towers are also found in many new suburban developments.

New construction techniques made building high-rises economical. The "flying form" (developed by Tridel Construction in Toronto) employed a pre-engineered forming system that could be moved quickly from floor to floor, allowing for speedy concrete pouring. The introduction of the climbing crane from Europe allowed prefabrication of some construction elements and easy movement of workers around the site (McKellar 1993, p. 149).

Some argue the necessity of high-rises because of the cost of land and the urge for higher densities. The image, says Murray disparagingly, "is that of the tall apartment house cramped in a congested urban scene as the inevitable answer to high land values and resultant high densities" (Murray and Fleiss 1970, p. 2). But moderate-density housing need not be built in a high-rise form, and most high-rises are not high density. Certainly, in places like Vancouver's West End or Toronto's St. Jamestown, high-rise buildings have created high-density communities, but most high-rises are built simply as a matter of style.

Do high-rise apartments provide good housing? The high-rise tower has many detractors, perhaps the most vociferous of which is Christopher Alexander:

There is abundant evidence to show that high buildings make people crazy.

High buildings have no genuine advantages, except in speculative gains for banks and land owners. They are not cheaper, they do not help create open space, they destroy the townscape,

Photo: City of Vancouver

Fairview Slopes is the successful outcome of planning policies adopted by the City of Vancouver in the mid-1970s to encourage high-density low-rise housing. Densities, as measured by person or unit per acre, are more than three times greater than Habitat, although the form is much more modest.

they destroy social life, they promote crime, they make life difficult for children, they are expensive to maintain, they wreck the open spaces near them, and they damage light and air and view. But quite apart from all this, which shows they aren't very sensible, empirical evidence shows that they can actually damage people's minds and feelings. (Alexander et al. 1977, p. 115)

These strong statements are then followed by the citation of a number of supporting studies. Alexander urges a height limit for residential accommodation:

In any urban area, no matter how dense, keep the majority of buildings four stories high or less. It is possible that certain buildings should exceed this limit, but they should never be buildings for human habitation. (p. 119)

Some argue that tall residential buildings are inefficient. Alice Coleman, the English housing critic, cites studies that apartment buildings are more expensive to build than houses and certainly more expensive to manage. She concludes:

> Up to 18 per cent of their floor space is taken up in common parts [such as hallways, lobbies and elevator shafts] that would be unnecessary for houses. This would make room for one extra dwelling in every four or five. Even allowing for normal garden space instead of shared grounds, a decision to build houses instead of [apartment buildings] could have resulted in 10 per cent more dwellings within the confines of the existing [housing] estates. (Coleman 1985, p. 120)

Others have noted that some features of high-rise buildings are constructed for no useful reason. The balcony fits in this category. With a standard depth of four feet, it is too narrow to use for almost anything but outdoor storage. Alexander notes, "Balconies and porches which are less than six feet deep are hardly ever used" (p. 782), but almost no apartment developers bend their plans to accommodate actual use of this amenity.

Coleman goes further in castigating the whole movement to house people in apartment blocks, particularly those that are part of council estates in London:

> Our vast housing-problems machine has committed one blunder after another in the name of social betterment. The betterment is often hard to find, especially if compared to what might have been, but the malaise and misery and tragedy are writ large as soon as one opens one's eyes to the facts. The brave new Utopia is essentially a device for treating people like children, first by denying them the right to choose their own kind of housing, and then by choosing for them disastrous designs that create a needless sense of social failure. (p. 184)

Some critics argue that high-rise buildings are not good places to house younger children. In 1972, Oscar Newman made one of the earliest definitive statements on this point in his renowned study of public housing, *Defensible Space*:

The following general guidelines seem to emerge: for low income families with children — particularly those on welfare or
suffering pathological disorder — the high-rise building is to
be strictly avoided. Instead, these families should be housed in
walk-up buildings no higher than three stories. Entries and
vertical and horizontal circulation corridors should be designed
so that as few families as possible share a common lobby. This
puts a density limit of about fifty units per acre on a housing
project composed solely of this housing type. (p. 193)

There is only a small amount of evidence on the effect of high-rise
living on children. One review notes that although "the evidence that
this housing form has detrimental effects on kids is inconclusive,"
parents believe otherwise (Johnson et al. 1993, p. 6). Studies show a
higher incidence of behavioural disturbance in high-rises and more
difficult play arrangements. It was estimated that in the late 1980s 6
per cent of the young people in Ontario, or 150,000 kids, lived in
apartment buildings of five or more storeys (Barnhorst and Johnson
1991, p. 187), which gives some sense of the scope of the problem.

While these criticisms have had no effect in halting the approval
or construction of apartment buildings, they did lead some to search
for residential forms that present alternatives to both the single family house and the high-rise building.

Can anything be said in favour of the high-rise apartment building? With its elevators and level floors, it provides good accommodation for the disabled; depending on location, it can provide
excellent views. But the high-rise apartment building seems to raise
more questions than answers and should be approached with considerable scepticism as the obvious answer to housing problems.

Repair, maintenance and conversions

Issues of repair and maintenance are significant for housing. Houses
are generally small enough and simple enough to be easily repaired,
although homeowners can recount marvellous renovation disaster
stories. Apartment buildings, both small and large, pose many more
problems.

The need for house repair is often a result of original construction
problems. Changes in the nature of the home construction industry
have aggravated these problems. At the end of the Second World
War, most new houses in Canada were built by small firms of fewer

than fifteen employees, building ten or twelve houses a year. Carver noted in 1948:

> The small speculative builder undertakes the erection of only a few houses at a time, saving the cost of managerial overhead and office space and protecting himself from market uncertainties by keeping his output in line with the immediate demand of prospective purchasers. (Carver 1948, p. 63)

Builders often knew whom they were building for, and they knew that next year's buyers would come on the recommendations of families they had already satisfied.

Carver thought that this kind of small-scale building would never produce the number of housing units Canada needed, and he argued for large-scale developments undertaken by large-scale developers building enough houses to achieve an economy of scale. The success of Don Mills in the mid-1950s pushed Carver's recommendation to the fore, and large house-building companies, which built hundreds of homes a year in a given locale, began to emerge. The emergence of large companies meant the disappearance of the personal relationship between builder and buyer. Further, the quickly escalating land prices meant that house builders were less able to make money on the land, and turned more and more to cheaper construction methods to survive in the market.

The crunch between declining new house quality and buyer expectations occurred in the early 1970s. Buyers complained mightily about the shoddy quality of the homes they had purchased — the drywall would fall off, or the trim wasn't proper, or insulation was missing, or the plumbing wasn't done right. They demanded home warranty programs that would protect buyers of new homes from faulty or unfinished houses.

Ontario is the only province with a mandatory warranty program, which it established in 1976. Home builders must register and pay a fee equal to $2 for every $1,000 of building value. The warranty covers defects in workmanship and/or materials for one year after purchase; water penetration and electrical, plumbing and heating systems for two years; and major structural defects for five years. Claims during the first year are made directly to the builder, or if the builder has gone out of business, to the program. After the first year, all claims are made to the program. By the end of 1992, the Ontario Home Warranty program had paid out $100 million for claims resulting from "uneven administration of the Ontario Building Code and poor fulfilment of approval and inspection mandates by municipalities," in the words of program's director, Barry Rose (Rose 1993), as well as from poor workmanship, builder error and defects in materials.

Governments have been more willing to establish programs to help homeowners with repair. Federal home repair loans were made available as early as the 1930s under the Home Improvement Loans Guarantee Act (Patterson 1993, p. 321). The current federal program is known as the Residential Rehabilitation and Assistance Program (RRAP). It provided assistance to more than 300,000 units from its introduction in 1973 until 1985 (Patterson 1993, p. 333), mostly in rural areas (Skaburskis 1993, p. 181).

The construction of high-rise apartment buildings is carefully monitored by municipal building officials; these buildings are generally free of structural or system defects. There are fears, however, that serious problems will eventually emerge because of the methods of construction used.

A comprehensive study has been undertaken of the state of repair of high-rise apartment buildings in the City of Toronto (Toronto 1986; 1992). The structures studied were built twenty-five to thirty years ago of poured reinforced concrete and brick non-load-bearing curtain walls. They are still fairly young, as buildings go, but still the study worried about defects becoming dangerous in the following areas:

- weather penetration through roof and walls
- structural integrity: missing expansion joints, balcony disintegration
- building systems: boiler failure, inadequate electrical supply; galvanized pipe replacement, ventilation controls
- parking structures: slab disintegration, missing waterproof membranes, leaking subgrade walls
- occupant safety: firemen's elevators, smoke detectors, fire alarm systems
- movement systems: elevator vandalism
- equipment and fittings: countertop replacement, cupboard replacement, retiling bathrooms.

Often, fixing one problem entails dealing with another, so it is not reasonable to attempt to do these repairs one at a time. The cost of rehabilitation to deal with these concerns is large — estimated at $7,000 to $15,000 per unit in 1992 dollars. The rent increases necessary to fund this amount would be 10 to 15 per cent per year for buildings in average condition. Rent controls prevent such increases, and Ontario landlords would be reluctant to invest their own money in this way. But even without rent controls, this increase is far more than the market can bear; tenants, most of whom have low to moderate income, would find it very difficult to manage. With or without rent controls the investment would be sizable, and if a building is feared to be crumbling, the investment might not been seen as a prudent one to make.

Since a sizable portion of the housing stock of any large city is in high-rise buildings, no city can afford to lose this stock. How can rehabilitation be ensured so that the housing becomes safe in the long run?

One suggestion is that controls similar to those imposed through the non-profit housing program should be used: high-rise landlords should be required to pay annually a sum equal to a specified percentage of building value into a reserve fund. This fund could be administered privately, subject to audit, or it could be administered by the province and disbursed to effect these larger structural repairs. While this may generate adequate funds to deal with repair in the long run, it will not be of much help in the first twenty years of the program.

A second proposal is for a government program to be established to help tenant-controlled non-profit or co-operative companies purchase these buildings, and then use imaginative mortgage arrangements, such as the graduated payment mortgage, to repair them. Supporters of this proposal argue that it can be done with government mortgage guarantees of the purchase price and the funds needed for repair, but without direct subsidy of any kind (TNPRC 1993).

Unless some general strategy is agreed to before the first high-rise apartment buildings are closed for safety reasons, one can expect a policy response to be made on the fly, as individual landlords try to cut deals on the future of their buildings.

The impending spate of conversions of high-rise buildings from office use to residential will intensify these questions of building repair. Across North America in the past twenty years, the amount of new office space built was staggeringly high, doubling, tripling and quadrupling the amount of office space available. As every city has since learned, the market has been unable to absorb all of this space, and vacancy rates of 15 to 20 per cent are becoming the norm in downtown cores. These high vacancy rates have meant that entrepreneurs have looked for alternative uses for second-class office space — and residential use looks attractive.

The first substantial conversion application made in Canada was for the B.C. Hydro building in Vancouver in 1993. This twenty-one storey structure was built 1957, using a central service core of reinforced concrete, floors cantilevered out, with a skin of glass and steel panels in an aluminum grid as a curtain wall. The floor plate, the usable area on each floor, is considered today too small for office uses, and the building now stands vacant; hence the application to convert it to 242 condominium units. The conversion application has been approved by Vancouver authorities, and when the units were offered for sale as condominiums, they were snapped up in two days.

Similar kinds of conversion applications are now being made in other cities. One possibility is that approvals be granted subject to the proviso that structural rehabilitation matters be addressed in a straightforward way now, to guarantee high states of repair for the next fifty years. Without such a condition, high-rise residential conversions may quickly spiral into blighted, unlivable projects.

Making a unit a home

Many would like the place where they live to feel like "home." As Witold Rybczynski notes in his thoughtful and provocative book, *Home, A Short History of an Idea*, home is a place expected to provide intimacy and privacy, comfort and ease. Too often the opportunities for these amenities are obscured by poor or inappropriate design, where style intrudes on comfort. He advocates "a return to furniture that is accommodating and comfortable; not chairs that make an artistic statement, but chairs that are a pleasure to sit in" (pp. 221-22).

A place feels like home because of the resident's feeling that he or she is in control of it. This might relate to the resident's status or tenure, or how the resident is treated by whoever is in charge. Christopher Alexander argues that it is next to impossible to feel at home in rental premises, and suggests a course of action:

Do everything possible to make the traditional forms of rental impossible, indeed, illegal. Give every household its own home, with space enough for a garden. Keep the emphasis in the definition of ownership on control, not on financial ownership.

Photo: City of Vancouver Archives

The B.C. Hydro building in Vancouver is one of the first large office towers to be converted to residential uses. Many expect such conversions to become more common, as it is recognized that the glut of office space in many cities will never be taken up with office uses.

Indeed, where it is possible to construct forms of ownership which give people control over their houses and gardens, but make financial speculation impossible, choose these forms above all others. In all cases give people the legal power, and the physical opportunity to modify and repair their own places. Pay attention to this rule especially in the case of high density

apartments: build the apartments in such a way that every
individual apartment has a garden, or a terrace where vegeta-
bles will grow, and that even in this situation, each family can
build, and change, and add on to their house as they wish.
(Alexander et al. 1977, pp. 395-96)

People cannot be genuinely comfortable and healthy in a home
which is not theirs. All forms of rental — whether from private
landlords or public housing agencies — work against the natural processes which allow people to form stable, self-healing
communities. (p. 77)

The link Alexander makes between housing form (particularly the
presence of a small garden) and good housing is as intriguing as his
proposals about control being more important than ownership.

The non-profit co-operative is one example of a tenure alternative
to ownership that is not simply a landlord–tenant relationship, and it
might satisfy Alexander since it does not allow speculative profits.
But how should these characteristics be secured in private rental
housing, where the relationship between the tenant and the landlord
is more adversarial? Most provinces have enacted security of tenure
legislation, which states that apart from non-performance of lease
terms, good tenants can be evicted only if the owner is personally
moving into the unit. Even this provision, however, gives no protection to many tenants who have made the unit into their home. This
is one of the unanswered questions of private rental housing.

A key question that arises in many forms of tenure is the idea of
community, to which we turn in the next chapter.

Conclusion

Housing forms have changed dramatically during this century, sometimes for the better and sometimes for the worse. However, it is not
possible to attempt to define the characteristics of "good housing"
apart from immediate questions of repair and safety, since the factors
involved are so numerous and often relate more to locational characteristics than to physical constraints. High-rise apartment towers
have not proved to be the solution hoped for, and indeed now pose
a worrisome repair problem for their owners, tenants and the community at large. Good housing is housing that a family feels comfortable in, given all the factors at play. Bad housing is housing that
is vacant when everyone has choices.

Chapter 4

Designing Good Neighbourhoods

For most of this century common wisdom has been that the less dense the housing, and the more it is protected from other uses, the better will be the neighbourhood. In reaction to the sometimes chaotic situations in nineteenth-century European cities, a number of new visions emerged, of which the Garden City vision has been the most pervasive. The Garden City idea proposed areas of discrete single uses intermingled with gardens and parks as a desirable aim. The profession of planning was largely invented to achieve that objective. Once the Depression of the 1930s and the Second World War were over, this planning approach flowered with very visible results: house lots became larger; "slums" were cleared away and replaced with housing schemes set in fields of grass; precincts of the city were devoted to one use, be it houses, apartments, retailing, offices or industry; and urban densities fell greatly (Sewell 1993; Hodge 1986).

The difference in the kind of neighbourhoods this change produced is astounding. Communities built in Canada before the Second World War generally are laced with straight streets intersecting each other at right angles — a grid road system. Retail shops are found on arterial streets in residential areas. No house is more than a block or two from a corner store and other local services, and public transit is equally close at hand. Many of these neighbourhoods are still as they were fifty years ago, mixing houses (many subdivided into two or more units), small walk-up apartments, restaurants, hardware stores and other shops, churches, social agencies, small factories and workshops, and various other uses. Some of these neighbourhoods have seen much renovation and rising house prices, while others have been damaged by redevelopment, which brought large apartment towers, public housing or other urban renewal.

Neighbourhoods built since the Second World War generally consist of vast tracts of houses on large lots set on winding streets with wide boulevards. Most homes are occupied by only one household, and often that household consists of two parents who have seen their children leave to establish their own families and homes. The winding streets mean that transit is relegated to the main arterials, a considerable walk from most homes, and the preferred method of transportation is the automobile. High-rise apartment towers are bunched together in specific locations, usually at the intersection of arterial roads. Commercial uses are restricted to large shopping complexes, spaced every four or five miles; industrial uses are confined to industrial districts.

Population densities in the post–Second World War communities are substantially less than in pre–Second World War communities, by a ratio of two or three or more to one. In the 1960s, densities might be 8,000 residents per square kilometre in the city core and 2,500 in the new suburbs. As the 1960s moved into the seventies and eighties, core densities fell as households became smaller; suburban household size modified only slightly, and the ratios moved closer to two to one. As suburban households age and their children move out, that ratio is again moving up, toward three to one.

A study of mid-sized Ontario cities such as London, Windsor, Kingston and Kitchener showed that just as the suburban explosion was getting under way in the 1950s, the average density of the developed urban area was 6,500 persons per square kilometre. By the mid 1980s, it had fallen to 3,200 persons per square kilometre. Each square kilometre of land occupied by the city was used half as intensely as thirty years earlier (Commission on Planning 1993). Populations had thinned out and Canada had become a predominantly suburban society (Bourne 1993, p. 274).

There are differences in densities between cities as well as within cities. Table 4.1 compares densities in the city cores — that is, in the part of the city built before 1945. Population densities in post-1952 parts of these cities are much less: in Montreal, 1,300 persons per square kilometre; in Toronto, 1,200. The remainder are all below 1,000; indeed, most are below 500 persons per kilometre.

Given these differences between and within cities, what is a good neighbourhood to live in? Are the newer neighbourhoods better than older ones? What does "better" mean? Just as some forms of housing are much more amenable to human behaviour than others, it would not be unreasonable to think that different kinds of neighbourhoods

Table 4.1	
Population densities in city cores, per square kilometre	
Toronto	6,500
Montreal	5,800
Vancouver	4,100
Victoria	3,800
Ottawa	2,900
Hamilton	2,600
Quebec City	1,900
London	1,800
Regina	1,600
Windsor	1,600
Halifax	1,400
Saskatoon	1,300
Sherbrooke	1,300
St. Catharines	1,300
Kitchener	1,200
Winnipeg	1,100
Calgary	1,000
Edmonton	900
Source: CUI 1993.	

have different effects on their residents. Ada Louise Huxtable noted: "You can create desolate wastelands of the spirit as well as of the environment. You can scar people as well as land" (cited in SITE 1982, p. 39).

Addressing the question of what makes a "good" neighbourhood raises some of the most contentious issues of contemporary values and exposes our cultural biases. But this question must be addressed, given its importance to creating good housing.

Stable neighbourhoods

The idea of the neighbourhood as the building block of good communities was first proposed in 1929 by Clarence Stein and Henry Wright, who were creating a regional plan for New York City. Many since have suggested that in large cities residents can find their identity only in the neighbourhood (Sewell 1993, pp. 40, 84). In a changing world, the home and the neighbourhood may be the only stable elements a family has.

One belief that seems to have gained wide acceptance is that neighbourhoods should be stable and not subject to change. Almost every municipal planning document in the country is based on this assumption. For example, the draft plan being prepared for the City of North York reads:

> Many of the City's residential areas function as stable residential neighbourhoods. Major changes in the amount and type of housing in these neighbourhoods is not desired or necessary. Accordingly, these areas should not be the sites of major redevelopment proposals. Rather, only minor changes, that serve to enhance the quality of these areas as stable residential neighbourhoods, should be permitted. The proposed housing policy is therefore based on the idea that stable residential neighbourhoods should be identified and protected from unwanted change. (North York 1993, p. 1)

The proposal goes on to note that "change will be directed to specific areas of the City where it is needed and away from stable residential neighbourhoods."

The strongest protection to "stable" neighbourhoods is zoning, the tool that allows a municipal council to determine which uses and densities are permitted and which are not. Zoning controls have been widely used in North America only for about fifty years. However, examples of the use of zoning powers can be found as early as 1904 when Ontario municipalities were given the right to control the location and construction of stores, laundries, butcher shops and factories (Moore 1979, p. 317). In 1924, Kitchener became the first city in the country to have a comprehensive zoning bylaw, but it was not until 1954, for instance, that Toronto's first comprehensive zoning bylaw was enacted (Hodge 1986, p. 222).

Thus zoning is a relatively new concept in city planning. Gerald Hodge notes that "zoning was variously justified in its early days in securing proper sanitary conditions or protecting land values, both of which aims had connection to the law of nuisance" (Hodge 1986, pp. 111-12). Walter Van Nus comments on "the tendency to use zoning to confirm the status quo" (Van Nus 1979, p. 236), and others talk about how zoning "concentrates mainly on the fixity of land values by preventing changes in the established usages within an area" (Bossons 1993, p. 114).

Toronto's Lawrence Park community, which was built just before the First World War, provides an example of how zoning has been used to maintain the status quo. In 1929 residents asked for zoning so "that the residential character of the Park should be preserved and the value of their property should not be depreciated or destroyed by ... semi-detached houses, duplex houses, apartments, stores" (Moore 1979, p. 323).

Now, at the end of the century, almost all residential areas in the country are covered by very tight zoning bylaws, which prevent virtually every use except whatever is existing and proscribe any change in the size of existing structures. In single-family residential neighbourhoods, second units are almost never permitted; nor is keeping lodgers or renting to roomers, or having a home business (although long-standing exceptions are often made for doctors, who once practised out of their homes). One case went all the way to the Supreme Court of Canada before a decision was made that five friends who wanted to share a house could not be prevented from doing so by a zoning bylaw restricting residential uses to a "single family" (*Bell v. the Queen*).

That residential uses would be restricted to single family, as is dictated by zoning bylaws in so many parts of Canadian cities, is a substantial change from traditional living arrangements. For many hundreds of years, families extended themselves to include relations and half-relations or friends, rooms or floors were rented out, and work was often done in the home. "Single-family" use as defined in zoning bylaws is but a small slice of the variety of successful living arrangements: it excludes the elderly, parts of families living together, and single individuals living together for convenience — be they people who share a common characteristic such as the disabled, or those who share an economic interest such as roomers. The potential and actual variety of residential households is considerable, and it seems presumptuous that a municipal zoning code should attempt to impose rules to order the ways in which people live.

Many municipalities have taken the idea of a stable residential neighbourhood so seriously that a whole code has been erected to control what buildings are allowed. Permissible dwellings are prescribed in terms of size of lot, building set-back from lot lines and floor area. Any attempt to build a smaller house, say on a lot with a twenty-foot frontage in a neighbourhood where most lots are thirty, forty, fifty or more feet wide, would require a rezoning. Any attempt to build a house with two separate units, or a building for families or individuals with lower incomes, would involve a rezoning. Planning processes can be byzantine and time consuming enough to prevent potential applicants from establishing such a use in a "stable residential neighbourhood." Zoning controls are usually effective at not allowing into the community anyone who wishes to live in a less costly home.

The monotonizing effects of zoning for single-family neighbourhoods are often augmented by development standards — that is, "technical" standards applied by staff to any development proposal. Some development standards applied in many communities are minimum lot frontages of thirty or forty feet, effectively excluding the building of modest houses such as the GROW home; minimum set-back requirements, often twenty feet from the front lot-line, requiring very large lots; minimum parking standards, such as two parking spaces per unit, whether or not residents can be expected to afford automobiles, creating an extra expense; minimum road widths, requiring unnecessarily wide roads, which add to the cost of the housing; boulevards between the road and the sidewalk; turning radii on cul-de-sacs to suit the longest fire truck in the city's fleet, creating a vast unneeded sea of asphalt, with unfortunate environmental effects; separate trenches for water and sewage service, adding considerably to expenses; attaching roof leaders to storm drains, which has a deleterious impact on the local water table. The list goes on. Development standards add unnecessarily to costs (they ensure that the housing built is never as economical as possible) and often have a perverse impact on the natural environment. The need for these standards is debatable, but because they are lodged at the staff level, as though they somehow encode professionally developed expertise which may not be questioned by mere amateurs, the bases on which they are established are rarely challenged. The effect of these standards is to reinforce zoning bylaws that maintain stable neighbourhoods.

The critics of the stable neighbourhood idea

The very precise and prescriptive zoning controls used by most municipalities may be criticized from two points of view: first, that they produce neighbourhoods that are exclusionary; and, second, that these neighbourhoods are homogeneous and boring. These arguments are most often made against zoning that protects low-density residential neighbourhoods from change. In fact, it is often difficult to separate criticism of zoning and criticism of suburban communities.

Photo: City of Toronto Archives

Not all pre-suburban neighbourhoods were without fault. This picture of Prices Lane in Toronto, early in the twentieth century, shows a relatively compact neighbourhood based on a street system with mixed uses, but is it really worth replicating?

The most powerful evidence in support of these critics is summarized by Laura Johnson, who reviewed literature on the experience of children in stable suburban residential communities. She concludes: "In fact, there is some evidence that in suburbs, characterized by lower density, young people's interactions with peers are less frequent, less spontaneous, with visits revolving less frequently around common interests. In short, high neighbourhood density may favour friendliness, spontaneous play activity, and contribute to a field of opportunity for children's interaction with age peers" (Johnson et al. 1993, p. 11). Albert Rose believes that integrated neighbourhoods are also more efficient in terms of public spending on social programs (Rose 1980, pp. 251-52).

Edmund Fowler analyzes the social implications of low-density suburban communities and comes to similar conclusions. He says that they discourage neighbourly contact; they allow for more vandalism and crime; they are costly in the provision of public services; they are bad for children; and on a private basis they are expensive. Fowler criticizes the suburb as "killing us with its pollution, cutting us off from meaningful contact with neighbours and destroying authentic politics, preventing our children from developing a sense of responsibility, turning our public spaces into fearsome battle zones where no one fears to venture" (Fowler 1992, p. 176).

The noted urban commentator Jane Jacobs states, after reviewing experiences in a number of American cities, that "the greatest flaw in city zoning is that it permits monotony" (Jacobs 1961, p. 237). She argues that good living environments need two things stable residential neighbourhoods lack — diversity and concentration.

> Flourishing city diversity, of the kind that is catalyzed by the combination of mixed primary uses, frequent streets, mixture of building ages and overheads, and dense concentration of users, does not carry with it the disadvantages of diversity conventionally assumed by planning pseudoscience (Jacobs 1961, p. 223).

> Dense concentrations of people are one of the necessary conditions for flourishing city diversity. And it follows that in districts where people live, this means there must be dense concentrations of their dwellings on the land preempted for dwellings. (p. 205)

Planners Ken Greenberg and Frank Lewinberg note other benefits, while putting the change in neighbourhoods in perspective:

> Before the spread of the automobile in North American cities, the fabric of urban areas tended to be very finely mixed, comprised of uses of all kinds in close proximity to one another. The automobile has opened up vast new areas for urbanization, allowing people to live much further from their place of work. Thus were born the first low density auto-oriented suburbs...
>
> In the auto age, the separation of land uses became an obsession with urban planners, transportation planners, builders, and residents alike, to the point where zoning even prohibited corner stores from residential areas. As the environmental consequences of this pattern of urban living are being recognized (such as air pollution and global warming), and as the quality of life implications become clear (we spend more and more of our valuable time commuting ever longer distances to work), it is valid to question the underlying rationale for the separation of uses.

A closer mixing of different uses within reurbanisation areas has many important benefits ... A mix of uses, on main streets and arterials, say, also promotes the vitality of an area, and improves safety by having more activity at all times of the day or night, and more "eyes on the street". It also strengthens a sense of local community, by providing local opportunities for residents to work, shop, or take time off in their own neighbourhood. Employment and residential uses together can better support local businesses, increasing the diversity of services available. (Berridge et al. 1991, pp. 21-22)

David Hulchanski thinks zoning for stable neighbourhoods is more insidious in its intent. He sees it as an attempt to exclude the disadvantaged from certain areas of the city:

While present-day zoning is not based explicitly on race, ethnicity, gender or disability, the effect of exclusionary zoning and planning practises is to violate human rights. The courts have ruled that discrimination occurs even where there is no intent to discriminate; that even an apparently neutral policy can have an "adverse effect on" or can "constructively discriminate against" disadvantaged groups. Restrictions imposed on social housing, accessory apartments and special needs housing are equally discriminatory. It is this kind of housing that disadvantaged groups rely on most. Excluding or limiting any of these housing types "constructively" discriminates against those dependent upon it. (Hulchanski 1993a)

What must be remembered is that zoning by its essence is a negative tool. It cannot be proactive, but only preventive. It cannot be made into the inclusive instrument that Hulchanski seems to favour. The American urban critic Oscar Newman suggests that the alternative is for governments to adopt programs that ensure diverse integrated neighbourhoods, even if that means paying middle-income families to live in otherwise poor neighbourhoods (Newman 1981, pp. 23-25). A less costly alternative might be to ensure that zoning does not prohibit the coexistence of various kinds of housing and related uses (such as retail), or to ensure that its definition of permitted residential uses is very broad.

In spite of its popularity, the "stable residential neighbourhood" may not be a good place to call home. Fowler thinks such neighbourhoods have very substantial shortcomings. Some changes to the model could produce real benefits.

The planning process

New neighbourhoods don't come into existence on their own; they are planned. The plans involve permissions and restraints decided on by the municipal council: within these controls the new neighbourhood is built.

Planning became a strong municipal function only in the latter third of this century: before then, many individual initiatives shaped by municipal decisions about services such as sewage and transit, combined to determine the shape of the city. Current planning wisdom calls for the preparation of plans for existing neighbourhoods to control whatever change might be proposed. Rarely do these plans go beyond describing the existing situation, allowing little physical change without substantial amendments — which take considerable time. Few plans look to the future, or describe what might or should happen. Usually plans assume that no change should be permitted without careful scrutiny: accordingly, they are helpful to neither developers nor community residents.

Thus, by its very nature, planning as it is practised enforces the status quo and makes change difficult. Stable residential neighbourhoods are well protected by this process.

The following planning tools are often employed by municipalities in Canada:

General plan: Many municipalities have a general plan, also called a municipal or official plan, which gives a broad-brush description of land uses in the municipality. All planning actions must be in conformity with this general plan.

Where the provincial government has established planning policy, municipal plans must have regard to provincial policy. Ontario has a number of such planning policies: one requires that 25 per cent of the new housing provided in a municipality be affordable to those with income in the bottom three quintiles; another requires the protection of significant wetlands; a third protects gravel deposits; a fourth restricts development in floodplains. These policies set a general framework within which general plans are prepared at the municipal level. Other provinces have not defined their policies so clearly; municipal planning occurs in a more unfettered manner, although provincial approval may be required for general municipal plans.

Zoning bylaw: The comprehensive zoning bylaw is more specific than the general plan in determining what is permitted where in the municipality. In many municipalities zoning simply describes what uses were there when the bylaw was passed and allows no new development or change in use without specific municipal approval. Thus, physical changes or changes in use usually require a rezoning (a change in zoning). Zoning must conform to the general municipal plan.

In western provinces, a development permit process is often used instead of rezoning. Development permits tailor permissions to particular applications (Bossons 1993, p. 118).

Minor zoning changes (sometimes called minor variances) are often dealt with by a committee of adjustment or other appointed body.

Plan of subdivision: Any proposal to take a large piece of land (such as a farm) and divide it into smaller pieces (such as housing lots) requires a plan of subdivision, which may be approved by a municipality, although often provincial approval is also required.

Some provinces allow a lot to be severed or divided into several parcels by what is known as a "consent" process, which is much less formal than the subdivision process.

Development review: Often municipalities will require approval of particular details of a development application, such as location of garbage disposal facilities and details of landscaping, car access points, electrical service vaults and so forth. These matters are secured by agreement between the municipality and the applicant.

Lot levies: Most municipalities charge a lot levy, or a fee on each lot, purportedly to cover capital expenses the municipality will be put to because of the development. The matters funded by the levy may include sewage treatment plants, libraries, schools and so forth. (Many other costs, such as new roads and sidewalks serving the development, are already the developer's responsibility.)

The effect of these levies is to pass on to the home buyer the capital cost of most government services. In many cases, municipalities require developers to fund the very best level of facilities — not just a baseball diamond, but a diamond meant for semi-pro ball, with lights and other frills that might not otherwise be obtainable. This practice is often referred to as "gold-plating."

Levies in some municipalities are anywhere from $10,000 to $30,000 a lot, or the equivalent of 10 per cent of the cost of a new home, which is simply tacked onto the price of the house, making the house that much less affordable. In an attempt to regulate municipal lot levies, the Development Charges Act was enacted in Ontario, requiring that levies be based on supportable professional studies. That legislation, however, has not reduced levies, but merely rationalized them. The development industry continues to complain that its product is being levied unfairly (Bossons 1993, p. 124f.).

Levies must be paid before a municipality will consider issuing a building permit, which often puts the developer in the position of agreeing to pay so the project can proceed.

Building permit: Once all other approvals have been given, the municipality may then issue the building permit. Indeed, if the application meets all requirements, the municipality must issue the building permit, and will be so ordered by the courts.

The process that must be followed by the proponent of a housing development is long and arduous. Often it can involve an amendment to a general or municipal plan and a rezoning, an exercise that can be accomplished within twelve months but in larger cities has been known to take several years. If the change is small and simply involves a rezoning, it might be accomplished in five or six months, although some cities seem to have difficulty accomplishing a rezoning within a year. After the plan amendment and rezoning are approved, the development review process can take another two or three months. (See Hodge 1986, generally on planning tools and processes.)

A typical process to achieve development approval would involve the following steps:

1. Preliminary review of the proposal with planning staff
2. Application to city clerk for rezoning and/or general plan amendment
3. Notification by the clerk to the public of the application
4. Application sent to council for information and preliminary debate, and staff asked to report
5. Application circulated to municipal staff for comment

6. Planning report prepared and sent to planning committee, where a public hearing is held
7. Committee decision recommended to council
8. Council decides on the application
9. If council has approved a development, legal documents prepared by legal staff
10. Council approves legal documents.

In some provinces, provincial approval is required for plans of subdivision, and in Ontario the whole matter can, if objections are received, be reviewed and reheard by the Ontario Municipal Board, an administrative tribunal established to review municipal planning decisions. The timing of provincial approvals varies from province to province. The Ontario Municipal Board in 1993 generally scheduled hearings about twelve months after an appeal had been made. (A good description of the process in Ontario is found in a booklet entitled *The municipal approval process for small non-profit housing projects*, by the Housing Development Resource Centre, August 1990.)

Some municipalities schedule additional opportunities for public input — such as at step 4, or just before step 6 — and council meetings often involve public submissions. In Vancouver, where provincial approval of city decisions is not required, council meetings on contentious development projects involve much public input and can last for many days.

The process is clearly a lengthy one, and not to be embarked on without good cause. Small applications are hardly worth taking through the process: it is too long, and with legal and planning advice, too costly. Thus, homeowners wishing to rent out part of their home as a second unit simply do it illegally, rather than apply for any needed rezoning.

The larger the project, the less the delay and cost actually mean in the total scheme of the development. Applicants wishing to develop several hundred acres as a housing subdivision are not particularly worried by the time and money. But those trying to accomplish something small — such as putting up a small building containing a dozen rental units — will find the planning process daunting.

The biggest challenge of the planning process is faced by a developer who would like to make a change in an existing neighbourhood. These developers must factor in the possibility that the ultimate decision of the council might be to refuse the application — leaving

the developer with a piece of land purchased for development purposes that now has little value, and with the outstanding interest
charges on the purchase. Given the risk, many developers have found
it easier to build on greenfields.

NIMBY

Developments proposed in existing communities usually require proponents to obtain rezonings and amendments to the plan. Given the
specificity of existing planning controls, approvals are needed for
quite simple proposals: projects for houses that differ slightly from
existing ones, such as infill houses; for two houses on a fifty-foot
lot; for a shop with apartments over it; or for a small walk-up
apartment building.

Residents of the communities where such proposals are made
often object to any proposed change. The objections can cover a host
of topics: the effect of increased traffic; overshadowing; the ability
of existing water and sewage services to handle the development; the
infringement on neighbourhood character; the inadequacies of existing schools or social services; a decline in property values because
of the development; the likelihood of crime increasing because of the
development; the shortage of park space; and so on.

The planning process gives residents a good opportunity to voice
their views and sometimes slow down the approval process. It pits
existing residents who elected the municipal council against development proponents who probably don't have a vote and against the
as-yet-undefined residents who might move in to the project. Existing residents clearly are in a very powerful position and can attempt
to claim that the stability of their neighbourhood is being challenged
by the proposed change.

In the 1960s, as neighbourhoods were demolished for high-rise
apartment towers, the arguments of residents were easy to sympathize with. Residents didn't want neighbourhoods demolished;
rather, they wanted development to proceed in a manner that
strengthened rather than ripped apart the physical fabric. Since then,
most existing neighbourhoods have been protected from such cataclysmic change with very tight zoning controls. Large-scale change
is strongly discouraged, but so is most small-scale change. As noted,
even modest proposals, in keeping with existing forms, are subject
to strong opposition.

Many developers make decisions on the assumption that residents
of stable residential neighbourhoods will fight any change of any

Photo: CMHC

Many older neighbourhoods faced this fate in the 1960s: a block of homes would be cleared out and a high-rise apartment building constructed. This process generated support for the idea of the "stable residential neighbourhood." This photo is of the Milton Park area in Montreal, which citizen opposition saved from further intrusion, when the developer's assembly was purchased and turned into a non-profit co-operative housing project.

kind. In these cases, objections are often categorized as the Not In My Back Yard (NIMBY) syndrome. Unfortunately, NIMBY has sometimes been applied to situations where residents have an understandable, and often resolvable, objection (much like residents in the 1960s who agreed with change, but not cataclysmic change). For our purposes, NIMBY objections will be defined as either those made in order to keep neighbourhoods exclusive, or those made because of a fear that housing for moderate and lower income families will destabilize the neighbourhood.

There is the sense, at least among many providers of non-profit and co-operative housing and other housing that serves lower income families, that the unspoken reason for opposition is a fear that households with incomes lower than current residents' incomes might move into the neighbourhood and decrease property values. Much anecdotal evidence exists for this sentiment. In the late 1980s, a Scarborough neighbourhood on the fringe of Metro Toronto fought a development of lower priced houses because of the social problems (including crime and prostitution) that residents felt were sure to ensue. Observers were amused to learn that the houses the neighbours were fighting would sell for $230,000 apiece, slightly more than the average price of new houses in Metro Toronto at the time, but slightly less than current values in the neighbourhood.

In the City of Etobicoke, in Metro Toronto, a neighbourhood fought hard against a non-profit housing project because of the infusion of low-income residents that it would bring — only to learn that a survey of local residents showed that most had incomes too low to qualify for the majority of units in the project, which would be rented at market rates.

According to the many studies undertaken, no negative impacts on the values of neighbouring properties result from non-profit, co-operative and even public housing. Many people are not aware of existing group homes or social housing in their neighbourhood, indicating that their mere presence is not socially destabilizing. Some studies show that people in general support the idea of halfway houses (HDRC 1990a).

One can understand some fears that a housing project may cause destabilization. In the early 1980s, as psychiatric hospitals were being closed, people feared the policy of deinstitutionalizing mental patients: it forced many vulnerable individuals into intolerable living conditions and did cause problems in some neighbourhoods. People do have an interest in ensuring that social facilities and social housing are well run. (Many neighbours who originally fight a group home on their street become after a few years active volunteers and serve on the board of the sponsoring organization, making it clear that knowledge and experience can lead to understanding and support.) Further, there are reasonable concerns about good and appropriate building form, concerns easy to understand given the many ugly buildings erected this century.

But NIMBY objections go beyond these concerns and aim right at the heart of housing that people can afford — the exclusionary aspect of NIMBY. A number of community groups now argue against new housing projects on the basis that their community "already has more than its fair share." Some municipal councils work out the percentage of social to other housing units in each ward, and then claim that wards with figures above the median should not see any further social housing built in them. One flier distributed in downtown Toronto in 1990 read:

> No one is against social housing. That isn't the issue. Everyone agrees that, as a society, we must care for the less fortunate. What we care about is the over-concentration in our part of the city. Why has our community been targeted?...
>
> It is no coincidence that, with this increase in social housing, there is an increase in our area of street crime, prostitution, crack and drug dealing. Recent TV shows on the subject of street crime and the increased use of guns by criminals observe that a great amount of drug trafficking occurs in the corridors and underground garages of SOCIAL HOUSING UNITS! (Don Community 1990 — flier)

This kind of opposition lends support for Hulchanski's argument that zoning is being used to keep certain people — those with lower incomes, for example — out of certain neighbourhoods.

Intensification

Economics has a way of driving issues and cultural values. As cities and individuals have found that money seems less and less available, they have looked for ways to economize. Many individuals have done this by renting out part of their homes as second units, thus getting extra money to help with the mortgage and other expenses. Municipalities that have spread to their borders now find that the only way to expand the tax base is to allow the redevelopment at higher densities of land that is already serviced. In short, there comes a time in a city's life when intensification seems a reasonable option. It is a constant phenomenon in cities — the explosion of downtown office towers in the last thirty years being but the latest and most visible sign. Intensification is now occurring in some neighbourhoods, and has become a major issue of debate.

The trend to segregated, single-use, low-density areas has already been noted. Reversing that trend has clear benefits:

Reurbanisation (intensification) provides an opportunity to achieve environmental goals, and to improve the social and physical fabric of the metropolis. For example, reurbanisation can reduce auto dependence in many ways, such as creating critical densities needed for walking, cycling, and the use of transit. (Berridge et al. 1991, p. 3)

Several successful new neighbourhoods with moderate densities have been built in the last twenty years. One example is Fairview Slopes in Vancouver. This area overlooks False Creek, just to the south of Vancouver's downtown, and in the early 1970s consisted of homes on large lots that were ripe for redevelopment. Under the leadership of Vancouver planner Ray Spaxman, new designations were established which encouraged development, but within a very constrained set of rules.

Permitted densities were relatively high — an fsi of 1.5x, which allowed some 65,000 square feet of floor space to be developed on every acre, which at a gross of 800 square feet per unit produced some 80 units per acre. But the plan also imposed strict height limits of 25 or 35 feet, depending on which side of the slope the property was on (to ensure views of False Creek from all units). A further requirement was that every 150 feet along the street front the architectural style would have to change, to ensure some variety in building form and detailing.

These new zoning controls proved felicitous, and a great deal of new housing within these parameters has been built on Fairview Slopes by private developers. The new community appears wonderfully successful: housing is in great demand (always a sign of success), with rents and selling prices high. The high densities support a strong and interesting local shopping strip on West Broadway, the main arterial road in the area, another sign of a healthy community.

Another example is the St. Lawrence community in downtown Toronto. This 45-acre site of old industrial uses was purchased by the City of Toronto in the mid-1970s for residential development. Although some parcels still remain vacant, most of the site has been developed. The number of units ultimately planned for is 3,500, or a density of about 90 units per acre. Buildings are either townhouses or apartment structures of six to eight storeys. Tenures are considerably mixed, by design: non-profit rental, non-profit co-op, condominium ownership, fee simple ownership and ordinary rental. The ground level of many apartment structures contains non-residential uses such as retail shops, restaurants, medical offices, schools, community facilities and other needed local uses.

While residents sing the praises of this new community, the real test of its success is the same as that for Fairview Slopes: the private development sector has been eager to build projects of their own on the edges of St. Lawrence.

Both Fairview Slopes and St. Lawrence ran contrary to conventional wisdom, but their successes indicate that they are viable models that might well be replicated, or at least studied well so that variations can be developed for other communities. They prove quite conclusively that intensified neighbourhoods can be very successful.

Where else will intensification occur? Given the strength of the idea of the stable residential neighbourhood, the most popular locale for intensification is the arterial street, where some shops and higher density residential uses might already exist. Intensification on arterials is often called Main Streets redevelopment.

The essence of a Main Streets program is permitting higher intensity development without involving the lengthy and expensive rezoning process. Instead, it would permit redevelopment as-of-right, or without rezoning. Such an arrangement means the developer faces no risk in getting through the planning process successfully: the whole risk is in whether what is built can be successfully marketed.

The key issues are how much development should be permitted without the need for planning approval and whether the development permitted is enough to entice some entrepreneurs to build. Should four- or five-storey structures be permitted? Should density controls be established or simply built-form controls?

Parking is a contentious matter. Approval for most urban redevelopment is given on the understanding that at least one parking space will be supplied for every apartment. But parking is difficult to provide on small sites on Main Streets, and expensive, often adding

$15,000 to $20,000 to the cost of a single apartment unit. Should developers be permitted to build small-scale housing projects without parking spaces? Main Streets advocates generally say "yes."

These kinds of approaches represent a radical change from the ways planning has been conducted and cities have been built in recent decades. They assume that rather than preventing development and change, zoning should help encourage and shape it. They assume that higher intensities are generally better than lower intensities of city life.

Further, these changes look to larger issues and benefits, such as public transit. If densities are low, then public transit is simply uneconomical for the municipality. The evidence now seems overwhelming that a population density of 30 to 40 people per gross hectare (about 10,000 per square mile) is the minimum needed for a public transit system that is economically and functionally viable (Newman and Kenworthy 1989). Most communities built since 1950 have densities well below that (which explains a lot about the problems faced by public transit), and thus will need to intensify to support transit. As well, uses must be more finely mixed than has been permitted in the past forty years, so that the direction, purpose and time of day of transit trips are mixed, and do not require that all trips happen in one direction in a certain time period. One report recommends as a goal for the intensification of urban centres a ratio of 1.5 residents for every job, whereas the mix in contemporary suburbs is now about 15 residents for every job. This would be a significant change (Berridge et al. 1991).

Developers across the country are now proposing that new "suburban" communities have higher densities, a mix of housing types, and a mix of uses, much like communities built before the Second World War (Sewell 1993, Chapter 8; UDI Pacific 1993). New styles are being devised by the industry to respond to new markets, and the "stable residential neighbourhood" model is perhaps losing some of the allure it once had.

Intensification of cities is certainly coming to the fore as a planning direction with support from many professionals. But it may not prove to be capable of doing battle with the idea of the stable residential neighbourhood. As one commentator notes:

> In spite of low income growth and the worst affordability crisis in recent memory, more people in the Greater Toronto Area and elsewhere are living in single detached units. Massive ratepayer

opposition to proposals to increase housing demand in any form continues to occur in most communities. (Simpson 1993, p. 6)

Intensification may be in for a rough ride politically.

The change created by "monster homes" should not be classified as intensification. Most often, one smaller house is demolished to make way for a larger house, with no net gain in dwelling units; the only change is that the new unit is much larger than the old. Of course, it is difficult to be precise about defining a "monster home." Size is only one aspect responsible for the unflattering name: other complaints include: 'overshadowing of adjacent gardens, overlooking and loss of privacy, blockage of views, loss of trees and landscaping, and designs that are inconsistent with "the character of the neighbourhood"' (Stanbury and Todd 1990, p. ii).

Monster homes invoke all the sentiments about stable residential neighbourhoods. Residents demand various kinds of zoning controls over physical characteristics of the structure: height of the building; eave height; set-backs from front and side lot lines; maximum length of the new house; a reduction in permissible floor space index (fsi). Often the regulation ensures that the only new houses that can be built are ones that mimic the characteristics of those already there. There appear to be no negative effects from these new controls on property values (Stanbury and Todd 1990, p. iii).

Gentrification

One noticeable change to older neighbourhoods in the last two decades is the influx of younger professionals. These new residents purchase homes and make wide-ranging renovations both inside and out. The process, a significant one, is called gentrification.

Gentrification results in two changes. First, the residents of the houses that are purchased and renovated are displaced. Often those displaced are tenants with lower incomes, living in the least expensive accommodation they could find. As gentrification occurs, it removes the lowest priced housing from the market so that the loss of inexpensive housing escalates and the number of displaced people grows. Often the houses that are gentrified had been occupied by a number of roomers or households who have great difficulty finding similar housing to replace what they have lost. Ley writes, "A direct relationship exists between inner city gentrification, the erosion of affordable housing, and tenant displacement in Canada's largest cities" (Ley 1991, p. 192).

Photo: Charlotte Sykes

Living in the heart of the city is again respectable, and gentrification, with its serious side-effects on the poor, is a fact of life. The photo shows renovated houses in Toronto's Cabbagetown.

Gentrification involves no real physical change except repair and renovation. It is change that zoning can't control, since zoning does not control property ownership. Thus the normal planning tools invoked to control change are not helpful in giving existing low-income tenants some security. In his review of the process over a decade, Ley notes, "Preservation, down-zoning, and improvement policies enhanced neighbourhood amenity, but could not check household transition" (p. 196). As an area becomes more attractive to young professionals, house prices rise, making selling even more likely, hence creating even more of a threat to low-income households. The only remedy is for social housing organizations to compete on the market with the gentrifiers (which is too expensive to maintain over the longer term without massive subsidies) or provide alternatives in the form of social housing.

Therein lies the paradox. The loudest cries of NIMBY come from those who have just purchased and renovated and are in their first throes of discovering the charms of living in an older area of moderate density and mixed uses. These residents are often the most vociferous in stating they already have their fair share of social housing in their neighbourhood. Those who as a group have done most to directly create a housing problem are the least likely to wish to see that problem addressed. Hence the insidious nature of gentrification.

The second result of gentrification is neighbourhood invigoration. Not only are older houses repaired and renovated, but new stores, restaurants and services are opened to serve a new clientele. New residents ask for improved municipal services — better paving, sidewalks, street-lighting, park facilities, and so forth — and help ensure that areas neglected in the past by the city receive reasonable attention. The city housing stock is retained and strengthened, which must be seen as a positive benefit.

Thus gentrification is a mixed blessing. No city has managed to create as much low-income housing as has been lost through this normal process of neighbourhood renewal. This loss considerably blunts the very positive aspects of regeneration, and turns gentrification into a serious housing issue.

Conclusion

There is a great deal of talk in the early 1990s about the need for alternatives to the stable residential neighbourhood with its segregated uses and low densities. New models of successful intensified neighbourhoods with mixed uses have been developed in Vancouver and Toronto, and these might be used as models elsewhere. As well, some developers seem receptive to innovation, and are proposing neighbourhoods much more mixed in uses and housing types than traditional neighbourhoods, developments which generally make better use of land with higher densities. Intensification proposals are receiving a more receptive hearing. One group of developers notes that

> the difference in people's incomes and lifestyles means that a variety of housing types must be available and at reasonable prices. And the communities and neighbourhoods where people are housed must provide them the opportunity for employment, transportation, recreation, and social/cultural interaction. (OHBA n.d., p. 2)

The consensus that has held for the last half century on what constitutes a good neighbourhood to live in is beginning to break, and new ideas are being greeted warmly. This may not be enough to create a change in cultural values, but clearly something is in the wind.

Chapter 5

Home Ownership Programs

Expanding opportunities for home ownership has been one of the key thrusts of government housing policy since the Second World War. This emphasis has a kind of logic to it: political parties want to offer popular policies, and offering voters the opportunity to own their own home is bound to be popular.

"Home ownership is a Canadian tradition," says one commentator. "Acquiring some land was a primary motivation of the early settlers from Europe, where private land ownership was rare" (Shaffner 1975, p. 7). Another sees it an expression of Canadian values:

> That the majority of households should be home owners and that young children ought to be raised in single detached homes are values which have always been widely held in Canada. Most families aspire to home ownership, and politicians and opinion leaders think this is a good thing. A nation of home owners is a stable, respectable, "thoroughly Canadian" nation. Housing policy in Canada ... has always accepted those values and indeed has probably done much to encourage and entrench them. (Fallis 1980, p. 81)

Two reasons stand out among the many advanced to support these values. Ownership gives the resident the maximum amount of control over the housing; and it plays a significant role in accumulating wealth and creating a large family asset (Steele 1993, p. 41f.).

But this thrust has limitations. Providing home ownership may not be a reasonable way of addressing questions of affordability, and thus may not help those who most need housing. In the rush to provide ownership opportunities, people with more serious housing needs may be overlooked. Hulchanski comments on ownership policies in the 1950s and 1960s: "Housing production objectives were achieved, though distributional and equity considerations were ignored" (Hul-

Photo: Avi Friedman

One joy of home ownership is the ability to create a garden in the backyard, as in this GROW home development in the Montreal area.

chanski 1988, pp. 17-18). Others agree (Dennis and Fish 1972; OAHA 1964).

Humphrey Carver, having spent much of his professional life advising on housing issues, was much more critical in retrospect of those policies:

> The only interested party in the housing scene which didn't seem to get much attention at the staff meetings of CMHC was the Canadian family which couldn't afford home ownership ... The criterion of success was the number of new housing units provided under the National Housing Act ... To give some humanity to these statistics the expression used was the "number of new front doors," suggesting the grateful smiling faces of the families who would respond to the postman's knock. A subject that did not appear on the agenda was the question of

what was behind the front door. (Carver 1975, p. 108, quoted in Hulchanski 1988, p. 18)

Almost two-thirds of Canadian households are owners, a small increase since the 1940s (CMHC 1985). This increase shows the effect of the many programs introduced from the 1950s through the 1970s to support ownership, including condominium ownership, mortgage insurance, savings plans, ownership for moderate-income families and other schemes discussed in this chapter. Marion Steele believes that ownership among families with children has increased considerably — from a range of 25 per cent in 1941 to almost 70 per cent by 1986 — while ownership rates for households without children, including those living alone, has fallen (Steele 1993, p. 47). Hulchanski shows that ownership has fallen considerably for households in the lowest income quintile over the past twenty-five years, remained generally constant for the second and third quintiles, and increased by 10 per cent or more for the top two quintiles (Hulchanski 1993b, p. 73). Both conclusions would lead one to believe that in the future programs are likely to focus on improving the lot of those who can afford ownership.

For purposes of analysis, policies and programs directed to the ownership market are divided into three major headings: those increasing supply in general; helping selected home owners; and other programs. The discussion sorts out the kinds of programs that have been considered or implemented, on the assumption that past programs provide a reasonable understanding of options for the future. The analysis attempts to put cost figures on programs and reviews their ability to address questions of affordability and need. As noted in Chapter 2, this latter task is a very difficult one indeed; the cursory remarks here are not made to belittle the difficulties involved in reaching intelligible conclusions. (Useful sources for this chapter are Adams et al. 1986, especially Section 2; Fallis 1980; Miron 1988, p. 242ff.; Hulchanski 1988, pp. 22-41; Canada 1986; CMHC 1985, particularly the Appendix.)

Increasing supply in general

Providing mortgage money: If housing is to be built for sale, then funds must be readily available to builders and developers. The shortage of mortgage funds was a significant problem before the Second World War. To address the problem, in 1936 the federal government passed the Dominion Housing Act, which authorized loans by the federal government for new construction and reduced interest rates — although the underlying purpose of the program was to stimulate a beleaguered Depression economy rather than provide housing. Within three years some $20 million had been loaned to approved private lending institutions to help finance 5,000 units. (For a detailed history of housing programs before the end of 1945, see Bacher 1993.)

In 1938 the National Housing Act (NHA) was passed — again with specific reference to stimulating the economy and creating employment — authorizing loans of up to 90 per cent on houses costing less than $2,500. Some 15,000 loans were made over four years. Loans were mostly made by insurance companies, since banks were not permitted to loan for housing purposes.

In 1944, amendments to the NHA established Central Mortgage and Housing Corporation (later Canada Mortgage and Housing Corporation) to administer the joint loans made for housing under the 1936 and 1938 legislation, and generally to take charge of housing matters.

Significant changes came with the new National Housing Act in 1954. This legislation first permitted banks to lend for housing purposes — loosing a large flow of new mortgage funds — and established a form of mortgage insurance on new housing (Poapst 1993, p. 94f.). The legislation required that all approved mortgages for more than 75 per cent of property value be insured so the lender would be protected from default by the borrower. The cost of the insurance would be paid by the borrower, and the program would be administered by CMHC. CMHC would have the right to establish the interest rates for which the loans were made, as well as the maximum loan per dwelling, minimum down payments, and a requirement that total carrying costs — principal, interest and property taxes — not exceed 25 per cent (later 30 per cent) of gross family income. The program would be run at no cost to the government.

Insured loans amounted to $378 million in 1954 and $600 million in 1955, before dropping to $387 million in 1956 and $261 million in 1957. The annual total has jumped and bobbled since that time, depending on housing starts and economic conditions (Fallis 1980, Tables 1 and 2).

There is no denying the effect of these changes on the supply of mortgage money. As a federal government report noted twenty-five years later:

> By creating a virtually risk free investment in mortgages and
> setting the charge for absorbing these risks below what lenders
> would normally incorporate in their calculation for making an
> insured loan, the loan guarantee and insurance program en-
> hanced the long run desirability of residential mortgage invest-
> ments. (CMHC 1979, pp. 6-7; cited in Adams et al., p. 148)

Housing starts, more than three-quarters of which were single-family
houses, jumped from under 75,000 a year in 1951 to 138,000 in 1955.

But starts then slumped. Interest rates began to rise, and banks
began to look for other investments. In 1959, market interest rates
rose to above 6 per cent, the maximum banks were permitted to
charge under the Bank Act; banks withdrew from NHA lending.
Sensing that sufficient funds would not be available to continue the
construction boom, the federal government intervened with direct
housing loans of its own. CMHC would lend mortgage money if the
applicant could verify that private funds were not available. This
direct or residual lending by CMHC amounted to $199 million in
1957 and $324 million in 1958. For the next decade annual amounts
lent out on this basis varied considerably until changes to the program in 1972 limited direct loans to very specific locations. In 1973,
for instance, direct lending amounted to just $38 million (Fallis 1980,
Tables 1 and 2).

In 1967 the Bank Act was amended to remove the 6 per cent
ceiling on interest rates for banks, and CMHC freed the interest rate
permitted for NHA mortgages, leading to significant changes in the
cost of mortgages. The conventional NHA mortgage rate jumped to
9 per cent in 1969, and fluctuated between 9 and 12 per cent for the
next decade, finally climbing to an astronomical 21 per cent in 1981.
Since the interest paid on the mortgage is such a significant part of
the cost of owning a home in the early years when little principal is
being paid down, these changes had a powerful impact on who could
afford to purchase a home. In 1969 the term of an NHA mortgage
was reduced to five years (presumably to account for fluctuating
interest rates), and in 1970 private mortgage insurance was authorized (Poapst 1993, p. 98).

The NHA mortgage insurance programs allowed the federal government considerable say over the kind and price of housing that
would be insured, and given the private sector's reliance on these
programs, considerable influence over what would be built. How-

Photo: Charlotte Sykes

A typical example of the fruits of the mortgage insurance program: the 1960s version of suburban housing as found in North York, Ontario.

ever, no unusual steps were taken to ensure that affordability was factored into insurance arrangements. It seems fair to conclude that the main impact of the mortgage insurance program was to finance moderately priced housing purchased by middle-income families (Fallis 1980, p. 81). Several attempts to have CMHC make the direct lending program more amenable to lower income families were successfully resisted (Fallis 1980, p. 83).

Was NHA mortgage insurance, in the end, of any great importance in broadening the class of people who purchased houses? Miron suggests that most of those who bought with an NHA mortgage would have purchased a home anyway, although probably a few years later in life (Miron 1988, p. 245). Steele reaches a different conclusion: she thinks NHA loans were a direct help for families with incomes in the bottom third, and notes that by 1965 18 per cent of families were in the bottom-third income grouping, compared to 6 per cent in 1954 (Steele 1993, p. 46).

What is not debatable is that the mortgage insurance program favoured and encouraged the construction of suburbs, resulting in cities that were considerably different from those Canadians were used to. Thus, massive development growth was accompanied by change in the ways cities looked and worked.

Managing interest rates: Interest rates can have a powerful effect on the availability of mortgage money. High rates entice those with capital to put it into mortgages rather than other forms of investment. This was the strategy in 1967 and 1969 when the government feared a possible slump in housing supply. Other effects of this approach may not be desirable: high interest rates increase housing prices and reduce demand. Further, a change in interest rates affects not just the housing sector, but other industries as well. It is difficult to target changes in interest rates to housing alone.

Strengthening demand to increase supply: Where adequate capital exists to support housing construction but not enough building is taking place, governments can look for other ways of increasing supply. One way is to increase demand, making potential buyers more eager, or giving them more reason, to buy. This could be done by giving a potential owner a financial benefit for purchasing a new home.

This thinking lay behind the federal government's Registered Home Ownership Savings Plan (RHOSP) in 1974. This plan permitted individuals who did not own homes to put up to $1,000 a year for ten years into a special RHOSP fund and to deduct this amount from income in calculating income tax. If the money in the fund was put toward the purchase of a house, no taxes would be paid on it. The RHOSP was extended in 1983 to permit to purchase of furniture. The program was ended in 1985.

The cost of this program was not in funds spent, but rather in tax revenue which was lost. These kinds of costs are usually referred to as tax expenditures. The cost of the RHOSP program — the loss of income tax revenue — was estimated at about $100 million a year (Hulchanski 1988, p. 31, citing Dowler 1983). No studies have been done to determine whether this program had the intended effect of increasing supply, or whether most of the money went to the purchase of existing, rather than new, housing. It cannot be concluded that the program was successful in spurring new construction.

Those with higher incomes clearly have more of an interest in plans such as RHOSP since they are more able to save and thus participate in the program. A higher income individual falling in the 30 per cent tax bracket would save $300 for every $1,000 invested, while a lower income taxpayer falling in the 15 per cent tax bracket would only save $150 for every $1,000 invested. The financial benefits of the program clearly flow to those with higher incomes. (An analysis of benefits from Registered Retirement Saving Plans, which are quite similar to RHOSPs, found in National Council of Welfare 1990, bears out this conclusion). While costly, the program did not address questions of affordability.

A second method of increasing demand is to make a grant to those who buy new houses. Several programs have been introduced with this in mind. In November 1974, when housing starts again seemed ready to slump, the federal government introduced the First Time Home-buyers Grant Program, giving every first-time home-buyer $500 for the purchase and occupancy of a new single-family home not exceeding CMHC price limits. The program continued for thirteen months until the end of 1975, cost $46.8 million, and contributed to almost 100,000 purchases, or about half of all single-family housing starts.

Several provinces introduced programs that topped up this grant. Ontario, for instance, provided a grant of $1,500 for first-time home-buyers purchasing any new or resale unit.

In June 1982, the federal government response to a worsening economy, a slumping house-building industry and soaring interest rates was the Canadian Home Ownership Stimulation Program (CHOSP). It provided a grant of $3,000 to first-time home-buyers. After almost $800 million had been poured into grants, the program was cancelled in April 1983 (Canada 1986).

For any government in Canada $800 million was a stupendous amount to spend in ten months on a housing program, about equal to the amount spent by CMHC on all social housing programs from 1979 to 1983 (Bacher 1993, p. 250). As noted in Chapter 1, average annual expenditure by the federal government during the 1980s was less than $1.4 billion, most of it going for operating subsidies for public and non-profit housing.

Almost nothing is left to show for this $800 million expenditure: the money was swallowed by the system. No analysis has been done of the effects of this program, but two general observations have been made. Some complain that the effect of the program was simply to allow builders to charge an extra $3,000 for each new house. Some say it put $3,000 more into the pockets of people who were going to buy a house in any case.

Clearly, CHOSP was directed to those buyers who would be approved by a mortgage lender in any case. None of the money went to households who rented their accommodation. It is fair to conclude that none of the money set in motion by CHOSP was directed to households who had problems affording a place to live. Some funds might have helped provide construction jobs for those in the bottom two quintiles — although there is no evidence to support even this surmise.

Helping builders: Immediately after the Second World War, the federal government introduced the Integrated Housing Plan to encourage the construction of speculative ownership housing. For builders who agreed to sell at set prices, CMHC undertook to buy back any unsold houses. Five thousand units were produced under this program in each of 1947 and 1948, amounting to approximately one-half of all NHA-sponsored housing in those years. Cost figures and information on who benefited from the program are not available (McKellar 1993, p. 137).

Helping owners

Helping new owners: As house prices rose faster than incomes in the late 1960s and early 1970s — new and resale house prices rose by 53 per cent between 1972 and 1974 — several programs were introduced to target groups that might not be reached with more general approaches. Prominent among these were grants to first-time buyers already discussed.

An "innovative low-cost housing program" was introduced by CMHC in 1970, aimed at low-income families. It was modified the next year to permit loans at below-market interest rates. These programs funded about 10,000 new units, and were then replaced with the Assisted Home Ownership Program (AHOP) (Steele 1993, p. 46).

AHOP, directed to moderate-income families purchasing a new home, was introduced by the federal government in 1973. CMHC set the permissible income levels and price limits. Qualifying families were offered mortgages covering 95 per cent of the purchase price, and to reduce housing payments (principal, interest and property taxes) to less than 25 per cent of family income, a five-year interest-free loan was available. If that loan failed to provide a reduction sufficient to allow the purchaser to qualify, a further grant of $300 was available. Over the five years the program was in place various changes were made, including increasing the grant to $750, ensuring that the effective interest rate was no greater than 8 per cent, and varying repayment arrangements. The program was ended in 1978.

AHOP was popular: 94,200 mortgages were provided under it, with total subsidization by the federal government of $125 million, or about $1,400 for each participating family. As Fallis points out, at a time when median income was about $8,000 per family, only 7 per cent of recipients in the AHOP program had an income below the median (1980, p. 97f.). AHOP benefited young middle-income families, and those who received the benefits were a very small number of those actually eligible (Fallis 1980, p. 100). Steele interprets the data differently, concluding that half of all AHOP borrowers had incomes in the bottom-third income group (Steele 1993, p. 48).

AHOP provoked a default rate of about 8 per cent. This rate may have been anticipated since the program was intended to appeal to those who did not have a lot of money (Steele 1993, p. 46). Consequently, CMHC incurred large deficits, estimated in the early 1980s at almost $800 million — although this sum includes deficits on other programs as well (Poapst 1993, p. 105).

Citing other critics, Miron questions AHOP's influence on the creation of new moderately priced units. He believes at least half, and maybe three-quarters of these units would have been built and purchased even if AHOP had not been in place (Miron 1988, p. 242).

Ontario enacted a program directed at a similar group of moderate-income families five years earlier, in 1967. Home Ownership Made Easy (HOME) had the same kinds of income limitations as AHOP, but it offered a subsidy by way of a fifty-year land lease so that families did not have to pay the full land cost immediately on purchase. Further, in most cases the land was owned by the provincial government, and the lease was set on book value of the land to the government rather than market value. Resales were restricted during the first five years, after which the land lease could be purchased at the market value established five years earlier. To further help owners, the Ontario Mortgage Corporation provided subsidy in the form of mortgages at below market rates.

About 30,000 units were subsidized under HOME before it was cancelled in 1978. There was much public outcry as families sold after the first five years and made what many considered capital gains at public expense.

Fallis notes the enormous benefits given those who managed to be accepted under HOME. They received a subsidy of $1,400 a year at a time when median income was about $8,000. The program chiefly benefited families in the middle third of income distribution, who received 75 per cent of all benefits; the remainder went to families in the upper third of the income distribution. Families in the bottom third received no benefits (Fallis 1980, pp. 92-94).

Hulchanski believes that ownership patterns across the country were hardly affected by these kinds of ownership programs. The high point for home ownership in Canada was 1961, when 66.0 per cent of households were owners. That fell to 60.3 per cent by 1971, then increased to 62.1 per cent in 1981 and 62.4 per cent in 1986. As noted previously, Steele believes that ownership among families with children did increase during this period, and it was to these households that these programs were directed. However, it is fair to conclude that generally these programs supporting home ownership just put more money into the pockets of families who were going to buy homes in any case.

Helping existing owners: Various programs have been introduced to help existing homeowners. The late 1970s and early 1980s were years of real difficulty for owners, when the economy was inflationary and interest rates were volatile, climbing to more than 20 per cent. The Graduated Payment Mortgage program, introduced in 1978, permitted shifts in the timing of mortgage payments. Owners of homes under CMHC-specified ceilings could reduce monthly payments by $2.25 for every $1,000 of principal, a reduction that would be offset by a comparable increase in capital owing. The effect of the program was to give some breathing room to those having difficulty meeting monthly payments by permitting creative cashflow solutions. No subsidy was involved in this program.

More significant difficulties were faced by owners attempting to renew mortgages, particularly in 1981 as mortgage rates rose above 15 per cent. The Canada Mortgage Renewal Plan (CMRP) was introduced that year, providing grants of up to $3,000 a year to qualifying owners. Almost $50 million was paid out under CMRP before it was cancelled in 1984. It is unclear which owners benefited from this expenditure and what their income was.

In early 1984 the federal government introduced the Mortgage Rate Protection Program (MRPP), a form of insurance managed by CMHC to protect against extraordinary mortgage rate increases. The program was not considered attractive — perhaps because interest rates quickly fell from 21 per cent to below 15 per cent — and by the end of 1984 it was estimated that fewer than a hundred people across Canada had taken advantage of it. Only twenty-six policies were issued in 1985 (Poapst 1993, p. 103).

Repair and rehabilitation: The federal and provincial governments have offered programs for home rehabilitation and repair for many years. In 1937 the federal government provided a loan guarantee program for home repair, making 126,000 loans before the program was shut down in 1940 shortly after the outbreak of war. A second loan program was started in 1954 (Miron 1993, p. 397).

In 1973 the Residential Rehabilitation Assistance Plan was introduced, permitting CMHC to make grants and loans for repair and renovation of many different kinds of residential buildings. Almost 200,000 grants were made to home owners during the next fifteen years, most to owners with moderate incomes. The Ontario government augmented this with the Ontario Home Renewal Program (OHRP), which ran on similar lines.

In 1977, the Canadian Home Insulation Program made available to owners a grant of up to $500 to help cover the cost of insulating their home. Almost $1 billion was spent on 2.5 million grants (some were for multi-unit buildings) before the program ended in 1986. Unfortunately, many grants encouraged the use of formaldehyde-based insulation which, when it was found to cause significant health problems, had to be removed, also with the partial support of government programs.

As a method of stimulating employment in the construction trades, the Canada Home Renovation Plan (CHRP) was introduced in 1982 to provide forgivable loans of up to $3,000, covering 30 per cent of the cost of renovation. Before the program was cancelled in July 1983, $230 million had been spent on 121,000 grants.

The Canadian Oil Substitution Program (COSP) was introduced in 1980 in reaction to very high oil prices, helping owners convert to natural gas and other energies for heating homes. The program was cancelled in 1985. Like CHRP and CHIP, COSP was not devised to apply only to those owners who had lower incomes. It is fair to assume that most benefits went to owners with incomes above the median.

Other programs

Of significant benefit to homeowners was the decision of the federal government in 1972, when a tax of 50 per cent was introduced on all capital gains, to exclude from the tax the sale of a personal residence. (In the early 1990s, the rate was increased to 75 per cent on capital gains.) Since this decision involved no cash outlays, to some it might not be considered a "program." However, the decision causes the government to forgo revenue that otherwise it would receive and the exclusion is referred to as a "tax expenditure."

Hulchanski categorizes the exclusion as a "popular housing subsidy" that permits owners to benefit fully from appreciation. "The capital gains tax break allows home owners to build up and shelter equity in their house, trade up to better houses, and eventually 'cash in' their equity at retirement (or at any time)" (Hulchanski 1988, p. 29).

The annual forgone tax revenue was estimated in 1979 at a high of $3 billion and a low of about $400 million, with more agreement on a middle figure of $1.5 billion annually (CMHC 1979, p. 127). Quite simply, by excluding personal residences from the capital gains tax the government agreed not to collect $1.5 billion in taxes each year. This benefit flows only to owners, not tenants, and most benefits those whose properties most increase in value. Evidence is clear that higher income households receive most of the benefits of this and other tax expenditure programs such as the Registered Home Ownership Savings Plan. It was estimated that in 1979 the combined benefit of the two programs to an individual with an annual income of about $25,000 (then just above the median income) was $964; the benefit to an individual with an annual income of more than $100,000 was $6,753 (Hulchanski 1988, pp. 31-32). Those involved in the non-profit housing field often argue that providing a subsidy of $1,500 per annum to a middle-income resident of a non-profit project is a far more efficient use of public funds than allowing owners to escape an annual tax of three or four times this amount on the enormous profits they make as housing prices increase.

Programs that have never been fully implemented in Canada are the deduction from income taxes of mortgage payments and property taxes. Both programs are in place in the United States; in the United Kingdom, only mortgage payments are deductible. These programs were promised by the Progressive Conservative Party in the 1978 election, but since the Conservative government was elected only with a minority of seats and fell within a year, the program was not implemented (Shaffner 1979).

A mortgage and property tax deduction program would not just benefit owners at the expense of renters. It would also benefit higher income owners much more than middle or lower income owners. Higher income owners generally own more valuable properties (generally with larger mortgages) which attract higher property taxes, so the deductions permitted by such a program would be larger. Further, higher income households are in higher tax brackets with higher tax rates, so the deduction would result in a much more significant saving than for someone at a lower tax rate. Shaffner concludes that the programs would have done nothing to improve the affordability of homes for first-time buyers and little for low-income households (1979, p. 21) The programs have seemed so inequitable to Canadians that they appear to have fallen off the agenda of all political parties.

Some argue that mortgage interest deductibility would be reasonable if personal residences were subject to capital gains tax, since it represents the cost incurred in acquiring the asset on which the capital gain is made. The difference, however, is that a personal residence is unlike other capital assets since it is used by the owner, who benefits from that use. Permitting payment deductibility would not fairly recognize the benefit accruing to the owner living in the residence.

However, some provinces have programs that help owners meet expenses. A program in British Columbia allows owners to deduct up to $720 a year from local property taxes. The program, which costs $470 million per year, has been recommended for cancellation (British Columbia 1992, p. 38).

A number of provinces have programs to help elderly or disabled owners. British Columbia defers their property taxes, and Ontario offers partial property tax rebates. Most programs do not define eligible owners on the basis of income.

Conclusions

Federal and provincial governments in Canada have enacted a number of programs to benefit current homeowners and those who wish to become owners. The amounts poured into these programs have been considerable, and in all likelihood represent a majority of the money spent on housing programs since the Second World War, even though owners and potential owners are not the Canadians most in need or with the most substantial problems of affordability.

Examination of these programs is important in assessing program options in the future. Details of ownership programs can be reworked in various ways to provide more precise directions in which benefits might flow. Thus, through design change it would be possible to ensure that more benefits from the AHOP program went to those with slightly lower incomes and fewer benefits of the RHOSP went to those with higher incomes.

But those changes would not much affect the general scope of who benefits: programs focusing on home ownership help those who can afford to be owners, generally households with middle or upper incomes, falling in the top two income quintiles and occasionally in the third. Given the cost of owning a home, those with incomes in the bottom two quintiles generally cannot participate.

In addition, the justification for many programs directed at ownership housing was often economic: to create jobs and get the economy rolling again. But this justification can be used for virtually any housing program, including one directed solely at those with problems of affordability.

At the same time, appealing to owners makes good political sense. Owners vote more often than tenants, and they hold positions of more power and influence in society. An overwhelming proportion of elected politicians at the municipal, provincial and federal levels are owners who can be expected to sympathize with others in the same position as themselves. It would be unusual if those representatives did not favour programs supporting home ownership.

Given the frequency of intervention by governments in the field of ownership housing, it is difficult to talk about the functioning of an unfettered ownership "market." The market is clearly influenced by incentives or disincentives placed there by government. The question for those interested in creating a housing policy around ownership housing is what that intervention is intended to accomplish, and at what cost.

Chapter 6

The Land Question

The title of this chapter implies there is one land question. In fact there are two, although they are as closely related as two sides of the same coin. First, is there enough land approved for development to meet the need and ensure that housing prices do not increase? Second, is there a monopoly or near monopoly on land likely to be used for new housing?

Answers to both questions lie at the heart of explanations for rising house prices and might help address the issues of affordability discussed in Chapter 2. During the boom of the 1960s and 1970s, as the number of suburban house starts mushroomed across Canada and prices mushroomed as well, these questions received much attention; they have received little attention since. Thus, while the questions and answers might still be relevant, there has been little data collection and analysis in the past fifteen years.

The classic study was prepared for CMHC by staff researcher Peter Spurr in 1974 and then buried until it was discovered and published in 1976. Spurr's book was followed by James Markusen and David Scheffman's study, which quarrelled with evidence that seemed to point to an oligopoly; by James Lorimer's *The Developers,* which implied a small oligarchy of developers; then by David Greenspan's study for the federal government, claiming that no one company had any particular amount of influence on the market for suburban land anywhere in the country; and finally by Clayton Research Associates' 1991 study for CMHC concluding that concentration of land ownership would give some owners "oligopolistic power over the availability and pricing of building lots."

Land was not always seen as a significant price component in housing that families could afford. In 1948, Carver analyzed the elements of housing costs, as shown in Table 6.1.

Given the large percentage of monthly cost consumed by the building itself, Carver thought it important to see how that compo-

Before Don Mills, suburban house styles were simple and repetitious. The style is reminiscent of that of Wartime Housing Limited: small one-and-a-half-storey houses with a common setback, central door and side drive, marching down the street. These homes were built in the Tower area of Scarborough, Ontario in the early 1950s.

nent could be reduced, and he proposed various design solutions. One of his proposals was building suburbs on a mass scale to effect cost efficiency through repetition and large numbers. This was the planning basis for Don Mills, Canada's first corporate suburb at just over

	Total cost	Monthly cost	Percentage/month
Building	$6,225	$22.94	39
Land	775	3.23	6
Money*		15.68	27
Maintenance		6.66	11
Property taxes		11.66	17
Totals	$7,000	60.17	100

Table 6.1

Components of housing cost, 1948

* Money: A 3 per cent interest rate on a $2,000 down payment is assumed, and a 4.5 per cent rate on a $5,000 mortgage.
Source: Carver 1948, p. 50.

Table 6.2

Increases in home ownership costs and incomes

Year	Home ownership cost for first purchasers	Income available
1961	100	100
1966	130.6	114.3
1971	197.2	141.6
1976	389.1	227.8

Source: Fallis 1980, p. 32.

two thousand acres, and other Canadian suburbs (Sewell 1993, Chapter 3). Carver also proposed careful house designs to reduce construction costs. He didn't spend time trying to reduce the land component since it was by far the smallest part of the cost of a new house.

But land quickly became a significant factor in housing cost. In 1968, land costs accounted for an average of 18 per cent of the total cost for a new house, although that average hid some significant variations: land accounted for 33 per cent of the cost of a new house in Toronto, 38 per cent in Halifax, and 12 per cent in Montreal (Spurr 1976, p. 20). In 1986, the building lot accounted for 49 per cent of the price of a typical house in Metro Toronto (Sewell 1994). In the early 1990s in large metropolitan centres the land component makes up between 30 and 40 per cent of the cost of a new suburban house.

Perhaps one reason why so few studies have been done to update the work done in the 1970s is that the significant changes in land prices occurred during that period and have remained relatively constant ever since.

House prices and incomes

Since the beginning of the suburban boom in the 1950s, the price of new houses has risen more quickly than the incomes of purchasers. This is evident in reviewing two kinds of analyses — comparing house prices to incomes of purchasers, and comparing new house prices to median incomes. Studies have been done on these increases only in the Toronto area, but there is no reason to suspect that the conclusions drawn from these studies would not apply to other metropolitan centres. In the case of house prices and purchasers' income, data are almost twenty years old.

Not all households are in the market to buy a new house. Some already own a house and have no intention of selling and buying again; some renters can't afford to buy; and some want to remain tenants. To capture these differences, Fallis compared the increase in home ownership prices with the increase in incomes of those who did not own a home and might be first-time buyers. As Table 6.2 shows, for first-time purchasers cost increases far outstripped income increases during this period.

A study prepared for the Urban Development Institute of Ontario bears out this position. It compared changes in the economic accessibility of new houses in the Toronto area in the ten-year period 1961-71. It concluded that 28 per cent of income earners could meet minimum income requirements for a new detached house in 1961 based on NHA statistics; the comparable figure for 1971 was 11 per cent based on NHA statistics, or, based on a survey of actual sales, a remarkably low 4 per cent (Derkowski 1972, cited in Sewell 1977, p. 32). Whichever figure is used, it is clear that many fewer families could afford to buy a new home in 1971.

This change in the accessibility of new houses is one that has not been reversed in the intervening twenty years. As noted in Chapter 2, CMHC concluded in the early 1990s that across the country only slightly more than one-third of families with children can afford to purchase a home, whether new or used.

A second comparison is between median incomes and new house prices, with data again coming from the Metro Toronto area. The

Table 6.3			
House prices and incomes in the Toronto area			
Name and year	*House price subdivision in suburb*	*Average house price offered for sale in Metro Toronto*	*Average family income in Metro Toronto*
Tower (1953)	11,600	14,000	5,400
Kellythorne (1963)	19,000	16,000	6,542
Cherrystone (1971)	35,000	30,426	11,841
Sandy Hook (1981)	120,000	90,203	31,238
Source: Sewell 1994. Notes on the methodology used in the study are found the Appendix.			

Photo: Charlotte Sykes

After Don Mills, low-slung ranch-style houses were the vogue. The garage has been pushed forward, making it more prominent, but the wide lots create a "country" atmosphere. This house in the Kellythorne area of Scarborough, Ontario was built in the early 1960s.

subdivisions compared all offered roughly the same mid-range housing, and when built, each suburb was "the next one out" and thus comparable in distance from the built city. Two conclusions are apparent from Table 6.3. First, prices increased relative to family income in the Toronto area. In the early 1950s, average house prices were slightly more than double average family income, rising slowly in the 1960s and 1970s, until in the early 1980s they were almost three times average family income. The change is clearer when we compare average family income and prices in the four suburban communities, where over the period the ratio changes from 1:2 to 1:4.

Second, the price of new suburban housing in the Toronto area, initially lower than that of other housing, became substantially higher. In the 1950s, buyers could look for lower priced housing in the new suburbs; by the 1960s that no longer held, and by the 1980s the price of new suburban housing was considerably above average. Thus, while in the early 1950s resale housing set the price at which suburban housing was offered, by the early 1960s the tables were turned and new suburban housing began to set the price for resale housing.

One interesting question flowing from these data is who the new house purchasers actually were. One answer is revealed in a review of the purchase arrangements of new owners. The following table compares average down payments with average family incomes:

Table 6.4		
Purchase arrangements in Toronto suburbs		
	Down payment ($)	Average family income in Metro Toronto ($)
Tower (1953)	2,400	5,400?
Kellythorne (1963)	3,500	6,542
Cherrystone (1971)	10,000	11,841
Sandy Hook (1981)	40,000	31,238
Source: Sewell 1994. Notes on the methodology used in this study are found the Appendix.		

What is clear from these data is the increase in down payment relative to income: it changes from a ratio of 1:2.5 to 1:0.75. The down payment required by the early 1980s could not readily be saved by an average household — and a lower down payment would mean monthly mortgage payments that ate up so much income the family would have difficulty surviving.

In all likelihood, the way most purchasers in Sandy Hook, and many purchasers in Cherrystone, generated the down payment was by selling a home. By way of contrast, purchasers in the early 1950s were likely to be first-time buyers. This represents a significant change in clientele: by the 1980s suburban houses had become second homes, affordable because purchasers had been able to sell previous properties. No longer was suburbia offering inexpensive housing for young families. Instead, suburbia was for the well established, those who already had managed to purchase a home.

This scenario is in all likelihood not peculiar to the Toronto area, but is reflected in all Canadian cities. Frank Clayton's study of the period 1986–1991 confirms this perception. He found that in Canada only one-third of all new homes were purchased by first-time buyers, and that only one in five home-builders even saw the first-time buyer as a main target group (Clayton 1992). His estimate includes the purchase of lower cost houses at great commuting distance from

After ten years, the ranch-style house of Don Mills has become both tired and cramped. No longer is there a "country" feeling to the street. This photograph shows the Cherrystone community in North York, Ontario built in the early 1970s. Garages are as dominant as houses.

concentrations of jobs as well as nearer suburbs, whereas the information cited for Metro Toronto deals with suburbs that are "the next suburb out" from built-up areas, where first-time buyers would have been even rarer. Further, prices for homes in "the next suburb out" were higher than prices elsewhere in the region, which explains the difference between the data produced by Fallis and by the Metro Toronto study.

Why did suburban house prices increase so much? Some think the increase had to do with the cost of land, which in turn might have something to do with who owns that land and the controls they are able to exercise in the market. A 1978 federal study chaired by David Greenspan agreed that there had been phenomenal increases in the price of new housing between 1972 and 1975: "on average in 25 urban areas across the country lot prices increased at a rate over 40 per cent greater than the general rate of inflation." The study noted that west of Ottawa, the increase was more than 50 per cent greater than general inflation (Greenspan 1978).

The Greenspan study concluded that "the land and house price explosion was not caused by either high profits or monopolistic developers," or by red tape, gold-plated services, citizen resistance or tax policies. None of these factors, the authors noted, "could sufficiently strangle supply for the short years of the boom to explain either price rises of that magnitude or their occurrence across much of this country. The reason is that they can restrict only new housing, not existing housing" (p. 6).

The study blamed the increase on demand factors; that is, such a large number of households wanted to purchase new houses that prices were pushed up. The authors provided a succinct outline:

> Inflation escalated.
> Real income exploded.
> The stock market dropped sharply.
> The baby boom of the 40's and 50's created a young families boom in the early 70's.
> The only major way for most people to beat the new federal capital gains tax of 1971 was to buy, occupy, and sell a home. Through changes in federal law, down payments became very low, and so the largest mortgages ever became possible. Because mortgage money was more plentiful than ever, mortgages became easy to get. Because the nominal interest rate on mortgages rose less than inflation, they became cheaper to pay for in real dollars. (p. 20)

> All our evidence points overwhelmingly to demand factors and changing expectations as the primary forces behind the 1972-5 land and housing price boom. (p. 21)

John Bacher calls Greenspan's study "manipulative" and chastises it for overlooking data that went against its conclusions. Whereas Greenspan claimed a shortage of serviced land, Bacher presents evidence that in most places no such shortage existed (Bacher 1993, pp. 242-43).

Land prices

A different explanation for the rising house costs was that the land component played a major role. Lorimer compares changes in construction costs, land costs and house prices for five cities between 1971 and 1976 in Table 6.5 (p. 105). Lorimer then estimates developers' profit on the land component of the house price, from the time the land was first purchased (usually as a farm) until date of sale with a house on it. Table 6.6 (p. 106) includes two of the examples he uses, both representative of others he provides.

Although in the 1990s it is difficult to believe that house lots ever sold for as little as $20,000 or $30,000, it is clear that the profit made was considerable. In 1993 in Vancouver, when the average house price was $290,000, a development industry report stated, " A new single family dwelling selling at $420,000 might have an underlying land value of $210,000, or 50 per cent of the value of the property"

	1971 ($)	1976 ($)	Percentage increase
	Table 6.5		
	The suburban house price explosion		
Vancouver			
house	19,178	37,196	94
lot	8,179	30,804	277
total price	27,357	68,000	
Calgary			
house	18,055	34,500	91
lot	5,848	35,400	505
total price	23,893	69,900	
Edmonton			
house	19,049	31,500	65
lot	6,663	29,600	344
total price	25,712	61,100	
Toronto			
house	20,539	30,061	46
lot	12,107	33,934	180
total price	32,646	63,995	
Montreal			
house	15,655	28,949	85
lot	4,483	9,339	48
total price	20,138	38,288	

Source: Lorimer 1978, p. 110. The lot figures for Montreal include an estimate for servicing. Title of chart taken from Lorimer.

(UDI Pacific 1993, p. 24). One wonders what the profit on a single lot amounted to.

Comparisons are also made by Lorimer with the sale of house lots from municipal land banks to emphasize the size of developers' profits on land. Like Hulchanski, Lorimer makes the point that many federal government programs in force during this period — reduction in the cash down payments required under the NHA, increase in allowable family income to be consumed by house payments, federal capital gains tax, RHOSP, AHOP — intensified already strong consumer demand (pp. 109-11). But the owners of suburban land were well able to take advantage of this situation.

Fallis analyzes the increase in housing components for a number of decades and comes to a similar conclusion about the increases in the cost of land. From 1971 to 1981, the cost of building materials increased by a factor of 2.36; construction labour, by 2.59; and land, by 3.18 (Fallis 1993, p. 88).

Some might say these years in the 1970s were exceptions. Comprehensive information is not generally available, but comparative statistics from CMHC for a number of cities make the point that the change in the land component differs considerably from the change in house prices. The increase in the land component is greater than the increase in house price for all cities in Table 6.7 except Vancouver. (In all likelihood the house price inflation in the 1990s in Vancouver has more than made up for its restraint in the 1980s.) Apart

Table 6.6		
Suburban land development costs and profits, 1976		
	Calgary project ($)	*Vancouver project ($)*
Raw land	138	757
Carrying costs	160	250
Taxes	60	150
Servicing	6,000 }	
Servicing carrying costs	400 }	13,800
Selling costs	1,000	1,000
Total cost	7,758	15,957
Selling price	20,400	30,804
Profit	12,642	14,847
Source: Lorimer 1978, p. 102.		

Photo: Charlotte Sykes

By the early 1980s, as seen in this photo of the Sandy Hook area of Scarborough, suburban houses have become even more cramped than in Cherrystone, and the street is lined with garages, little different than a back lane. The house now faces to the rear, and the street is a place of no interest or activity except for cars.

from Vancouver, where housing prices were almost unchanged, in all cities the cost of land rose more than did the total house price. At a minimum, one can conclude that land costs are a matter worth some study on their own.

Land supply

One possible explanation for the increase in the land component of new house prices is a shortage of supply. Obviously, if demand outstrips supply, then house prices will increase.

Studies of housing need are undertaken to get a handle on how much land will be required to accommodate anticipated growth and development. CMHC provides much information in this regard, including semi-annual estimates of lot supply in all major urban areas in Canada. If supply is greater than demand, then prices will remain relatively constant, but if for any reason demand outstrips supply, land and lot prices can be expected to rise.

Unfortunately, determining how much new land is available to meet demand for new housing is not always a straightforward task. One contentious issue in estimating supply is the size of the market

Table 6.7
Changes in price components, selected cities, 1981–1989

City	Land component (%)	Total house price (%)
Vancouver		
1981	100	100
1989	85.3	100.5
Calgary		
1981	100	100
1989	141.1	99.8
Winnipeg		
1981	100	100
1989	173.0	138.2
Toronto		
1981	100	100
1989	232.4	204.5
Halifax		
1981	100	100
1989	176.0	125.9
Source: Canadian Housing Statistics 1989		

area. As large cities have expanded and as house prices have increased, commutersheds (the distance commuters are willing to
travel) have grown enormously. In the Vancouver area, it is not
unusual to find residents of Abbotsford and Mission commuting 90
minutes to work in the downtown; similar commuting times and
distances are found in other cities. Settling on the size of the housing
market area depends on the length of the commute one can expect
new home-buyers to make. Which municipalities should be included
in an estimate of lot supply in Vancouver? In Toronto? In Montreal?
In Halifax? Does the distance of the commute depend on the difference in housing prices?

A second difficulty in estimating supply is determining whether a
lot is available for development. Some argue that if a municipal plan
has designated a lot for residential purposes, then it is available for
development. Others argue that simple designation is not sufficient,
since water and sewage services may not be built for some years, and
clearly houses can't be built and occupied until those services are in

place. Others suggest the only land that can be included with any certainty is land with approved plans of subdivision; that is, with all approvals in place, including water and sewage allocation. Still others suggest that even some land with plans of subdivision is for various reasons not particularly marketable.

A third question is the reasonable period for which supply should be available. Is a three-year supply reasonable? Is five years a better planning horizon to account for unanticipated changes in housing need? Could Montreal really have a thirty-three year supply of land, as claimed by Greenspan (Bacher 1993, p. 244)?

These questions have no agreed-upon answers, but are the fuel for the battles about whether the supply of land is adequate. One Ontario example indicates how different perspectives lead to different conclusions. In 1988, when housing in the Toronto area was booming and about 30,000 new units a year were being built and sold, many in the development industry feared there was a shortage of land, and that this would lead to price explosions. They pushed for more and faster approvals. Yet an unpublished study concluded that 45,000 acres of land that had received plan approval and designation, as well as water and sewage allocation, lay vacant. At an average density of 6.7 units per acre, this land would permit construction of 303,000 units — enough to meet supply for nine years.

Two significant factors affecting supply on which there is some agreement — infrastructure and the planning process — deserve mention.

Infrastructure: As already noted, one factor in land supply is servicing — sewers, water and roads. Building a sewage treatment facility is often beyond the financial capability of a municipality, and so will require some provincial funding. If such funding is not available, then lots may not be approved. (In municipalities where servicing is not available, developments have often been proposed on private septic systems. However, septic systems require large lots of an acre or more, and some soils are not able to absorb septic effluent.)

Before the construction of Don Mills, Canada's first corporate suburb, infrastructure expenses were met in two ways. Municipalities could pay for them directly, borrowing money on the open market for a twenty- or thirty-year term and then securing the funds needed to repay the debentures through property taxes. Alternatively, municipalities could levy a local improvement tax, a special tax on those properties deemed to benefit from the improvements. Larger projects, such as sewage treatment plants, would often be funded by municipal debentures. Smaller projects, such as local sewers and sidewalks, would be funded by local improvement taxes.

The developer of Don Mills agreed to guarantee debenture payments for the sewage treatment plant expansion, putting the municipality in a no-risk situation. The example was quickly followed, and many of the capital costs of infrastructure moved from being funded by the public to being funded privately. Some infrastructure costs, such as local roads and sidewalks, were assigned directly to the developer. Others were funded by municipal lot levies (called development cost charges, or DCCs, in British Columbia) established to cover at least the capital costs of large infrastructure, including libraries, schools and community centres. In the late 1980s, as developers complained about what they saw as capriciousness by municipalities in setting lot levies — sometimes they amounted to almost $20,000 per lot — Ontario moved to regularize lot levies through the Development Charges Act. This legislation required municipalities to do studies justifying the lot levies charged. Complaints similar to those that led to the Ontario legislation are being voiced in other provinces, although the Development Charges Act has been no panacea: the development industry has challenged its constitutionality, and the dispute continues to wind its way through the courts.

But even with levies or DCCs there remains a financial shortfall for servicing; all provincial governments provide municipalities with funds for new infrastructure. These funds are provided by way of regularized programs specifying the shares each government will pay, but often the programs are topped up by special grants for certain municipalities or certain projects. As provincial budgets grow more strained, these grants and subsidies can be expected to decline, raising worrisome questions about how infrastructure costs will be met.

Determining when sewage and water facilities are close to overload and when new facilities are required is very difficult. Governments have complicated formulas to determine capacity, involving expected sewage flow per person, pipe capacity, rainwater flows and other factors. In most provinces, provincial ministries determine whether municipalities have the capacity to service new development.

These questions are of utmost importance to developers, since if the municipality does not have sewage capacity, chances for development approval are slim. Accordingly, in some municipalities developers are very careful about securing sewage allocations. In the late 1980s, allegations were made that some developers were involved in questionable activities to secure allocations in the Toronto area, including gifts to municipal politicians and special friendships with senior staff (Ferguson 1988). Similar kinds of allegations are made wherever there are servicing constraints.

Clayton makes a link between the shift of servicing responsibilities from municipalities to the private sector and concentration in the development industry (Clayton 1991). That there should be such a link is understandable, for to pay for servicing costs developers need financial leverage, and larger developers will be able to obtain more leverage from lenders than smaller developers.

In many municipalities, particularly in Ontario and Quebec, sewage and water allocations have been moved from the local municipal level to the regional level, since water and sewage facilities are managed regionally. It has been suggested that in these cases centralized allocations may result in developer concentration and higher land costs: instead of many different municipalities making decisions there is only one set of decision-makers, and a developer able to influence it can achieve significant power and control (Ferguson 1988).

The planning process: The second significant factor influencing supply is the amount of land that has been approved for development. Approvals occur under a planning régime, usually involving several steps, as noted in Chapter 4. For the construction of new suburban houses the biggest planning step is the designation in a municipal plan of the site for development. Before agreeing on designation for development, most municipalities undertake a lengthy planning process that reviews major issues such as environmental constraints and consequences, effects on agricultural land, servicing abilities and transportation options. These studies often coincide with, and occur within, the framework of studies about housing need.

After the municipality has decided to designate new land for development, a second and more detailed planning study is done to arrive at the terms and condition for a plan of subdivision, whereby a large parcel of land will be divided into smaller parcels for development. The plan of subdivision, when approved by the municipality, is usually accompanied by an even more detailed control — a zoning bylaw, which specifies where particular uses will be permitted and the size and scale of structures to be built.

For the developer, these approvals are crucial since they determine the value of the land. A farmland designation is worth nothing to a developer, whereas a residential designation can be worth millions of dollars. Many of the allegations of municipal corruption or undue influence surround the granting of these approvals. Developers frequently insist that unless approvals are granted as requested the supply of lots will be insufficient and the price of housing will escalate unnecessarily. Municipal politicians often feel that unless they grant the approvals as requested, they will be responsible for increased housing costs. Yet developers often seem successful in demanding approvals when there is more than sufficient land available to satisfy demand, which brings us to the crux of the argument.

Control of land

Can the increase in land costs as a component of new house prices be explained in terms of who owns the land and puts it on the market? This question was widely debated in the 1970s, but has received little attention more recently. Thus the data are twenty years old, although they continue to be relevant.

Greenspan concluded that ownership and control of land was not a reasonable explanation for high prices, but others have questioned this conclusion, given the evidence that Peter Spurr had provided in his 1974 study. Spurr's evidence is tantalizing, but not conclusive. One problem is the difficulty of deciding whether land owned corporately should be considered ripe for development, or whether some parcels are so distant from development opportunities that they should be excluded from any calculation of market influence or control. One instance of the dilemma is the 1955 purchase by E.P. Taylor of 6,500 acres of land to the west of Toronto. Taylor bought this land just three years after work began on Don Mills, and it remained as farmland for twenty years. By 1969, a plan was proposed to develop the land as the Erin Mills community. Development began in the early 1970s and continued for more than two decades. In 1955, few would have considered this as land that would be added to the urban fabric, and thus the holding would not have been considered as one that would influence the market. Yet in retrospect, it was a key parcel.

Spurr produced land ownership data for six regions in the early 1970s. In Ottawa, eight firms owned 12,450 acres (p. 91). In Toronto, nine firms owned 36,484 acres (p. 112). In Kitchener, five or six major firms owned substantial areas (p. 132) that were expected to constitute as much as 60 per cent of developable land in ten years (p. 134). In Winnipeg, three firms controlled from 10 to 44 per cent of developable land, depending on the municipality (p. 138). The situations in Edmonton and Vancouver were less easy to summarize.

Lorimer considers Spurr's report, summarizes some parts of it, and augments it with other information to come up with the following snapshot for Winnipeg and Calgary in 1976 (Lorimer 1978, p. 90):

- In Winnipeg, four developers owned 12,878 acres: BACM 5,219 acres; Qualico 2,950; Metropolitan 1,763; and Ladco 2,946. With about 750 acres absorbed every year for development, this represents about seventeen years' supply.
- In Calgary, seven developers owned 13,110 acres inside the city limits: Nu-West and its closely related company Carma, 4,070; three Genstar subsidiaries 2,780; Daon 1,600; Qualico 1,220; Melton 2,250; Jager 1,010; and Premier 170. These companies owned a further 28,470 acres outside the city limits. This corporate land bank, according to Lorimer, would meet the need for suburban lots for thirty-five years.

Lorimer concludes that "by the early 1970s in most Canadian cities a few large developers held substantial acreages of land well suited for suburban development" (p. 89), land that was "sufficient to supply all the lots that will be required over the next five, ten or fifteen years" (p. 91).

There is no monopoly, but Lorimer believes it is fair to conclude that there is an effective oligopoly. The practice has been to divide up sections of the city so that one company works the western part of the city, another the east and so forth. A Calgary study noted: "Some sectors of the city are virtually controlled by one or two developers, and therefore, although there may be competition between developers on a city-wide basis, very often there is little competition in a development area" (Lorimer 1978, pp. 94-95). Developers wield strong market influence, maybe even market control. This influence obviously would be seen in rising prices, which were eminently visible in the 1970s.

One should be aware of the distinction between developers and house builders. Until the late 1980s, house building was usually carried out by small independent companies that purchased lots from the developer. Thus, new houses were actually marketed by a number of different companies, although the land itself was held by one or two companies before construction began. In the mid-1980s one large house-building company emerged in the Toronto area, Greenpark Homes. It was very closely related to the major developer group consisting of Marco Muzzo, Alfredo de Gasperis and Rudolph Bratty. It has been suggested that Greenpark was responsible for about one-half of the new homes built annually in the late 1980s and early 1990s in the Toronto fringe (Ferguson 1988).

A study by Markusen and Scheffman in 1977 disputed that market control was the explanation for rising prices of land for new houses in the Toronto area in the early 1970s. The study concluded that "the monopoly power theory did not hold up in Toronto during this period and that while there was an excess of speculative activity ... in the long run speculators cannot cause prices to deviate from competitive levels" (pp. 130-31). The study found that the land market was competitive, and that there was a great deal of uncertainty involved in the future use of many parcels, and the timing of that use (p. 123). It accounted for price rises by an increase in demand that the market was not able to respond to quickly (the same conclusion Greenspan had arrived at) and an influx of foreign real estate investment (p. 56). Since Markusen was also heavily involved in the Greenspan study, the parallel conclusions of the two endeavours are understandable.

Even with this conclusion, the study provides interesting data on major development companies, confirming large and significant land holdings by companies that often had related boards of directors. Although it rejects the conclusion that any group has effective control, the study supports the case made by Spurr and Lorimer: a few developers are very large and very powerful even if it cannot be proven that their size and power resulted in higher land prices.

The Markusen study also touches on the effectiveness of the Ontario Land Speculation Tax imposed in 1974 to respond to rising land prices. The act imposed a 20 per cent tax on any transaction that seemed speculative: sales under plans of subdivision were exempt, as were sales where the land continued to be farmed; therefore, the legislation wasn't intended to focus in on anything other than random trading of possible development sites. The study concludes that the effect of the legislation would probably be to increase the concentration of holdings, and that little tax would be collected. What remains unsaid is that a tax on the profits made on land might have been a more effective tool if the object was to dampen land prices for new houses.

A 1989 study of Mississauga, a growing suburb on the edge of Toronto, concluded there was a significant concentration of land ownership. The percentage of residential land registered by the four largest developers in Mississauga was as follows: in 1971, 59 per cent; in 1981, 46 per cent; in 1985, 37 per cent; in 1986, 59 per cent (Zubowski 1989, p. 32, cited by Clayton 1991). Other studies have cited comparable instances of concentration in other cities (Munro 1987).

Clayton concludes, in a study for the Canadian Home Builders Association carried out with financial assistance from CMHC, that concentration seems to be the wave of the future. Implying that the change that occurred in the 1970s was reasonable and perhaps natural, the study confirms the approach taken thirteen years earlier by Lorimer:

> The trend toward increasing concentration of the residential development industry during the 1960s and 1970s continued in the 1980s and is forecast to persist in the 1990s. In some urban centres in the 1990s, this is expected to result occasionally in the largest developers attaining, at least temporarily, some oligopolistic power over the availability and pricing of building lots. (Clayton 1991, p. 1)

This conclusion might provide the basis for governments to take fresh initiatives to reduce the price of new housing. The land question may indeed be one single question, not two, since the matter of industry concentration seems now to be a fait accompli.

Municipal land banking

One proposal to avoid large increases in land costs is public land assembly or land banking, often carried out by the municipal government. To attract industry, land banking has been frequently employed by municipalities as they create industrial parks which are then used as an enticement to new industries. Less frequently, land banking has been pursued for housing purposes.

Spurr notes five municipalities that have banked suburban land for new housing: Kingston, Peterborough, Hamilton, Saskatoon and Red Deer (Spurr 1976, Chapter 4). Land banking offers a municipality the chance not only to control price, but also to direct growth, establish and achieve planning objectives, and meet social goals that otherwise might not be met. Unfortunately, with the exception of Red Deer and, for some years, Saskatoon, these cities used land banking to fuel growth with little regard for securing other objectives.

While in each case the program was successful at getting house lots into the market, Spurr notes, the key issue is the pricing policy decided on by the municipality. It can sell at cost, which would often be much less than the private market price, or it can sell closer to the market and make a profit that the municipality then can use for other purposes. With the exception of Red Deer, where the municipality's land was virtually the only land available for new housing, the decision has most often been to sell for a profit. Apparently the attraction of easy money is greater than the pressure to offer less expensive housing.

CMHC offered land-banking and land-assembly opportunities for municipalities until 1978, when Greenspan's report was used as the excuse to kill those programs. As in noted in Chapter 9, land banking was often used by municipalities in the 1970s to buy land that was then used for non-profit housing programs: it was not used to promote suburban house building nor to ensure that its cost was the lowest possible.

Conclusions

The relationships between corporate land ownership, effective market control and land prices received considerable attention during the 1970s as land prices rose quickly. Since that time, however, these questions have received little attention, although there is reason to believe that effective oligopolies of suburban land have been established in many metropolitan centres. These questions require contemporary analysis and debate. If the experience of the 1970s is any guide, one can expect land prices to again rise sharply with negative impacts on house-buyers, and these issues to again come to the fore.

Chapter 7

Private Rental Housing Programs

Support for private rental housing and renters has never been at the forefront of housing policy in Canada. As Hulchanski says, "The aim of Canadian housing policy has been to make ownership of a detached house, and more recently, a condominium apartment or townhouse, a feasible option for those able to qualify for a mortgage" (Hulchanski 1988, p. 18).

Various reasons account for the limited attention received by rental housing. Tenants are generally less well off than owners, and thus have less political leverage. Most elected officials and senior civil servants are owners, not tenants, so tenant experiences and problems are not as well known to these decision-makers. And across the country only one-third of households are renters, although in many larger cities tenants account for more than half the population. In Montreal, they make up almost two-thirds of the population.

Rental housing has often been regarded as housing at the bottom of the heap. Thus, while the 1938 National Housing Act contains provisions permitting the implementation of rental programs directed at families with low incomes, only those parts of the act directed to ownership questions were implemented (Hulchanski 1988, pp. 18-19).

The filter-down approach has also played a role in taking the focus away from rental housing. It assumes that less expensive housing will become available or filter down as families move into more expensive housing. Assuming that housing problems are addressed by building expensive, mostly ownership, units, the filter-down approach emphasizes the top of the market, not inexpensive housing. While discredited by almost everyone who has looked hard at it, the filter-down approach has proved to have a long political shelf life.

Rental housing initiatives for low-income families have suffered as a result.

Two triggers have helped put private rental housing programs on government agendas. One trigger is the case made by landlords that subsidies will help deal with rental housing problems. A second is the thought that new construction will help stimulate the economy. In rare instances, concerns about affordability and the plight of low-income tenants have brought rental housing to the fore. The different approaches employed in both areas are discussed in this chapter under two headings: encouraging rental construction, and helping tenants. A third heading touches briefly on questions of repair.

The programs discussed here relate to privately owned rental housing. Programs directed at rental units that are publicly owned, or owned by not-for-profit companies, are reviewed in Chapters 8 and 9. Rent controls are discussed in Chapter 10.

Encouraging an increase in rental units

Governments have a number of ways of encouraging more rental units. They can offer tax benefits or they can offer outright grants and loans. The former do not involve a cash outlay since they are accomplished by not collecting taxes that otherwise would have flowed to the government. These costs are known as "tax expenditures," and since to the unsuspecting public they do not seem to represent an expenditure of new money, they have proven to be considerably attractive to governments. In the case of rental housing this is where major sums have been spent, often without good reason.

Rental units can also be created by governments relaxing zoning controls that smother small-scale change that could lead to more rental units. These techniques are discussed after a review of financial instruments.

CCA: Capital Cost Allowance: The most significant program encouraging landlords to build more rental housing is a tax expenditure program, the Capital Cost Allowance (CCA). The program was introduced for rental housing in a general fashion in 1954, and amended in 1981 and 1987 (Dowler 1983, especially Chapter 3).

CCA permits a landlord to depreciate an apartment building at a certain percentage per year (in 1977 the rate was reduced to 5 per cent for brick buildings) much as an industrial company may depreciate a machine on the assumption that one day it will have to be replaced. The difference, of course, is that the apartment building in all likelihood is increasing in value (not decreasing), so the effect of the CCA is to offer the owner a tax break or subsidy: some of the building's value can be deducted as an expenditure, even though the expenditure has never been incurred.

Lorimer gives a number of examples of how the profits of a development company are offset by CCA deductions, with the quite fictitious result that the company must "struggle" to keep itself in the black. He concludes:

> The effect of the CCA concession is that the developers show huge paper losses on the income properties business on their corporate tax returns, even though their audited financial statements show that they earned profits on income properties. These huge paper losses offset the profits the developers earn and report in other aspects of their business. The result is that, on their income tax returns, the corporate developers are telling Ottawa that they are break-even or near break-even operations and hence have to pay no tax on profits, since they have little or no profits to tax. (Lorimer 1978, p. 65)

CCA is formally only a tax deferral: the taxes are still said to be owing, pending ultimate disposition of the building. Financial statements of development companies show the sum as "deferred taxes"; Lorimer demonstrated that the thirty-five largest public development companies in Canada showed $382 million on their books as deferred taxes at the end of 1975 (p. 66).

Needless to say, owners found many ways of ensuring that the tax was never paid — including demolishing the building just before sale and so claiming the building had no value whatsoever. It would not be unfair to characterize CCA as a straightforward subsidy to landlords of rental housing.

Dowler estimates the annual loss to the government from CCA at about $100 million in the early 1980s (Dowler 1983), but this may have decreased with the 1987 amendment (Fallis 1993, p. 85). Since CCA is available to all landlords, it is unclear whether it has any effect on lowering the cost of rental housing. Apart from the recognition that CCA subsidizes residential landlords (compared with other kinds of investors), it is unclear what influence CCA has in encouraging the construction of more rental housing. CCA has no relationship to the income of the tenant or the monthly rent, and thus does not address questions of affordability, although Steele, citing

Clayton, believes that in principle it does reduce rents (Steele 1993, p. 42).

It is difficult to conclude that CCA helps provide housing for lower income families or that it adds many new units to the private rental stock.

MURBs: Closely related to the CCA is the Multiple Urban Residential Buildings (MURBs) program introduced in 1972, which continued (with a brief interruption in 1980) until the end of 1981. It was introduced at a time of high demand and high interest rates, and Minister of Finance John Turner saw it as a method "to provide a *quick and strong* incentive to the construction of new rental units" (spoken in May 1974, cited by Dowler 1983, p. 26). The MURBs program permitted the CCA deduction against all taxpayer income, not just revenue from the rental units, and it was combined with the deduction of "soft costs" incurred in construction, such as legal and marketing fees, interim financing costs and insurance. Miron argues that MURBs compensated for 1972 changes to the Income Tax Act that limited the writing off of rental loss (Miron 1993a, p. 16).

The savings to investors under the MURBs program are enormous. Taking an example from *CA Magazine* in 1977, Dowler shows that on an investment of $700,000 in a 267-unit MURB development, a taxpayer can claim tax losses of $2.5 million over ten years while still garnering a cash return of $1.3 million (Dowler 1983, p. 37).

On a per unit basis, Dowler estimates the 1983 subsidy to be between $5,600 and $7,200, or 15 to 20 per cent of the capital cost of the unit. As can be imagined, it was an enormously popular investment. Over the seven years it was in place, the cost of the program, through lost revenue, was very high. One claim puts the cost at $2.4 billion (Hulchanski 1988, p. 36), another at $1.3 billion (Anderson 1984). The number of units used as tax shelters was just under 200,000 (Hulchanski 1988, p. 36).

It is questionable whether this program actually resulted in any more units being built than would otherwise have occurred. While the subsidies involved must certainly have attracted money to the rental housing market, there seems no conclusive evidence that any extra units were built when the program was in place: the housing stock did not expand beyond what was otherwise contemplated (Dowler 1983, p. 44).

There seems general agreement that MURB units were costly units, priced at the high end of the market. Deductions permitted were greater if costs were higher, and the greatest market potential in the 1970s was at the luxury end of the market (Dowler 1983, p. 48). One can argue that tenants benefited generally from MURBs because of possibly increased supply, but any benefit to low-income tenants would only have occurred as a result of a filter-down hypothesis, with the limitations already noted. A study of the Vancouver market observed that the amount of subsidy from MURBs that reached renters was limited at best (Gau 1982).

Thus, for all of its expense, one can conclude that the MURBs program did not address issues of affordability and did little or nothing to benefit low-income tenants.

Limited dividend rental: One program to encourage construction of rental housing for lower and moderate-income households was in place for almost forty years. While the idea had been around since 1938, only with changes made in the early 1960s did it become widely effective, until it was ended in 1976. It was known as the "limited dividend" (LD) program since it assumed that the developer's profit should be limited to a fixed rate of return in exchange for the government loaning funds at below current interest rates. The 1960s revision removed the limitation on return and in its place had CMHC set rents, allowing what was considered a reasonable return while still ensuring affordable rents for low-income households. As long as the mortgage loan remained outstanding, CMHC was able to set rents (Adams et al. 1986, pp. 175-76).

With the mid-1960 amendments, the LD program loaned 95 per cent of the capital cost of the project, at rates below what the market would charge. It was an attractive program for developers who were otherwise unable to secure financing, particularly for sites or projects that mortgage lenders feared were not commercially viable. The program gained something of a reputation for funding projects on second-rate sites, such as those bordering industrial areas or close to railway tracks, or projects that might be a trifle too large or not attractively designed. The considerable variation in the amount loaned on an annual basis indicates that the LD program was taken up when private funds were not otherwise available (Fallis 1980, p. 18).

Over its lifetime, the program funded slightly more than 100,000 units, most between the mid-1960s and mid-1970s. It was aimed at households "with incomes ranging from the middle of the lower third to average income, forming a stratum between those who live in public housing and those who purchase housing unassisted in the private market" (Fallis 1980, pp. 69-70).

Since CMHC often waived income limits when a developer had problems renting units in LD financed buildings (Dennis and Fish 1972, p. 238), data on who actually was housed by this program are somewhat unclear. Further, there has never been a thorough study of the effectiveness of the program or of its cost. Fallis concludes that in general the program benefited the targeted group of low- to moderate-income households.

Developers were able to benefit handsomely from the LD program, apart from their ability to manage the buildings and make a return on investment (even if it was "limited"). The easiest profit to be made was at the front end of the project. Having purchased the land and then obtained a rezoning to build the new apartment structure, the developer was able to borrow up to 95 per cent of the capital cost of the project. That capital cost included not only the cost of construction, but also the cost of the land as determined by the developer for the project.

Thus a developer might have assembled land for a project, in the process spending $1 million. Once assembled and rezoned, the land might then be appraised at $3 million. If the construction cost were $5 million, the developer would apply for a loan under the LD program of 95 per cent of the value of the land and the cost of construction — $8 million — and immediately receive, much like a windfall, 95 per cent of a $2 million profit on the land. Tenants, of course, would pay rent based on the value of the land being $3 million, rather than the $1 million actually paid.

This method of making a very quick capital gain on the land is not restricted to the LD program, but can occur in any situation involving land assembly, rezoning and reappraisal. Lorimer calls the monies generated this way "appraisal surplus profits" and considers it a basic method by which developers make profit. Thus while low-income tenants might benefit from a program encouraging rental construction, there is a very clear benefit accruing up front to the developer. Imagine the interest if the tenants moving into the building, rather than just the developer, had the chance to share in this windfall.

Loans and grants: A number of programs to create new private rental units have involved loans and grants of various kinds on a per unit basis.

The *Assisted Rental Program (ARP)*, begun by the federal government in 1974, is perhaps the best known program in this category. ARP was designed to stimulate rental construction by attracting more private capital (Adams et al. 1986, p. 182). It provided developers with loans of up to $1,200 per unit per year (at a time when many units rented for $300 per month), to reduce the rent to the level of existing market rents for similar existing units. The loan was for fifteen years, and depending on certain factors, could be interest free for the whole period.

By the time ARP was cancelled in 1978, loans had been provided to 122,650 units at a cost to the government of $300 million (Hulchanski 1988, p. 36). Since the effect of the program was to bring in units at rents comparable to existing market rents, it is fair to assume that the main beneficiaries of the program were moderate-income tenant households. The program was never intended to help tenants with problems of affordability.

N.H. Lithwick believes that ARP had little effect in creating extra rental units, and that the rental units would have been built in any case. Lawrence Smith, however, sees ARP as an effective spur to construction, and argues that without it the dampening influence of rent controls introduced in 1975 across the country would have prevented the building of new rental units (both cited in Miron 1988, p. 255).

The *Canada Rental Supply Program (CRSP)* was a similar but more limited program, introduced in 1981. By the time CRSP was cancelled in 1984, $61 million had been spent on just 21,700 units (Hulchanski 1988, p. 36). One can assume that even though CRSP was more expensive on a per unit basis, it did nothing to benefit low-income tenants.

Various similar grant and loan programs have been introduced by provincial governments in aid of new rental housing. Ontario, for instance, has seen a number of such programs over the years: the Ontario Rental Construction Grant program offering grants up to $600 per unit per year to top up ARP loans (1977); the Ontario Rental Construction Loan Program offering interest-free loans of up to $6,000 per unit, secured as a second mortgage (1981); and the Innovative Rental Construction Loan program to encourage innovative financial and development arrangements, which was not well promoted and quickly lapsed. These are only a few. All involved grants and loans for the purpose of encouraging new rental housing for moderate-income tenants. British Columbia also established a rental

Photo: Charlotte Sykes

Canada's contribution to house-form structures might well be the semi-detached house, such as those shown here from the Riverdale area of Toronto. Built early in the twentieth century on twenty-foot lots, these houses have a basement and three floors. The house on the left has been divided into two units, one occupying the basement and first floor, the other the top two floors; the house on the right is occupied by four different households.

supply program subsidizing interest rates when market rents were well below economic rents, although the program has been recommended for cancellation (British Columbia 1992, p. 64).

These programs generally cannot be designed in ways that allow them to reach low-income tenants. For obvious reasons, developers have no interest in constructing units for tenants whose income is so low they will be unable to meet the rent on a continuing basis. At best, loan and grant programs to encourage new private rental construction can be expected to be targeted to moderate-income tenants who can pay their own way in the world. Whether or not programs lead to the construction of more rental housing than might otherwise occur is an open question: given the views of Lithwick already noted about the limited effect these programs had on creating extra units, such a positive result should not be assumed.

Second units: One method of encouraging new rental units is to permit owners to create a rental unit — a second or accessory unit

— in their own home. The idea of renting out part of one's home is hardly novel: it was common practice throughout Canada until zoning bylaws emerged in mid-century to prevent it — a matter discussed in greater detail in Chapter 4. (Useful information on this question is found in the 1992 Ontario Ministry of Municipal Affairs publication *Apartments in houses: some facts and figures*. This booklet provides most of the data that follow.) With the difficulty many families face in affording a new home, some developers are now building houses with a self-contained unit all ready to rent out, to help the family meet mortgage payments.

Zoning bylaws in most municipalities in Canada prevent owners from establishing a second unit within their home. Obtaining a rezoning for this small change is time-consuming and often sets neighbour against neighbour. But these constraints have not stopped some owners from creating a second unit: estimates are that as many as 10 per cent of owners in many larger cities now rent out an illegal second unit. Indeed, up to 20 per cent of all new rental units in Vancouver in the late 1980s was supplied by second units (British Columbia 1992, p. 94). These units are often created without any changes to the exterior of the house. The owner's incentive to disregard the law is clear — a monthly rent cheque to help cover the cost of the mortgage.

Second units are unlikely to attract households with children; mostly they are occupied by one or two adults. The incidence of car ownership by tenants of these units is about 40 per cent of that of homeowners. There is no evidence of any adverse impact of second units on property values.

In spite of the tough zoning restrictions enacted by municipal councils, surveys in many Ontario municipalities show, surprisingly, that two-thirds or more of the population favours or has no objection to second units. The Ontario government has used this support as the basis for legislation introduced in 1992 to prevent municipalities from stopping an owner from creating a second unit. In British Columbia, it is the basis for proposed changes (British Columbia 1992, p. 97).

In general, second units are offered at rents significantly below those for units in apartment buildings. American data show rents for traditional units at $308 per month — and rents for second units at $227. A 1989 study in Vancouver found rents for second units to be 37 per cent less than those for traditional units; a similar situation is apparent in Toronto. Thus, second units are more generally afford-able to households with lower incomes than are other units.

The number of new units that could be created through a second-unit strategy is impressive, if the conclusions of a study in Vancouver are any indication (Stanbury and Todd 1990). The study found that from about 1976 on, the City of Vancouver "withheld enforcement" of bylaws restricting second units. The number of illegal units grew from fewer than 6,000 in 1976 to 26,000 in 1986 — an increase of more than 20,000 units. By way of comparison, during that same period 31,800 new housing units, both ownership and rental, were constructed in the city. (Of course, many new units were also built in municipalities outside the city of Vancouver during that period.) Thus the number of second units created was almost two-thirds of the number of traditional units created in the city. Clearly, a second-unit approach can add a significant number of new rental units to the housing stock. In many cases, second units are created in neighbour-hoods that have lost population as a result of shrinkage in family and household size, leaving extra capacity in sewage and water services, which these units can utilize without any additional public expenditure.

A second-unit approach, although not yet tried on a large or consistent basis, seems to hold considerable promise. It can create a considerable number of units; those units will generally rent for less than traditional units, and thus be more affordable to households with lower income; the creation of these units does not generally involve public expenditure on new infrastructure; and the program has no costs associated with it. For a government wishing to address questions of affordability in an effective manner, it seems like an excellent option.

All that lies in the way of its implementation is the cultural bias against mixing different incomes and families. In some cases it is a not insignificant barrier.

Some provinces have adopted programs that help owners create units in existing buildings through various grants and loans. Ontario's "Convert-to-Rent" program introduced in 1982 is one such example. However, the problem rarely lies in obtaining the funds needed to create the unit: the problem is the difficulty in securing zoning approval. The program has met with little acceptance.

Helping tenants

The best way to help a tenant is to pay some or all of the tenant's rent. Two kinds of programs attempt to do this: rent supplement and shelter allowances.

Rent supplement: Since 1971, the federal government has been sharing in the costs incurred by provinces involved in rent supplement programs. The designated provincial agency makes an agreement with a landlord to meet the rent on a unit, then selects a tenant for the unit and sets the rent for the tenant on some basis geared to the tenant's income. The tenant pays the geared-to-income rent to the landlord, and the province supplements that to reach the rent the landlord requires. Agreements with landlords are signed for varying periods of time.

In the 1980s, some 32,600 units were being subsidized under rental supplement programs with costs shared generally equally by the federal government and provinces. More than half these units were in Ontario, one-quarter in British Columbia, and the rest spread throughout the country. The cost to the federal government for the fiscal year 1984/85 was $44 million, implying an average subsidy from the federal government of about $1,300 a unit, or a total public subsidy of $2,600 a unit (Canada 1986, p. 51ff.). By 1985, the rent supplement program was winding down, and new agreements were not replacing expired agreements.

There are two obvious merits to the program. First, by taking a small number of rent supplement units in a large number of buildings, the province can ensure that there is no undue concentration of low-income families, a criticism that some have laid at the door of public housing. As Albert Rose notes, "The great advantage of this program is that low income families are interspersed in the community with other families" (Rose 1980, p. 120). Second, unlike many of the units made available under programs that increase the rental stock, the housing made available under rent supplement is clearly intended for lower income households. If affordability is the issue, rent supplement can be assured of addressing it, since the program is well able to direct the benefits to specific tenants. The federal task force study noted, "The private landlord rent supplement program is the most effectively targeted of the federal social housing programs. The average income of program clients in 1984 dollars was just under

$9000 a year [which would put them in the country's bottom two income quintiles]" (Canada 1986, p. 53).

But the rent supplement program has some limitations. "The obvious disadvantage of a rent-supplement program is that it does not add to the total housing stock — it allocates a portion of the existing stock to lower income groups. At a time of inordinate tightness in the housing market, when vacancies in multiple dwellings are ... low ..., there is little or no incentive for landlords to enter into such agreements" (Rose 1980, p. 120). The rent supplement program works best when there is a large supply of rental units and the main problem being addressed is affordability. The federal task force noted that "landlords are not likely to participate in the program if they can rent their unit on the market" (Canada 1986, p. 53). As vacancy rates plunged in the early 1980s, the demand from landlords for new rent supplement units vanished.

Some note a third problem with the program: when the lease expires, the tenants must move on. Since leases under the program have generally been for less than ten years and many for only three years, the tenant has no security. Further, as with many other programs, including loan and grant programs like ARP, there is no continuing benefit from the money spent: all benefits end when the lease ends. Some suggest that public funds would be better spent securing equity in units.

Given continuing low vacancy rates in most Canadian cities and the general collapse of interest in new rental units by the private sector, there seems little future to a rent supplement program in the private sector. However, it will continue to be used by non-profits and non-profit co-ops.

Shelter allowances: Rent supplements are attached to the unit rented. When the subsidy is portable and related directly to the tenant rather than to the unit, the arrangement is referred to as a housing or shelter allowance, or in an American context a housing voucher. This subsidy is used in a number of provinces, often for low-income senior citizens (Streich 1993, p. 267).

The allowance is a cash payment or transfer to a family, often paid on a monthly basis. The family selects its own accommodation, making its own arrangements with the landlord.

The specific arrangements can be worked in various ways. For instance, the tenant can be told that the allowance will only be paid for units meeting certain standards of repair, or within a certain cost ceiling. Further, conditions can be laid down as to who gets the allowance, based on income or family size. Some American cities — Cleveland, for example — have limited the number of available allowances, awarding them on a lottery basis in the same way that Ontario in the 1970s provided subsidies for new ownership units to moderate-income families on a lottery basis.

The merit of a shelter allowance is that it goes entirely to help a low-income tenant meet the rent of a unit the tenant wants to rent. In short, it permits low-income tenants to operate within a market system of housing. The benefits all flow to that end. Hulchanski has been a strong critic of shelter allowances, stating:

> The most serious concern about a full-scale shelter allowance program is rent inflation ... because [allowances] directly and immediately stimulate demand rather than supply, [and they] permit more of the population to compete for the existing rental units. Unless there is a healthy vacancy rate and supply of new affordable rental units coming on stream, normal market dynamics will lead to increased rent levels in general, i.e. for all tenants. (CUCS 1983, p. 46)

Hulchanski believes that the benefits of shelter allowances will flow not to the tenant but to the landlord in the form of higher rents — just as first-time home-buyer grants were said to result in a price increase in new homes equal to the amount of the grant.

Some have disagreed with this criticism, notably Steele, who draws on Canadian evidence as well as an American study on housing allowances. The American study (described fully in Chant 1986, Chapter 4), begun in 1970, cost $160 million: $80 million was spent on various kinds of housing allowances, and the other $80 million was spent studying the results of the expenditure. Hulchanski argues that the very high vacancy rates in the cities involved in the U.S. study make the findings not useful for Canadian cities (also see Kjellberg 1984). Steele, however, comes to different conclusions about the validity of shelter allowances. Reviewing a small housing allowance program in Manitoba, she found that rents did not rise even as quickly as inflation. Steele has proposed a shelter allowance program for all of Canada at an annual cost for 1984 of about $300 million. Other estimates run as high as $700 million annually (see Chant 1986, p. 238), depending on the size of the allowance and whom it would go to. Clayton estimates an annual cost in Ontario in

1993 of $274 million, or about $1,000 for each of the families in core need taking advantage of the program (UDI 1993, p. 4).

While there has been a strong debate about shelter allowances, and much support from developers and landlords who see it as a way of readily housing low-income households in existing vacant units, a sizable shelter allowance program has never been introduced in Canada. The reluctance to try the program might not relate to the criticisms of Hulchanski, however valid those criticisms might be: rather, it might simply reflect what governments see as limited political benefit from helping low-income tenants.

Maintaining good repair

Ensuring that housing is in good repair has been a public concern for more than a century. This concern has been addressed most directly through municipal building codes and health bylaws, which gained favour early in the century. Like other public health measures, this approach has had considerable positive impact on the problem.

However, some rental property has continued to fall below acceptable standards of repair. Government programs have included financial incentives through loans and grants since 1937, although usually these programs are directed more to homeowners than to landlords.

In 1954 the federal government established a Home Improvement Loans program, guaranteeing loans for the repair of ownership or rental property. The Residential Rehabilitation Assistance Plan (RRAP) was established in 1973, with special emphasis on repairs in areas that a year or two earlier would have been called "blighted" and ready for bulldozing through the urban renewal programs cancelled just the year before. RRAP included a forgivable loan to owners with low income. Participating landlords had to agree to have their rents controlled — a condition that made RRAP unattractive to many landlords.

Serious repair problems for high-rise apartments appear to be on the horizon as discussed in Chapter 3, although programs have yet to be devised to respond to them. Numerous tenant groups have threatened rent strikes to achieve a reasonable standard of repair, and while examples can be cited where the strike or the threat of strike has been successful, such tactics have never been sanctioned by any province in Canada. Tenants continue to rely on the vigilance of municipal building inspectors, which sometimes leaves much to be desired.

In Ontario, municipalities are permitted in limited circumstances to enter property and make repairs the landlord refuses to make, then to levy the costs against the property and collect them through property taxes. This is an extraordinary remedy, and available only through a cumbersome procedure. Like a rent strike, it seems to function better as a threat than in practice.

Conclusions

Programs in support of private rental housing have rarely been directed to those with the most significant housing needs. The beneficiaries have often been those already wealthy enough to build new units. The rent supplement program has been able to target low-income recipients effectively, but the program has not been widespread, and the amount spent on it compared with that spent on increasing the supply of units unaffordable to low-income households is small. The shelter allowance program, while attractive in principle, may not be able to generate enough political support to be implemented, and in any case it could only be effective in cities where vacancy rates are high — and such cities are difficult to find in Canada.

"Despite the political and economic imperatives for government action which stemmed from early and continued documentation of rental housing problems," Joan Selby notes, the response has "been minimal, piecemeal and reactive ..." (cited in Hulchanski 1988, p. 33).

Chapter 8

Public Housing

Fifty years ago, public housing was considered the most significant answer to accommodating families with low incomes. Today, it is reviled. Like other issues in the housing field, public housing is shrouded in misunderstandings and preconceptions. Public housing projects are frequently portrayed as high-density jungles occupied by mother-led families on welfare. And the solutions often advanced to remedy public housing problems — more community facilities, tenant management, tenant ownership, a mix of low-income and middle-income families — are rarely relevant and in most cases do nothing to address real problems.

"Public housing" is a precise term, meeting two criteria: it is housing owned by a government or government agency; and rent paid on all units is calculated according to household income. Public housing does not include the various kinds of non-profit housing (as discussed in the next chapter), even if it is owned by a government agency.

A history of public housing in Canada

The housing shortage of the Second World War led to the first direct government involvement in house-building in Canada. Wartime Housing Limited was established by the federal government in 1941 to build housing for workers in government industries. The results of WHL can still be seen in many cities: modest one-and-a-half storey bungalows with steeply pitched roofs. At the beginning these were rented at moderate rates. When Wartime Housing merged with the Veterans' Rental Housing program after the war, even more homes were built; by 1949, 49,530 units, mostly single-family houses, had been constructed. Then, as the war fever wore off and the federal government decided that the provision of housing would generally be left to the private sector, the program was wound down and the housing was sold off (see Rose 1980, pp. 28-30).

Photo: City of Calgary Archives

Canada's first public housing was built by Wartime Housing Limited, during and after World War II. The style was economical, making the best use of interior space to effect the greatest cost savings. This example is from Calgary.

The continuing challenge for governments to intervene directly to meet housing needs was picked up by city governments. In 1947, voters in Toronto endorsed the expenditure of $6 million to build Regent Park, a city-owned public housing project covering half a dozen blocks of cleared land. The 1,300 units were to be rented on a geared-to-income basis, and the design was quite similar to the first public housing project built in North America, the 1934 Cedar-Central project in Cleveland — brick, three-storey, cruciform buildings spread on a sea of grass. The name mimicked John Nash's 1812 plan for luxury homes in a park-like setting in London, Regent's Park (Sewell, 1993, pp. 66-73).

Several other cities such Saint John, St. John's and Winnipeg proposed housing developments of their own, although on a much smaller scale (OAHA 1964, p. 40). The federal government responded with amendments to the National Housing Act in 1949, which authorized a federal-provincial partnership to build and manage rental housing for low-income families. The new legislation required the federal government to cover 75 per cent of capital costs and operating losses; the remaining 25 per cent would be covered by the province. The province would manage the housing.

Central Mortgage and Housing Corporation established an architectural division, which prepared plans for a number of large projects in the 1950s such as Lawrence Heights, Regent Park South and Warden Woods in Toronto; Skeena Terrace and McLean Park in Vancouver; Mulgrave Park in Halifax; and Jeanne Mance in Montreal. The plans were well praised by other architects (Rose 1980, p. 34). Some projects were in the suburbs, on the edges of the city; others were in city centres where older houses ("slums," as they were designated by the planners) were demolished to create vacant land on which to build.

The idea of slum clearance was not new — it had received much attention among planners and social critics in Canada for several decades. The Halifax explosion in 1917 led to the unexpected introduction and implementation of new planning ideas on the demolished site, and the Bruce Report, documenting slum conditions in Toronto in 1932, gave legitimacy to slum clearance as the way to deal with housing problems (Sewell 1993).

By the late 1950s, about 12,000 units had been built under the 1949 public housing program, representing something less than 1 per cent of the total housing units built in Canada during that period (Hulchanski 1988, p. 19). Ironically, this new public housing was less than one-quarter of the 50,000 moderately priced units that Wartime Housing had built and rented, but had then sold off — perhaps the largest squandering of a low-income housing resource ever seen in Canada (Miron 1988, p. 253; Bacher 1993, p. 181).

By the end of the 1950s public housing activity had slackened considerably. Municipalities had difficulty finding the money for the new infrastructure required for these developments (Rose 1980, p. 37), and provincial governments had little interest in contributing 25 per cent of capital costs. Although the original impetus for public housing had come from municipalities, the 1949 program had removed any role for municipalities, so the push for new projects had been taken away (CMHC 1990a, p. 6).

In 1964, amendments to the National Housing Act revitalized the program. Under the new program CMHC would provide 90 per cent of the capital costs, reducing the provincial contribution to 10 per cent. Operating losses would be shared equally, not 75/25 as in the 1949 program, but ownership of the projects would remain with the provinces.

Albert Rose, one of the progenitors of public housing in Canada, calls the legislation a "turning point," putting all the questions about whether low-income families would be offered decent housing "squarely in the laps of the provincial governments" (Rose 1980, pp. 40-41).

In May 1964, the same month the NHA amendments were approved, Ontario introduced and approved legislation to establish the Ontario Housing Corporation (OHC) as its public housing arm. OHC immediately began an aggressive program of acquiring small buildings and municipally sponsored projects, and encouraging new construction. OHC's basic policy was that it would act only at the request of local authorities: it would not build in a municipality without that municipality's approval (Rose 1980, pp. 102-5).

Other provinces established comparable agencies for the same purposes in the next few years. The building activity was remarkable. In 1964 there were about 10,000 units of public housing in Canada; by the end of 1974 that number had risen to 115,000.

But this activity generated criticism, as Rose notes:

> The house-building industry displayed increasing alarm at the significance of public housing in [Ontario] and the rising proportions of annual completions which were in the public sector. The municipalities were more critical than in the past of the growing public housing presence in their midst. Moreover, local governments were receiving demands from tenant groups for increases in local services: recreation, public health, daycare and other social services. Elected and appointed officials tended to blame the activity in public housing for concentrating the needy and the demanding in large projects and for involving citizen involvement in public affairs. For their part, however, tenant and citizen groups ... were critical of the social management in public housing programs, critical of admission procedures, critical of the rent scales and all manner of rules and regulations governing social behaviour. (Rose 1980, pp. 105-6)

A further problem was that the construction of new public housing often was predicated on slum clearance, or the destruction of existing neighbourhoods through urban renewal plans, clearing land to provide a place where the new housing would be built. Residents of these neighbourhoods quarrelled with designations that classified their communities as blighted and tried to stop these plans at City

Hall, in the process criticizing the shortcomings of public housing. These neighbourhood struggles were fought in Halifax, Montreal, Toronto, Hamilton and Vancouver (Fraser 1972; Sewell 1972, 1993).

To deal with these and other criticisms, Prime Minister Trudeau established a Task Force on Housing and Urban Development in 1968, and appointed cabinet minister and former home-builder Paul Hellyer to head it. The Task Force's report was released in January 1969. It caused a sensation. Regarding public housing, Hellyer concluded:

> The big housing projects, in the view of the Task Force, have become ghettos of the poor. They have too many "problem" families without adequate social services and too many children without adequate recreational facilities. There is a serious lack of privacy and an equally serious lack of pride which leads only to physical degeneration of the premises themselves. The common rent geared-to-income formulas do breed disincentive and a "what's the use" attitude toward self and income improvement. There is a social stigma attached to life in a public housing project which touches its inhabitants in many aspects of their daily lives. (Hellyer 1969, pp. 53-54)

Ironically, these criticisms are alarmingly close to those aimed at the blighted areas that many public housing projects had replaced and were meant to improve. They were repeated by Dennis and Fish in their report for CMHC published in 1972. They note that "CMHC architects were eager to prove that they could produce award-winning housing which would make the poor not only as well housed as the average Canadian, but better housed" (Dennis and Fish 1972, p. 185), but conclude that the architects and the program failed:

> ... the poor locations found for residual housing; problems of design caused by cost cutting or attempts to build outstanding housing for the poor; high density, high rise housing dictated by cost concerns; insensitive management that treats public housing tenants as welfare clients; the negative attitude of administrators, surrounding neighbourhoods, and the public generally. All are aspects of the stigma inherent in a program aimed only at the poor. (p. 218)

Photo: CMHC

The Jeanne Mance public housing project in Montreal was typical of the early 1950s: large scale "slum" clearance, followed by the erection of a structure which bore little relationship to its surroundings, and lots of open green space.

Their report indicates that many projects in cities were large, containing more than 200 units apiece, and that by far the largest number of units built in 1968, 1969 and 1970 were apartments, not units in house-form buildings. They recommended that the public housing program be abandoned, and that a new non-profit and co-operative program be introduced.

The urban renewal program, which enabled municipalities to assemble land in downtown neighbourhoods and demolish its housing for the large public housing projects many complained about, was ended in 1972; the non-profit and co-operative program was introduced by the federal government in 1973; and the public housing program was scaled down and finally terminated in 1978, except for the Northwest Territories, where it remained in effect for five more years.

By the time the 1964 public housing program was generally cancelled in 1978, it had resulted in the building of 164,000 new units. The total stock of public housing, some 205,000 units, today represents about 2 per cent of Canada's total housing stock (Hulchanski 1988, p. 19).

Canada's public housing portfolio

In 1988, there were 4,801 public housing projects in Canada, containing 205,692 housing units. (The data in this section come from CMHC 1990a). Almost 90 per cent of the projects contain fewer than 100 units; less than 4 per cent of the projects contain 200 or more units, and some of those projects are exceptionally large — such as Regent Park North, with 1,300 units (p. 13). The image of the large projects has contaminated our understanding of the bulk of public housing in Canada.

Slightly more than two-thirds of units are located in cities of more than 30,000 people: the projects in smaller centres are generally small in size, consisting of ten to fifteen units apiece. Half the units in Canada were built for, and are occupied by, senior citizens (p. 20).

The projects are distributed across the country as Table 8.1 shows. Projects cannot be segregated into either just seniors or family projects, as the chart implies: about 200 projects comprising almost 15,000 units house seniors *and* families with children (p. 20).

About 430,000 people live in public housing. Precise information on who these people are unravels several myths. The age groupings of public housing residents do not reflect those of society at large. One-quarter of residents are under the age of 15 years; another quarter are 65 years of age or more. But in family projects, one-third of the residents are children under 15 years of age (compared with one-fifth in the general population). In seniors' projects one-half of the residents are 75 years of age or older (compared with 4 per cent in the general population). Thus in the family projects the young are overrepresented and in the seniors' projects the over-75s are overrepresented (pp. 26-27).

Average annual income of public housing households in 1988 was $10,632, compared to average renter household income in Canada that year of $25,892. This means average public housing household income is 40 per cent that of renter households in general. Further, 60.7 per cent of public housing households have an annual income of less than $10,000, compared to 18.2 per cent of all renter households. The poor are substantially overrepresented in public housing (pp. 33-34).

Fully 96.1 per cent of public housing households have incomes at or below the core need income thresholds (p. 120). This might be

Table 8.1

Public housing portfolio across Canada

Province	Number of projects	Number of units	Number of units for seniors
Newfoundland	176	4,710	199
P.E.I.	90	951	671
Nova Scotia	477	10,228	6,702
New Brunswick	157	3,892	1,700
Quebec	630	35,632	14,527
Ontario	1,329	96,582	49,770
Manitoba	336	12,808	6,363
Saskatchewan	577	12,353	8,991
Alberta	531	16,899	8,769
British Columbia	100	7,978	3,342
Yukon	22	261	24
N.W.T.	376	3,338	205

Source: CMHC 1990a, pp. 18, 21.

seen as the ultimate proof that the public housing program has successfully targeted low-income families.

Only 18.7 per cent of households list employment as the major source of income, while 30 per cent list social assistance. However, these figures must be kept in a reasonable perspective: 61.5 per cent of all public housing households are retired or unable to work because of disability, and some of these households receive social assistance. Excluding this 61.5 per cent, almost half the remaining households (most of which are families) show employment as the major source of income. Thus, of those who can work, half have found regular work. Given the very low income of public housing tenants, it is clear that those who do work are paid very low wages (pp. 32, 36).

In spite of original intentions that public housing would provide short-term accommodation, about 60 per cent of residents have lived in public housing for five or more years — and one-quarter have lived there for ten years (p. 175). It is generally thought that, on average, tenants in Canada move once every three years; that average obviously doesn't apply to public housing tenants.

In conclusion, the traditional assumptions about the size of public housing projects and who lives there are incorrect. Many projects are small, half the households are senior citizens, and about half of all family heads who can work, do.

Rents are determined in relation to income, but there are a variety of ways in which this is done across the country. Generally, rent calculation is a complicated matter, and a tenant would be lucky, using management manuals, to successfully arrive at a rent calculation that management would agree with. The percentage of income required as rent varies from about 25 to 30 per cent, calculated on gross income (although in Quebec for families it is calculated on 90 per cent of gross income). Some provinces permit a rent reduction based on the age and number of children. To entice tenants with higher incomes not to move out, some provinces have stated that the rent payable should never be more than comparable market rents. Rents for families receiving social assistance are usually set with regard to the shelter allowance portion of social assistance monthly payments, rather than simply as a percentage of income. Provinces differ on how much of the income from working children or spouses should be included in gross income to calculate rent. They also differ on whether the costs of any or all of heat, water and electricity are included in the rent, or whether they are extra charges (pp. 123-31).

Once everything is factored in, about one-third of tenants pay more than 30 per cent of their income in rent (p. 136), so the rent charged is actually above the guideline established for defining when a tenant is in "core need." That this occurs is probably a result of the complexity involved in calculating all of the factors used to determine how much rent should be paid. Thus, while public housing helps, it does not completely address problems of affordability for all its residents. As the 1990 CMHC *Evaluation* report notes, "Overall, 39.9 per cent of households surveyed remain in core need, despite the assistance provided through the public housing program" (p. 145).

Day-to-day management of projects is provided by local housing authorities in many provinces, although direct provincial manage-

Photo: CMHC

McLean Park in Vancouver, a project of the 1950s, mixed townhouses with a high rise, on land which had been cleared of all traces of the past. The townhouses are all straight lines: a less graceful design would be hard to imagine. The yards are open areas marked by boundary fences, just to make clear that this is no one's space in particular.

ment is provided in British Columbia, Newfoundland, and much of New Brunswick, Yukon and P.E.I. There are 1,092 local housing authorities across Canada. Two-thirds of these authorities manage fewer than 50 units; only 242 authorities manage more than 100 units, and a relatively small number of authorities manage large projects (p. 23). For instance, in Vancouver, the average size of ten projects is 216 units; in Winnipeg, two projects average 280 units apiece; in Toronto, five projects average 488 units apiece; in Montreal, one project had 796 units; in Halifax, ten projects averaged 160 units apiece (Dennis and Fish 1972, p. 182). On the whole, however, public housing projects are small, and managed locally.

The average operating loss for every public housing unit in Canada in 1986 was about $3,100: revenues were $2,450 per unit, expenditures $5,545 (CMHC 1990a, p. 272). From a subsidy point of view, the larger projects with apartments are more cost-effective than smaller projects. In 1986, operating losses per unit were higher for smaller projects than for larger projects, and higher for townhouse units than apartment units.

After amortization, the largest expenditure item is property tax, which between 1979 and 1986 averaged $760 per unit annually. Property taxes in Ontario, Quebec and Manitoba were much higher than elsewhere, averaging $853, $866 and $826 per unit per annum, respectively (p. 256). One interesting question is whether public housing receives local services of equivalent value to the property taxes actually paid. Many large projects do not receive municipal garbage pickup, street cleaning or lighting (all are handled by housing management, since streets are often private), and some would argue that other municipal services such as recreation do not meet the needs of public housing residents. It is easy to conclude that public housing pays more in property taxes than is provided in municipal services.

Generally, the public housing stock is in good condition. A 1988 survey found that 94 per cent of public housing units met NHA Minimum Property Standards, and that those in most need of repair were built twenty-five or more years ago (p. 58).

In summary: most public housing projects are small and are managed locally. Public housing contains an abundance of both older and younger residents, all with very low incomes, and half of those capable of working do so, often at very low paying jobs.

Public housing criticisms

Several criticisms of public housing have already been cited. Often the critical conclusions people have come to about large projects are applied to all projects, even those which are quite small. Since there are more than 1,000 housing authorities, it is unfair to tar them all with the same brush. Complaints made against social behaviour in large projects rarely hold in smaller projects. Thus, it is important to be as specific as possible in criticizing public housing, since most criticisms apply to only large-scale projects.

For our purposes, the criticisms discussed are those that apply to large urban projects — that is, the 3.6 per cent of projects with more than 200 units. The smaller projects rarely exhibit the kinds of problems found in these larger ones, and the prescriptions for change are accordingly generally inapplicable.

The problems with large-scale projects are widespread, and not restricted to Canada. At a 1984 conference on problems in public housing held in the Netherlands, Hugo Priemus of the Netherlands said:

In a number of countries great problems have arisen with the management of post-war dwellings. As a result we are in danger of losing much that we had taken for granted ...

We do not know what to do. Vacancy and vandalism. Financial losses. Dissatisfied tenants ... (Prak and Priemus 1985, pp. 7-8)

At the same conference, Robert Kolodny of the United States observed, "Public housing in the United States has been in trouble for at least 20 years" (p. 11). The list of problems was augmented by speakers from France, the United Kingdom, Sweden and Belgium.

The problems in Canada, it seems, are small compared to those in United States. There, a number of public housing projects have been abandoned and ultimately demolished. The most spectacular demolition was of the Pruitt-Igoe project in St. Louis. Pruitt-Igoe was designed by Minoru Yamasaki, architect of the World Trade Centre in New York City, and was built in 1955. It consisted of seventeen eleven-storey buildings containing a total of 2,764 units. Each floor of each building included covered walkways for resident use, giving reality to Le Corbusier's idea of "streets in the air." The American Institute of Architects recognized the design with an award.

But, as Newman recounts in *Defensible Space*, the design had everything to do with architects' preconceptions, and nothing to do with how people lived. Within fifteen years Pruitt-Igoe had been internally destroyed by residents, and in July 1972 it was demolished in staged explosions. One critic notes in a caption to the now-famous photo of the demolition: "Mankind finally arrives at a workable solution to the problem of public housing" (Wolfe 1981, p. 81).

The fact that many countries experience public housing problems makes it all the more important to be clear and specific about the exact nature of the problems with large-scale public housing projects in Canada. The numbers are quite high: Canada has 330 projects with between 100 and 199 units, and 148 projects with more than 200 units (CMHC 1990a, p. 185). Large projects which everyone admits have problems stretch from Halifax (Mulgrave Park and Uniacke Square) to Vancouver (MacLean Park, Raymer Gardens — now named Stamps Place, and Skeena Terrace).

The Metro Toronto Housing Authority (MTHA), the largest in Canada, will serve as an example to explore the criticisms of public housing in some depth. It will also serve as an example in discussing solutions to problems that are generally applicable to public housing and to large projects across the country. (Further information and detail can be found in Sewell 1988.)

MTHA is responsible for the management of 110 projects consisting of about 29,000 units in Toronto. MTHA's portfolio is almost entirely large projects, any one of which would contain more units than the whole portfolio of many housing authorities in Canada. These large projects are generally representative of large projects in other Canadian cities.

Some 24,000 units of MTHA projects are managed directly by MTHA staff; 5,000 are managed by private firms under contract. MTHA has responsibility for tenants in a further 4,000 units for which MTHA holds a rent supplement agreement with the landlord.

The total resident population in 1988 was estimated at 100,000, although it was thought that serious housing and affordability problems in Toronto in the late 1980s had probably led a further 25,000 people to occupy units as guests and relatives of the registered tenants.

Some problems and criticisms are common to all authorities across the country, since they relate to management practices and operating policies. These issues — management, rents, maintenance and repair — are discussed first, followed by comments pertaining to large projects.

Administrative issues: MTHA faces one problem that is common to all public housing authorities in Ontario, but may not be present in the same degree for housing authorities in other provinces: it is an authority without authority. Quite simply, it has responsibility for responding to all management problems, but not the authority to act as it sees fit. In Ontario, public housing was first owned and managed by the Ontario Housing Corporation. In the mid-1970s, as criticism of projects grew, the provincial government wanted to distance itself from day-to-day management in order to avoid criticism. It was then decided to establish separate housing authorities in municipalities where there were public housing projects. These local authorities would provide day-to-day management. The local housing authority would consist of representatives of the province, the federal government and the regional or county government. The chair would be appointed by the province. Some fifty-six local housing authorities were established.

While there was an interest in assuring more local control than under direct OHC management, the province and OHC remained interested in keeping a firm grip on the general issues surrounding public housing: how applicants were selected; how rent levels were established; general operating policies; and since the province remained responsible for sharing any operating loss with the federal government, the operating deficit of each authority. Budgetary concerns meant OHC and the province would approve annual budgets (including proposals for major repairs), and would also oversee staffing arrangements, including the selection of each general manager, total staff complement and rates of pay.

Agreements were entered into with each housing authority to reflect this distribution of power. They state that authorities can only change the staffing complement with the consent of the Ministry of Housing; can fill senior positions only with individuals approved by the Ministry; and cannot alter wage rates without the consent of the Ministry. Further, agreements state that authorities must abide by all OHC policies and are not permitted to substitute their own policies.

In essence, MTHA does not have the authority to control any of the matters that concern it. It must abide by province-wide policies set by ministry personnel and by an appointed OHC board, none of whom have any responsibility for running projects. MTHA has all the responsibility to run a very large housing portfolio, but none of the authority to do so. As any manager will note, the arrangement is a recipe for disaster. Effective management occurs only if responsibility and authority are lodged in the same place. Thus, in MTHA and other authorities in Ontario, management action is often filled with a sense of powerlessness and resignation, limitations that underlie the many problems in public housing: the difficulty tenants have in transferring from one unit to another; the strange point-rating system used to select new residents; the Draconian and ineffective policy that prohibited MTHA tenants from having pets; and so forth.

Rent policy is another area of contention for many housing authorities. Rents at MTHA, like rents in other public housing projects across Canada, are geared to income to meet federal requirements, and details of rent policy are set by provincial ministries. As already noted, rent-setting policy is extremely complicated, involving a number of factors pertaining to income and family size, and rents change whenever household income changes. Calculating rent

Photo: CMHC

Halifax's problem project is Mulgrave Park, a mixture of high rise and townhouses. This photo makes clear that the townhouses face onto a private walkway (bounded by a high cement retaining wall), rather than a public street. Note the graffiti on the wall; Alice Coleman would draw conclusions from it.

payable by each household takes up a considerable amount of staff time and energy in MTHA as well as in social agencies working with tenants.

At MTHA, a committee established by the MTHA Board concluded that the rent system discriminated against tenants who were employed, and discouraged tenants on government assistance from taking jobs. The complexity of determining the rent due also meant some tenants were vague (some claimed dishonest) in reporting their exact income to MTHA.

Working with tenants, staff and other interested parties, the committee reviewed alternatives and sought permission to implement a new rent policy that called for a three-year lease. At the beginning of the lease, the rent would be determined on the basis of income, and, subject to an annual rent increase equivalent to the increase in industrial wages in Toronto, the rent would not vary on the basis of income for three years: the tenant could earn whatever income he or she was able to earn, but the rent would not change. Provision would be made for situations where income decreased from that on which the calculation was made (Sewell 1988).

This proposal, according to the estimates made, would raise the same amount of revenue as the old rent system; would cost significantly less to administer; would free up staff time to deal with other matters; and would clearly inform tenants of their rental obligation during the term of the lease. Further, it would mean that tenants would not have continually to report changes in family income and status to MTHA staff. MTHA could become a hands-off landlord, just like other landlords.

The proposal was not agreed to by the Ministry of Housing, and thus was never put to CMHC for its agreement. Rents have continued to be mired in confusion and to be calculated according to a policy that discourages those tenants who wish to move from reliance on government income assistance to employment.

Maintenance and repair are a third problem area for many housing authorities. MTHA and other housing authorities are among the few landlords in Canada that do not have on-site superintendents responsible for day-to-day management and repair. On-site superintendents, whether resident or simply with a daytime office in the building or project, can be called in to review needed repairs, and make minor repairs or call in contractors for major repairs; make annual inspections of all units; and ensure cleanliness of the premises; and ensure good staff–tenant relations. This is normal practice in most privately owned buildings.

Across the country, two-thirds of public housing projects with more than 200 units have on-site offices; only one-third of projects with between 100 and 199 projects do (CMHC 1990a, p. 185). MTHA is one of those which does not generally have on-site offices. Consequently, tenants requesting a repair must phone a central number, which will then relay the request to staff at a nearby office, which will then dispatch someone to look at the request for a repair. It is a cumbersome method of dealing with tenant repair requests and it led MTHA to establish a goal of trying to respond to requests within ten days — a figure that is considered laughably long in the private sector.

MTHA's inability to deal with requests for repair carried through to other aspects of maintenance: up to one-third of the vehicles in many MTHA parking lots were visibly derelict; heating facilities were in very poor repair, with significant cost implications; elevators frequently broke down; fire alarms constantly rang when there were no fires; grounds and corridors were messy and littered with garbage, often smelling of urine.

MTHA apparently has not been alone in maintaining poor states of repair. One-third of tenant households in family projects across the country are dissatisfied with the repair of their units and with the speed with which requests are handled, and one-fifth with the maintenance of the grounds (CMHC 1990a, p. 155).

These are all signs of serious management problems, some stemming from management's lack of authority, some stemming simply from bad management that tenants experienced. And if management doesn't care about the condition of the project, why should tenants?

Social problems: Many references to social problems in public housing are made on the assumption that public housing creates and accentuates these problems. Many feel that crime rates are higher in public housing projects than elsewhere; that there is a sense of desperation for the people who live there; that projects are overcrowded; that there are too many children, and too many mother-led families; that the concentration of poor people drags people down; that security problems are immense. These are the main reasons for hostility to public housing.

Tenants themselves are worried about these issues. In family projects across the country, 42 per cent of households are dissatisfied with their personal security (CMHC 1990a, p. 155). A CMHC survey states, "The emergence of security as a major concern of tenants is a reflection of the problems with crime in family public housing projects." (CMHC 1990a, p. 281).

What accounts for these problems, and what can be done to address them? An emerging body of literature attempts to link social behaviour with physical design. One author writes:

> If design features can be really disadvantaging, then the worse the design, the larger the percentage of people who will have their lives blighted by it. It is a tragic thought that Utopian designers, with their idealistic intentions, have tipped the balance sufficiently to make criminals out of potentially law-abiding citizens, and victims out of potentially secure and happy people. (Coleman 1985, p. 22)

Oscar Newman's 1972 book *Defensible Space* was the first to make a correlation between design of public housing and security and crime, showing how security could be improved and crime levels could be reduced by different design of public housing to make space "defensible." Some of the design suggestions made by Newman are not to house families with children in buildings more than three storeys high; to restrict any apartment entrance to no more than 200 families; to modify the fire stairs in high-rise buildings; to design for natural surveillance of common areas.

Alice Coleman documents social problems as well as security issues and criminal behaviour in council housing projects in London, England, and looks at how design affects those problems. Coleman notes that it is very difficult to obtain good information on social problems in public housing projects, since data are usually gathered on a census basis not co-terminous with the project, and in any case some of the data are unreliable. Instead, as a basis of analysis she chose "types of malaise that leave behind visible traces: litter, graffiti, vandal damage, and excrement" (p. 23). All are visible and measurable.

Coleman's research measured these four factors in a number of blocks of council housing projects in London, then related them to design features of the blocks, making liberal use of Newman's studies, which were largely done in New York City. Nearby areas were used for comparison purposes. A total of fifteen different design elements were considered in respect to the four factors noted, and she concludes that the "ringleaders of the anti-social design gang" are a high number of dwellings using a single entrance; a high number of dwellings in any block; a high number of storeys per block; the presence of overhead walkways; and what is called "spatial organization," or the extent to which spatial arrangements allow good surveillance in and around the blocks. These are the elements that substantially determine the presence of litter, graffiti, vandal damage and excrement.

Coleman then examines other culprits often blamed for aggravating the four variables of malaise. She dismisses the following factors as contributing not nearly as much to anti-social behaviour as the five anti-social design elements: size of the project; age of the project; poverty; unemployment; concentration of "problem families"; administration; and presence of recreational facilities and shops. Regarding the "problem family" hypothesis, for instance, she notes, "We have been unable to find any properly tested evidence that substantiates the hypothesis, which is in stark contrast to the wealth of evidence we have assembled on how badly-designed blocks make it difficult for normal people to cope" (p. 92).

She believes that "child density contributes to high levels of abuse in badly designed buildings," and puts a density target for problems at no more than one child under 15 years of age for every six adults (p. 180). She believes population density to be irrelevant to social problems, as is the amount of nearby open space (p. 178).

Thus, Coleman comes to the conclusion, as did Newman, that the substantial influences on criminal and anti-social behaviour, on feelings of personal security, and on the ability of residents to "self-police" the places where they live have more to do with project design than with the often-blamed social characteristics of the inhabitants. What is innovative and helpful in Coleman's approach is that it does not blame the residents, who by and large would be hard to change: it blames a physical environment that can be modified in a relatively easy fashion.

There seems no reason to doubt the relevance of the findings of Coleman and Newman to large projects in the MTHA portfolio or elsewhere in Canada. Local circumstances must be taken into account in applying these findings, of course. For instance, the fire stair system in New York buildings is not standard practice in Ontario, and public housing projects in Canada make much more limited use of overhead walkways than do council housing projects in the U.K. Both are sources of danger. But generally it is probably fair to conclude, as Newman and Coleman do, that modifying the design of large public housing projects can substantially reduce anti-social behaviour and fears for personal safety.

Housing for low-income families will always be predominantly occupied by low-income families, some of whom are unemployed and some of whom receive social assistance. Units with several bedrooms will usually be occupied by households with children. By themselves, these characteristics should not be surprising, nor should they be a cause for general concern. What is discouraging is that the design of large public housing projects can create and aggravate social problems among such families. Coleman has shown that by taking corrective measures and rehabilitating public housing projects, the incidence of the four factors of malaise can be reduced so they are no more common there than anywhere else in the city.

Thus the perception that social problems are aggravated by large-scale public housing projects is often correct. But the reason for this has more to do with design of the projects than with those who live in the housing. Coleman concludes:

All these discoveries add up to the fact that it is Utopian design that has been imposed upon post-war Britain that appears to be the chief factor in many aspects of social decline in new or redeveloped areas. (p. 180)

Instead of blaming the architects and managers of public housing, neighbours too often blame the residents, who are the victims of poorly designed projects.

Of course, management can take other steps to respond to social problems. Hiring more security guards may have a very limited impact, since throwing more bodies at bad design can hardly be effective. MTHA found that security improved if management showed it cared about problems faced by residents by attempting to respond to complaints rather than ignoring them. If management does not seem to care about a project, residents will not either: but if management does care, resident behaviour improves (Sewell 1988). In the few instances where attempts were made to change staff attitudes, the results were quite positive for staff and tenants alike. Of course, changing corporate culture is never easy.

A variety of other responses are often made to anti-social behaviour and questions of resident security. For example, many suggest public housing would be considerably improved with more parks and recreation facilities — but as Coleman has shown, the absence of these facilities has little to do with aggravated social problems.

The suggestion of more green space might spring from an assumption that public housing is generally too dense, with too many units and families for every acre of land. That perception has little to support it. Most large public housing projects have densities in the range of 25 to 35 units per acre. This density is significantly more than new suburban subdivisions (about 7 units an acre), but significantly less than successful new housing schemes mentioned in Chapter 4, such as Fairview Slopes in Vancouver (at about 60 units an acre) or St. Lawrence in Toronto (at about 100 units per acre). Halifax's most notorious public housing project, Mulgrave Park, has a density slightly under 30 units per acre (349 units on 11.5 acres), although its design (two ten-storey towers, a walk-up apartment structure and a series of townhouses) makes the density seem much higher. (Mulgrave Park won a Canadian Housing Design Award when it was built in the 1960s — as some now say, a sure sign that it does not work well.) Vancouver's problem-ridden Little Mountain project, which consists almost entirely of townhouses, has a density of less than 15 units per acre. One of MTHA's most problem-ridden projects, Lawrence Heights, has a density of 10 units per acre, which is much lower than successful neighbourhoods such as Centretown in Ottawa or the Beaches in Toronto. The problem is not "high" density, and the solution is not more parks.

There are no data to indicate that children who live close to a recreation centre are socially better adjusted than those who live farther away, and without such data, it is difficult to argue that to solve social problems large sums should be spent on recreation facilities. Residents themselves acknowledge this: 90 per cent of families thought recreation facilities were available "nearby" (CMHC 1990a, p. 159).

One significant problem with providing more recreational services is that they are often located within public housing projects to better serve the residents. That kind of location further isolates residents in the project from the surrounding neighbourhood. If they attempt to use other neighbourhood recreation facilities, they are often told they have "their own" facilities that they should use. Recreation facilities do not help knit public housing communities together, but are another example — much like the private dead-end road system found in many large projects — of how the project is different than what surrounds it.

Experience in Toronto with a recreational facility built in Regent Park South in the early 1980s after countless demands by residents and local politicians teaches that it is used only by project residents. Worse, it has become a focus for criminal activity (drug dealing) rather than a means of alleviating social problems.

A second proposal often made to improve social life in large projects is to mix in higher income tenants with lower income tenants. Many suggest that one benefit of this change is that lower income children will pick up better social skills and educational and work habits. However, there is no hard evidence to support this commonly held notion. (Income mix lies at the heart of the non-profit housing programs that replaced public housing; the issue is discussed in more detail in Chapter 9.)

While the absence of income mix does not ensure the existence of social problems, the presence of income mix implies certain things about the community. Of most importance, it implies that people live there by choice, always a sign of a successful neighbourhood. Income limits force tenants who exceed those limits to move out (often those tenants are the very ones who have been economically successful), thus preventing long-term residency except for those with stagnant income. To help a create a community where neighbours have long-term relationships by choice, income limits should not be imposed.

Income mix, then, is one sign of a successful community, although trying to mandate it through a new set of rules will not result in success.

A third suggestion commonly made to improve public housing is to allow or require tenant input into management decisions. The more involvement residents have in the management of their housing, the better that housing will respond to their needs. But not all tenants wish to be involved in management questions: many simply want to pay their rent and receive good management in return.

The problem in most public housing is poor management or an unsatisfactory living environment, and it is often suggested that tenant involvement will ensure better decisions. There seems to be no reason to doubt such a proposal, and all possible avenues should be devised to elicit tenant views of alternatives.

But tenant involvement should not be seen as any great panacea for deeply rooted problems. Too often tenants are chosen by management to sit on committees or the board of a housing authority without regard for whom the tenant might represent, whether the tenant has skills to participate fully in meetings or whether the tenant has the skills and resources to consult with other tenants to ensure that their opinions are fairly represented. Admittedly, others who are appointed to the board may not have these skills, but that lack hardly qualifies a tenant appointee. Many instances of tenant participation smack of management paternalism, with no attempt to ensure that the appointee is anything more than a token representative.

Successful tenant takeovers of the public housing projects in the United States are often cited as examples that should be followed in Canada. American public housing must deal with problems not often experienced in Canada, including questions of race, guns, dying downtowns and persistent underfunding, and solutions there might not be applicable here. Further, the successes cited often seem so police- and rule-oriented in their outcome that they are frightening (Osborne and Gaebler 1993, p. 59f.).

The scope of the problems in large projects does not seem solvable through better tenant representation alone. Better tenant involvement in decisions might be a good start, since it may bring a needed focus and new energy, but it is hardly a final answer.

Another idea that is sometimes proposed is that housing authorities offer units for sale to tenants. In the United Kingdom, local housing authorities were authorized in 1976 to sell tenants the unit they occupied. Tenants were offered substantial discounts from market value — discounts of up to 30 per cent, changed in 1980 to 50 per cent, and then in 1983 to 60 percent — as well as mortgages covering 100 per cent of the purchase price (Howenstine 1983). Only a quarter of British public housing is in apartment form: three-quarters of the six million public units are house-form or terrace style, making them quite attractive to purchase. However, in spite of the very substantial subsidies offered, only 800,000 units, or one-eighth of the total stock, had been sold to tenants by 1983.

Other countries — Denmark, Finland, Germany, France — tried other tenant-purchase schemes, none with great success. One big problem is that public housing tenants are poor: they don't have the money to be able to buy and maintain a home. If the housing unit is sold to someone who can afford it, then the low-income tenant will be evicted but will still require housing, and the shortage of low-income housing will have been aggravated.

There are differing opinions on the financial effects of these sales. Some argue the public will lose financially because of the discount in disposing of public assets; others suggest there will be a public benefit since public subsidies will no longer be needed for the units sold. Some say low selling prices dampen the real estate market generally, although others respond that the niche for public units is so small that other kinds of sale housing are not affected.

Some consequences of these sales are generally agreed on. The most desirable units are sold first (for obvious reasons), so the housing authorities are left with the least attractive. In addition, many buyers may face mortgage default when the economic situation changes and they find they have no work and no resources to fall back on. A purchase might simply be the first step into deep water, followed by speedy eviction. Successful purchasers who do not default take a unit that is forever lost to other low-income families, diminishing the stock of housing for low-income families.

Other purchase arrangements have been suggested, including condominiums, and equity and non-profit co-operatives. All suffer similar kinds of problems and limitations. Selling public housing units is no solution to any kind of problem involving public housing.

Redesign and redevelopment: There is a larger sense beyond resident security and anti-social behaviour in which physical design problems should be viewed. The redevelopment of public housing projects has been suggested as one way of dealing with their social and physical problems. In many cases, redesign can alleviate the worst of the "utopian" characteristics reviewed by Coleman.

Large public housing projects occupy several or many acres of land, and are designed to operate on private roads and walkway systems. The consequences of this design feature are considerable:

- Since there are no public roads in the project, and since whole projects are private property (unlike other parts of the neigh-bourhood), there is no regular police patrol. (Police are not permitted on private property unless they have a search warrant or unless a crime is in process.) Thus incipient criminal behaviour and deviant behaviour must be monitored and controlled by housing authority staff rather than by a public police force.
- Since there are no public roads in the project, the municipality is not responsible for regular street-cleaning, snow-ploughing, street maintenance, street-lighting and garbage collection. These functions all become the responsibility of the housing authority.
- Since there is little distinction between outdoor space that is privately controlled by a tenant family and space that is the responsibility of the housing authority, all outdoor space becomes the responsibility of the authority.
- Since there are no public streets in projects, there is no publicly understood system for numbering units, making home delivery very difficult.

These design elements all come with substantial costs: the housing authority must carry out all of this work itself, often at high cost, with no benefit from efficiencies of scale available to municipalities. According to many tenants, service provided is often poor, but unlike other residents, public housing tenants cannot complain to their elected councillor to ask for services comparable to those available to everyone else. Further, projects were often constructed at less than city-required standards, so that roads and street-lighting in projects are often of inferior quality.

What makes things worse is that the local property taxes paid by every unit of public housing is considerable and, as already noted,

Photos: CMHC

Part of the redesign of Halifax's Uniacke Square involved giving units character and a public face — as was clearly accomplished in the different kinds of front porches attached to units. It is apparent how much the sloping roofs of the porches soften the harsh lines of the original buildings.

municipalities probably collect more property taxes from large public housing projects than they spend.

Several attempts have been made to redesign large projects. Regina's Regent Court, a townhouse project of less than 100 units, was rehabilitated in the 1980s. The physical design changes made were relatively small — landscaping was added and traffic flow was altered, and the units themselves rehabilitated.

Changes made to Halifax's Uniacke Square in the late 1980s were more ambitious. Uniacke Square was built in the mid-1960s, and consisted of about 250 townhouse and maisonette units, many facing onto those hallmarks of modern planning, private courtyards. The redesign took out several housing units, reconfigured other units, and was able to ensure that most units faced onto a public street, and were given a street address. Some public open space was converted into backyards, some paving was pulled up in favour of grass. A daycare centre was added, as well as a local housing office. All units were renovated, and some units received new front porches.

Thus the changes at Uniacke Square were more than simply cosmetic, and consisted of more than just rehabilitation. The way the space worked was regularized, so that the houses faced onto public streets, and had front and back yards.

The cost of these changes was substantial — about $41,000 per unit. If nothing had been done but the rehabilitation of existing units, the cost would have been $16,400 per unit (CMHC 1990a, p. 94). These kinds of costs have not made public housing officials amenable to redesign proposals as a way to address social problems.

Ottawa's Strathcona Heights project has also undergone a successful redesign. It was an eighteen-acre project of 404 units in walk-up apartment buildings, originally built for veterans in the late 1940s. While it was in the same form as public housing, it was not built or operated under traditional public housing programs. In the mid-1980s CMHC sold it to the City of Ottawa's non-profit housing company, City Living. It was hoped that about half the units could be rehabilitated, but experience on the first renovations showed that this could not be done: the units were too small (tenants now think that a three-bedroom unit of 750 square feet is too tiny to live in), and the cost of renovation was more expensive than new construction. Only 60 old units could be saved; 640 new units were built.

The redesign reconfigured circulation routes, which included making a cul-de-sac into a through street, and a new building for senior citizens was built on land that had been previously been a

Photos: City of Ottawa Housing Department

Ottawa's Strathcona Heights project was originally built in the 1940s for veterans, as shown in the top photo. In the 1980s it was purchased by the City of Ottawa's non-profit housing company and redesigned. The lower photo shows how substantial renovation was on the older buildings which were retained: new entrance ways, new wings to enlarge units, new porches, and new facings and a sloped roof to soften the structure.

parking lot. The addition of new units (density was almost doubled from 22 to 39 units per acre) meant that the changes could be paid for without recourse to the taxpayer, by generating revenue from the land price allocated to the new units. This is an example of a redesign of a project much like public housing, which was generally able to fund itself.

In the late 1980s an attempt was made to redesign Mulgrave Park in Halifax, but the site was very difficult to reconfigure successfully, in part because of the significant slope on which the project was built. The redesign was abandoned. The only change was a decision to move families with children from one of the apartment towers and use the building to accommodate households without young children.

In Toronto, three MTHA projects were considered for redesign and redevelopment in 1987 and 1988. Architect Alan Littlewood proposed a redesign of one section of Edgeley Village, consisting generally of townhouses. The section studied by Littlewood contained about 300 units, some in a twelve-storey tower, but most in townhouse form. The redesign had four objectives:

1. Streets: The introduction of public streets and lanes in order to create a sense of normality within the neighbourhood, provide better vehicular and pedestrian access, and increase security.
2. Public and private spaces: A clear definition and development of public and private space aimed at improving the general appearance of the neighbourhood, the provision of usable private spaces and safer public ones, and the clarification of what was private and what was public.
3. Car parking: A reorganization of car parking by providing, wherever possible, a car-parking space directly related to the dwelling with which that car is associated.
4. More dwellings: An increase in overall density aimed at revitalizing the neighbourhood, increasing diversity, providing much-needed housing and generating income from land value in order to pay for the rehabilitation program. (Sewell 1988, Key MTHA Documents, pp. 121-22)

Littlewood's scheme increased the number of units in that section of the Edgeley project from 298 to 520, while putting almost all units onto a public street and giving them street addresses. Since the development was now on a public street system, it was no longer a "project," but rather an integral part of the city which anyone could drive through, including police on normal patrol and municipal garbage trucks on their usual rounds. Many of the new units were in house-form structures, and could be a mixture of non-profit or private, rental or ownership units. The revenues garnered from selling or leasing land for new units would more than pay for needed renovations of existing units and services, and for new facilities meeting municipal standards such as roads, sidewalks and street-lighting (Sewell 1993, p. 225).

Tenants of Edgeley showed a very strong interest in the redesign prospects, as did neighbouring residents and local council members. However, Ministry of Housing officials decided that there was no mandate to proceed with the project and that CMHC might have objections to this kind of change. The initiative was unceremoniously shelved.

Plans were also prepared for the redesign of the Finch/Birchmount and Moss Park projects, generally following the same guidelines laid down for Edgeley Village, although the Finch/Birchmount redesign also included reworking a twelve-storey apartment building in the ways suggested by Oscar Newman for New York high-rises (Sewell 1988; Sewell 1993, p. 229f.). These redesigns all proposed to fund costs internally from the sale of land for new units, so that taxpayer money would not be involved. However, neither scheme proceeded further than the first preliminary study. The Moss Park proposal held much interest because of vacant unused land that could be developed without changing the project in any way, and provincial officials had other studies prepared, although nothing has yet been agreed to. Favourable talk of redevelopment at the staff level has not resulted in any projects coming to fruition in Ontario. The considerable expense of the Uniacke experience has not popularized the redesign and redevelopment approach, and housing staff generally seem to fear undertaking the necessary rezonings and embarking on struggles with neighbours, who are known to dislike public housing.

But redevelopment provides excellent opportunities to address many problems with public housing. Since new units can be supplied on land that is already publicly owned and serviced in a manner that alleviates existing problems in large housing projects — with neighbourhood approval, it is hoped — it seems a likely direction in which housing proponents might move.

Conclusions

Most public housing projects do not deserve the bad reputation that public housing now holds: most projects are small, while the problems are in the large projects. Public housing has proven the most economical of programs to address low-income housing needs, and it may have been much more popular if it had not come about in Canada at the exact moment when modern planning ideas were at their peak. In any case, those many public housing units not found in large projects seem to have raised little ire, and are a strong resource that provides good housing at modest public expense. As for the large projects, the design problems should be addressed without delay, and the opportunities presented by redesign should be seized.

Chapter 9

Social Housing

From their birth in 1973 to their demise in the early 1990s, non-profit and non-profit co-op housing programs followed a circuitous route. With the public housing program under attack in the late 1960s and middle-class Canadians facing mounting difficulties in meeting housing costs, the federal government turned to a number of different approaches to respond to issues of affordability: AHOP and first-time home buyers' grants for owners; MURBs for investors; and non-profit housing for renters. Programs for owners and investors had a relatively short life, but non-profit initiatives lasted for two decades. During that time, the non-profit programs were amended several times and given three different names according to how those changes were seen: assisted housing; social housing; and community-based housing.

"Assisted housing" was the term in vogue in the 1970s. That name showed that the housing was not being proposed for market reasons, but was assisted by government programs to serve purposes other than making a profit. It was then pointed out that all housing — private, public, ownership and rental — was assisted in some way by government programs, public funds or tax expenditures, and that what distinguished this housing was its social purpose and the manner in which it was managed for the residents who lived there. Thus the common term became "social housing" in the early 1980s.

Social housing programs soon became subject to strong attack from some neighbourhoods. NIMBYism raised its head. The programs were accused of allowing housing for low-income households into neighbourhoods simply because some government-run or financed non-profit company had found a site there, or because some bureaucrat thought there was a housing need. Social housing was said to be just another government program foisted on an unsuspecting public.

Attempting to better define what they said they were doing, in the early 1990s some non-profit proponents began calling their movement "community-based housing." They were, they said, community people trying to meet housing needs in the places where they lived. In this chapter, for purposes of simplification, the term "social housing" will be used to refer to non-profit programs in general.

There have been two strains to the non-profit housing movement. One provides rental housing on a not-for-profit basis, retaining most aspects of the traditional tenant–landlord relationship. Non-profits have been established by social, community and religious organizations, by municipal governments as well as by private companies who see some advantage (such as selling land, or making a profit on construction, or holding the management contract) in taking the initiative to pull together a group to set up a non-profit company.

The other non-profit approach creates a co-operative, where members of the group share in decisions about building the co-op and residents share in management decisions. The traditional tenant–landlord relationship is abandoned in favour of co-operative ownership. Co-op shares have no value, and cannot be bought or sold: they are one aspect of residency.

Housing built under these non-profit programs shares similar characteristics:

- It is not built for profit, but for social reasons.
- Financial support comes from government, and without that support the projects would not be viable in the first instance.
- Housing projects are generally conceived and delivered by groups of people interested in meeting housing needs, not by a company that has lined up a number of financial backers and investors.
- Project management is usually hands-on, and tailored to the target resident profiles; in the case of co-op housing, management is resident controlled.

Thus social housing is an alternative both to market housing and to government-controlled public housing.

In general, social housing has obtained mortgage funds for land purchase and construction as a result of government programs, either with direct loans from government or with loans from private sources guaranteed by government. Further, social housing has usually been supported by operating loans and grants to help ensure that some

Willow Park was one of Canada's first housing co-operatives, sponsored by the farm co-op movement in Winnipeg. Its 200 townhouses were located in a park-like setting, as dictated by modern planning ideology, with a cold and hard architectural style.

Photo: CMHC and Co-operative Housing Federation of Canada

percentage of units are available to households with low incomes. Since the introduction of social housing programs in 1973, policies and regulations concerning capital and operating funds have changed considerably, as governments reacted to various pressures and perceived problems. It is in reviewing these changes that many of the key issues about non-profit housing emerge.

The 1973 programs

In 1973 the National Housing Act was amended to allow for a vastly expanded non-profit and non-profit co-operative housing program, as advocated by the Hellyer report in 1969 and the Dennis/Fish report in 1972. Provisions had been made in the 1964 amendments for non-profit activity, and had been used by groups such as Rotary and Kiwanis to provide 18,000 units by 1973, mainly in small housing developments for senior citizens (Hulchanski 1988, p. 20).

The 1973 program signalled a major new initiative in housing direction. It provided loans covering 100 per cent of capital costs of a project. To ensure that rents were reasonably affordable, the pro-

Photo: CMHC and Co-operative Housing Federation of Canada

Abbotsford Housing Co-operative in British Columbia was one of the first built under the newly evolving co-op legislation. It consists of 106 units in ranch-style townhouses.

gram also provided a grant — technically a loan that was forgiven — equal to 10 per cent of the capital cost. The 100 per cent loan and the grants had an open-ended quality to them, and to set some spending limits CMHC established Maximum Unit Prices (MUPs). MUPs set the maximum amount a non-profit company could pay for a unit, acting as an effective upper limit on the cost of the land that could be purchased and on design and construction costs. MUPs varied from community to community, reflecting different land and construction costs.

Rents were carefully monitored by CMHC, but there were no income restrictions on tenants, nor were there any requirements to specifically house those with low income.

This was the era of community activism in Canadian cities, and non-profit companies were formed by church and community groups as well as institutions such as the local YMCA and labour councils, and by many municipalities. Since these groups had no expertise in housing development, the program provided start-up funding (of up to $10,000) to help undertake the initial planning of the project. Grants were readily available to meet the onrush of community energy.

Prior to 1973, only a few non-profit housing co-ops had been established in Canada. There had been some building co-ops in the Maritimes in the 1930s, where members loaned their skills and time to build homes for each other. Students on some university campuses had formed housing co-ops, such as Campus Co-op near the University of Toronto, which has co-operatively owned and run a number of houses since the Second World War. There had also been a few member-loan co-ops across the country, where members were required to make a loan to meet costs not otherwise covered in the mortgage — such as the Willow Park Housing Co-operative in Winnipeg, sponsored in 1964 by the strong co-operative farm movement on the prairies (Bacher 1993, p. 232).

The Hellyer report suggested a demonstration co-op program. This spawned half a dozen co-ops in the early 1970s in Toronto, Mississauga, London, Windsor and Abbotsford, British Columbia. These co-ops received loans from CMHC equal to 95 per cent of the capital costs, with members' loans covering the remainder.

The 1973 amendments changed the co-op from a struggling idea to a growing enterprise, particularly since now 100 per cent of capital costs were covered, and it was not necessary for members to contribute equity. The program funded acquisition and rehabilitation as well as new construction. Thus there was no need for a site to be cleared so that new housing could be built: older buildings could be renovated, where feasible.

One of the first projects to be funded by the new non-profit program, then transferred to a non-profit co-op established by residents, was the Bain Avenue project in Toronto, which had begun sixty years earlier as a non-profit project owned by a private board of directors, which included public interests. When the major private shareholder of that company tried to convert the project to condominiums in 1974, the City of Toronto stepped in to purchase it, and after pressure from tenants, agreed to transfer it to the residents' co-op. Later in the decade Bain's sister project, Spruce Court, also was purchased by a resident non-profit co-op, closing the loop set in motion 65 years earlier (Bacher 1993, p. 51).

The new programs instigated considerable activity — more than 4,000 new non-profit units were under construction in 1974 alone. The atmosphere was reminiscent of the early days of the public housing program, when municipalities took the lead. Toronto purchased 45 acres of land for its St. Lawrence community and then leased sites to a number of different non-profit and non-profit co-op

Photo: CMHC

Toronto's St. Lawrence Community took forty-five acres of industrial land on the edge of the downtown and turned it into a residential area of low-rise apartment buildings and townhouses. This photo shows the David B. Archer Co-op, designed in a form which became typical in the area. In the foreground are the beginnings of The Esplanade, a heavily treed street, which is one of the area's defining characteristics.

housing groups; Vancouver did the same in False Creek. Ottawa established an active non-profit housing program, as did dozens of other municipalities. Many municipalities supported non-profit housing groups by providing sites and helping with planning questions. Within a few years several score non-profit co-ops had formed, and a number of co-op housing support groups became established to help them with developments.

In 1974, amendments were made to institute a rural and native housing program. Within the next fifteen years, some 17,000 units were constructed under this program.

One change that distinguished the non-profit program from public housing was not covered by legislation, but was very significant: the physical design of projects. Not all projects reflected this shift, but it was very clear in Toronto, Ottawa and Vancouver, led by each municipality's non-profit housing company. The new design stressed some rather old-fashioned values: buildings and building entrances faced directly onto the street, not onto grass or private walkways; buildings were built on public streets with normal municipal services such as municipal garbage collection, street-lighting, and street-cleaning; plans called for very little common open space, preferring instead clearly defined front and back yards; household sizes and ages would be mixed, and units for the disabled would be integral to projects. These design elements meant that non-profit housing shared the characteristics of many other buildings in the neighbourhood. There was no attempt to be different or new — rather, the aim was to make buildings seem ordinary, to fit in with what was already there (Sewell 1993, p. 191f.)

These design changes meant that non-profit and co-op projects were not unwelcome in neighbourhoods. They were not always greeted warmly (see, for instance, Dineen's 1974 book *The Trouble with Co-ops* for the description of one Toronto fight), but they raised none of the serious hackles that greeted public housing.

From 1973 to the end of 1978, the program funded about 8,000 non-profit co-op units. They were largely located in Ontario, Quebec, Manitoba and British Columbia.

The 1979 programs

In the mid-1970s, governments embraced restraint, led by the federal government's imposition of wage and price controls in 1975. The federal government decided that direct lending was a likely source of savings. A 1978 report for CMHC, "New Directions in Housing," suggested that instead of direct lending, which showed up on the government's books, the government should encourage non-profit groups to borrow on the private market, then guarantee those loans. An explicit statement was made that the non-profit approach would replace public housing, and requirements would be set in place in respect of who would be housed. Further, provincial authorities would be given responsibility for housing allocations and program administration — an arrangement that also gave recognition to the sharing of power under the current constitutional legislation, the British North America Act.

These amendments were contained in Section 56 of the National Housing Act, and projects funded under it are often referred to as "Section 56.1 projects." Projects would contain a mix of incomes, with one-quarter of the units reserved for households with low income. Provinces administered the program on the basis of global

Photo: CMHC

When Montreal residents stopped urban renewal and the inevitable high rise towers that followed, they were able to purchase the properties the developer had assembled and convert them into a co-op. One of the gems saved and renovated is this powerful and graceful building, which is now included in the Milton Park co-op.

funding agreements with Ottawa. Rents were required to be set at the same level as the lower range of market rents in the area.

The subsidy provided was in two parts. On the one hand it set the interest rate on the mortgage at 2 per cent for a number of years; on the other, it covered the difference between what low-income families could afford (with rent set according to income) and the market rent charged for the non-profit units. The subsidy was intended to cover both matters, but after ten or fifteen years it was expected that the need for subsidy allocated to keeping the project generally affordable (the 2 per cent interest rate) would wane as inflation lowered fixed costs, and the subsidy would increasingly be spent on housing low-income families.

Pegging rents to the market signalled a significant shift in the purpose of non-profit housing. The attraction of the non-profit approach originally was that rents could be set on the basis of cost: as inflation continued but mortgage payments remained constant, rents would remain relatively flat and become more and more affordable each year. But with the new program, non-profit groups were told they had to set rents based on what private landlords in the neighbourhood were doing. The economic attractiveness of non-profits was immediately wiped out.

This was a major challenge for non-profits. Rents set simply on the basis of cost were too high to attract tenants — one reason that private rental housing construction had come to a standstill, even with the tax advantages discussed in Chapter 7. The problem, quite simply, was that land and construction costs had risen so much that unsubsidized new housing of any kind was not affordable to the vast bulk of the population.

The non-profit co-op sector fought this change, and after a stormy battle, got the federal officials to agree that rents for co-ops could be set on the basis of costs, as before. This signalled a two-stream approach for the federal program, since the non-profits had agreed with the new market basis of rent-setting.

The amount allocated to start-up grants was raised considerably, to $75,000, but as these grants grew in size they became less available to community groups, who had to spend more on the costs of getting the development proposal (not the development group) together. This was a good example of the design of the program affecting the nature of the development proposals, since government officials, less willing to risk these large grants on younger, less-experienced groups, favoured support for existing groups and their development schemes.

At the same time, the federal government ended the land-banking program. This had been a main part of the program for many municipalities that had formed non-profits; it had allowed municipalities to buy land not only for their own development, but also for development by private non-profits and co-ops.

The amendments changed some basic rules, but the non-profit and co-op programs continued to flourish. By the end of 1982, commitments for 65,000 units had been made under the Section 56.1 programs. Half were to private non-profits, 28 per cent to public non-profits, and almost 20 per cent to co-ops (CMHC 1983). There was strong municipal support: by 1984, in Ontario non-profit units had been built by 34 municipalities (Ontario 1985). In Vancouver 90 per cent of the social housing units built between 1978 and 1982 had been built on land leased from the city, usually at less than market rates (McAfee 1983).

But the high interest rates of the early 1980s — pushing above 20 per cent — provoked concern at the cost of the program and at who was being served by it. With high interest rates, federal government subsidies to achieve an effective 2 per cent rate for non-profits were enormous, and there were fears that within ten years the annual subsidy, then in the $250 million range, would reach $1.3 billion (CMHC 1983). Another problem from the federal viewpoint was the way subsidies were shared. Data in Ontario showed that for municipal non-profits in 1984, total expenses of $48.5 million where shared as follows: tenants (through rent) paid $21.6 million; the federal government, $24.3 million; the province, $2.6 million (Ontario 1985). The federal government was carrying almost 90 per cent of the subsidy, compared to the 50/50 operating deficit arrangement with public housing a decade before.

A CMHC evaluation was undertaken, and its conclusions published in 1983. The main focus was on those served by the program. The evaluation began by explaining the attractiveness of the income mix proposed as one goal of non-profit housing, first endorsed by Hellyer and Dennis/Fish:

> The achievement of a mix of income groups in Sec.56.1 projects was viewed as desirable for two reasons. First, a mix of assisted tenants with tenants paying market rents would contribute to the financial viability of the projects. Second, social problems associated with projects which contained high concentrations of low-income households would be reduced. (CMHC 1983, p. 162)

While these objectives might have been met, it was at considerable cost, according to the report, and the targeting was poor.

It was clear that the non-profit providers were effectively housing those with lower incomes. More than half the units of private non-profits, which included many church and social groups, for instance, were occupied by the poorest two quintiles in Canadian society, and the other providers had clearly met the target of providing one-quarter of their units for those with low income. But local politicians in cities such as Toronto and Vancouver, where non-profit programs had been extensively used, were complaining that the wrong people were benefiting from the non-profit program, and this study supported their argument. They noted that some units were occupied by higher income households in the top two quintiles. Rather than in-

Non-profit housing comes in all shapes and sizes, including this series of townhouses (which some have unkindly referred to as a saw-tooth design) in St. John's, Newfoundland. There are twenty-six units in the project.

Photo: Gerry Boland Studio Productions Ltd. and CMHC

terpreting this as a sign of success in achieving income mix, some thought that higher income people were securing a benefit they weren't entitled to. "The Section 56.1 programs are ineffectively targeted to those most in need," concluded the CMHC report (p. 8).

Table 9.1				
Income distribution by quintile, Section 56.1 program projects, by percentage				
Lowest				*Highest*
Quintile	1	2	3	4	5
By program				
Public non-profit	8.2	20.4	36.5	23.9	10.9
Private non-profit	28.7	29.9	20.7	13.7	6.9
Co-op non-profit	12.2	19.1	26.1	28.8	13.8
By type of unit:				
Family	14.7	21.5	28.1	24.0	11.6
Seniors	46.5	40.5	9.3	2.4	1.3
Source: CMHC 1983, p. 164.				

Supporters of the program disagreed. A Vancouver study showed that 95 per cent of households in non-profit housing had low to moderate income, and only 10 per cent would be able to find housing elsewhere in the city for less than 25 per cent of their income (McAfee 1983, p. 20). Studies for the Co-operative Housing Federation of Canada argued: "The average income of co-op households is approximately 29 per cent below that of other Canadian families. Approximately 66 per cent of co-op households had incomes of less than $30,000 in contrast to just over 50 per cent of all Canadian households" (CHFC 1990).

Questions of targeting had not been seen as important with MURBs, AHOP, CRSP or other programs, but in the mid-1980s, as governments struggled with deficits and a stagnant economy, they seemed to bubble to the top when talk turned to social housing. Attempts were also made to compare per unit subsidies under Section 56.1 programs and other federal programs, but not convincingly — simply comparing subsidies on a unit basis said nothing about who was being housed.

1986 and beyond

In 1986, the federal government decided it would fund housing only for those in core need, generally interpreted as households paying more than 30 per cent of their income for housing. Global agreements with provincial governments made it clear that if housing mix were to be achieved, the funds for the market units would have to come from the provinces. Non-profit providers accordingly made submissions to participating provinces for funds based on proposals with a high percentage of low-income units. Whereas 25 per cent of the units had generally been reserved for low-income families under the 1979 amendments (although some non-profit proponents asked for higher ratios, some even building only for households paying rent on a geared-to-income basis), under the 1986 changes, 66 to 75 per cent of units in non-profit and co-op projects were for those in core need.

In 1986 a cost-cutting change was made at the request of the co-ops — the index linked mortgage (ILM), where interest rates paid on mortgages changed monthly with the market, rather than remaining constant for the term of the loan. The co-op movement argued that allowing an ILM with a variable interest rate meant that the lender would not have to factor in the uncertainty of future interest rates, and so could potentially realize savings.

But these changes in finances and in focus were something of a diversion: what the federal government was really signalling was withdrawal from funding allocations for non-profit and co-op programs. After funding 50,000 co-op units and 90,000 non-profit units since 1973, the annual federal allocations shrank to a few thousand in the early 1990s.

Non-profit and/or co-op programs were continued under global agreements between the federal government and some provinces — notably Ontario, Quebec, British Columbia and Manitoba — but the federal government reduced its share dramatically. Ontario responded with the Homes Now program in 1988, funding 30,000 new non-profit and co-op units during the next three years without federal contributions, a program that it renewed in 1991.

The national program withered. Of the 18,506 social housing units on which construction started in Canada in 1992, 15,718 were in Ontario, and were funded entirely by Ontario ; 1,146 in Quebec; and 1,305 were in British Columbia. That left a rather insignificant 337 social housing unit starts in the rest of the country in 1992 (Canadian Housing Statistics 1992).

As the chart below shows, the federal government has substantially reduced its role in non-profit and co-op non-profit housing since the early 1980s. In 1992, it announced that 1994 would be the last year in which any new non-profit or non-profit co-op units would receive federal support.

Table 9.2

**Total social housing starts receiving federal funding
(under the National Housing Act)**

Selected years	Social housing starts	Total housing starts
1977	20,805	245,724
1980	14,518	158,601
1983	12,539	162,645
1986	6,854	199,786
1989	6,547	215,382
1992	5,649	168,271

Source: Canadian Housing Statistics 1987, 1992.

Some were pleased with the federal decision, seeing it as an inevitable finale to a program they thought was too costly and not helpful enough to the private sector (Clayton 1993a).

The downturn in the economy following the explosion of housing prices that ended in early 1989 meant that in Ontario, where non-profit programs had been most pursued, vacancy rates soared in the early 1990s. Non-profit and co-op projects found they were unable to rent all of their units assigned to be leased at market-rate rents. The province allowed many of these units to be rented at a rent-geared-to-income basis, which pushed the low-income ratio in some projects even higher.

The tightening of the noose on non-profit and co-op housing programs in the early 1990s left social housing advocates scrambling for new approaches. The real challenge was finding funds to replace those being withdrawn by the federal government in a situation where only one province, Ontario, seemed willing to provide social housing support. The most likely source of money was from new residents, and much thought went into equity schemes where residents would provide a loan or investment. Three models seemed possible: investment with a return of principal; investment with a return of principal and interest; investment with the right to sell (Poulin 1991). A number of experiments were tried.

One proposal that underlay a project of the Metro Toronto Housing Company Limited, the non-profit housing agency of Metro Toronto, was to provide moderate-cost housing for senior citizens who invested at controlled interest rates and agreed to a controlled sale price. This scheme appealed to seniors willing to sell the family home and move into a smaller apartment. As the project rented up in 1993, it appeared to be successful.

A half-dozen limited equity schemes in British Columbia found that empty-nesters (couples whose children had left home) were willing to sell their home, and then invest varying amounts in a shared equity project. The older the couples, the more willing they seemed to treat this investment as a way of securing a permanent place to live. The younger the couple, the more they saw it as an investment that had to compete with other investments.

Several equity co-op arrangements for moderate-income families were also tried in Quebec and Ontario, but they suffered from a general problem: if people have a chance to make a profit when they move out, they seem quite willing to pay a high percentage of their income as rent, but if there is no chance of a profit, they are much more wary about how much of their income they are willing to pay.

Some saw the hiatus in funding as not entirely bad, since it has given co-ops and non-profits a chance to catch their breath and review how far they have come in twenty years. There are projects old enough to begin exhibiting signs of wear and tear, and those problems need addressing, particularly as in some cases it has been found that reserve funds are not adequate to meet expensive capital repairs. Projects built in the mid-1980s, when CMHC squeezed Maximum Unit Prices so tightly that construction quality suffered, need careful attention. Projects from the late 1980s experienced problems in filling units renting at market rates after the boom of the late 1980s busted; imagination is needed to find ways out of this dilemma. The hiatus has given housing support groups the opportunity to address these questions before problems become unmanageable.

Special purpose social housing

The rise of homelessness and the recognition of special housing needs emerged in the early 1980s as the social housing program was in full flight. Social agencies created non-profit companies to serve clients with these housing needs. Client groups included ex-prisoners, unwed mothers, unprotected children, victims of family violence, alcohol and drug abusers, the physically disabled, the emotionally disturbed and mentally disabled, transients, and the elderly needing special nursing care.

Provinces gave different priorities to these housing needs, as Table 9.3 shows. In many cases the money spent on housing might in other circumstances have been taken from health and social service allocations — indeed, the federal government received a recommendation to do just that (Banting 1990, p. 157). The global agreements between the federal government and some provinces following the 1986 changes permitted up to 10 per cent of allocations to be spent on special housing purposes (Banting 1990, p. 155).

One private housing program should be mentioned, and while it doesn't qualify as a social housing program, it may be considered special needs housing. Habitat Canada finds housing lots and, through "sweat equity," builds houses on them, which it then deeds to low-income families at whatever little cost it has incurred. The construction is done for free by volunteers, as often as possible with donated materials. Volunteers include well-known individuals such

Table 9.3

Special purpose housing by province, 1979–84

Province	Number of units	Percentage of all social housing
Newfoundland	562	19
P.E.I.	283	38
Nova Scotia	696	16
New Brunswick	1,091	40
Quebec	2,239	6
Ontario	2,079	6
Manitoba	764	19
Saskatchewan	833	11
Alberta	760	7
British Columbia	5,161	29
Canada	14,468	12

Source: Banting 1990, p. 156.

as former American president Jimmy Carter. In 1993, Habitat expects to build forty houses across the country. The program is very small, but it offers some people direct physical involvement for a few days in creating new housing.

Municipal initiatives

As noted, many municipalities became actively involved in non-profit housing, both creating their own non-profit companies and sponsoring programs to assist private non-profits and co-ops. The local nature of non-profit housing invigorated some municipalities into other kinds of action to support affordable housing of one kind or another.

Montreal, for instance, undertook "Opération 10,000 logements" in 1979. The municipality was in the fortunate position of owning many small parcels of land throughout the city. The program encouraged small-scale rental projects by private entrepreneurs on this

Photo: CMHC

The Winnipeg Core Area Initiative program undertook urban rehabilitation on a large scale, buying and converting industrial structures, sponsoring new non-profit housing, and renovating downtown houses such as this one.

city-owned land. The city took submissions from developers for proposals on the different sites, and offered grants of up to $2,000 a unit for projects it chose to be built. The projects remained in private ownership, and without controls on rent, which leads to questions as to how long the housing will remain affordable.

The program managed to fulfil three objectives: it helped the construction industry; it increased the amount of rental stock in the city; and it generally made housing available to those with lower incomes. It was so successful that in 1982 it was expanded to "Opération 20000 logements."

Some cities undertook significant schemes for new communities within the existing built-up area. Toronto's forty-five-acre St. Lawrence community and Vancouver's seventy-acre False Creek site are good examples of this approach. Each city made sites in these large land holdings available to local non-profit groups. Similar proposals were made to develop old railyards in Winnipeg and Edmonton, but they fared badly and never became a reality. Toronto's attempt to repeat St. Lawrence in the mid-1980s with the planned Ataratiri community ran headlong into unresolved environmental and soil contamination problems, and a lack of political will, and was abandoned after $250 million had been spent to purchase land.

Cities played supporting roles in leasing land to non-profit groups at below-market prices; doing advocacy work; and helping with the education of various players in the housing game. (For a general overview of these initiatives see Carter and McAfee 1991.)

Many cities made special planning provisions for social housing. Recognizing that the incidence of car ownership in lower income families was much less than in moderate-income or higher income families, parking requirements in zoning bylaws were often reduced for social housing projects. The City of Toronto allowed social housing projects to receive a density bonus of 25 per cent over other housing, raising the ire of those who felt social housing was receiving too much attention, at least in their neighbourhood.

A more significant change was the idea of linking development approval to the provision of social housing. In its raw form, a municipality might state that a development application for an office building could earn an increase in density if it was accompanied by a certain number of social housing units on or off site, or land where the municipality might build such units. In the United States, such action by cities was called "linkages" or "equity zoning" (Krumholz and Forester 1990); in Canada, it was often referred to as "bonus zoning." It was not limited to the provision of social housing; in some cases it was extended to other social facilities such as daycare centres.

Bonus zoning is usually contentious. It accompanies large projects which on their own often raise questions about a city council's wisdom in development approval matters. Some argue that this specific linkage makes no sense, since the market cycle for office space bears no relationship to the cycle for affordable housing needs. When the rush to build office space is highest, the economy is at its hottest and housing needs often seem pushed to the background. When the economy cools, housing needs become more evident, but the strong push for new office space, on which social housing can piggyback, is gone. Many developers argue that they simply can't afford to bear the extra costs of providing affordable housing as well as meeting their own business needs. The idea behind bonus zoning, thus, may be seriously flawed (Toronto 1993).

The case for co-ops

Non-profit housing projects continue a somewhat traditional relationship between landlords and tenants, but remove the profit motive. Co-ops attempt to change not only the profit motive but also the landlord to tenant relationship by putting residents, acting as a group, in the place of the landlord.

A 1990 CMHC study found that "co-operatives had been highly successful in achieving income-mixing without polarisation of income groups. Income was basically a non-issue for members ... Mixes of family types, age, race and people with various backgrounds was perceived as healthy and a strength of co-operative living" (CMHC 1990b, p. 139). As already noted, income mix has been a significant objective of housing programs since the Hellyer report in 1969. Along with ideas of inclusivity, it has been a thorn in the side of many communities, often expressed as the NIMBY syndrome (discussed in Chapter 4). Co-ops appears to provide a more supportive environment to house diverse groups than do other kinds of housing (CHFC 1990b).

Co-op data indicate that co-ops house twice the percentage of families with children as other landlords; house a high percentage of disabled; on a unit basis, house more than twice as many single parent families, mostly female-led, as the private rental sector; and take significant initiatives to house the disadvantaged, including battered women, people living with AIDS and ex-psychiatric patients (CHFC 1990b, pp. 18-20).

As co-op supporters boast, "while any form of income-mixed housing will achieve a social mix, co-operative housing achieves social *integration*, that is, households from varying backgrounds actively meet and associate with each other. In a society so burdened with the costs of social divisions and concerned by the phenomenon of deteriorating race relations, this is no small achievement." (CHFC 1990b, p. 21)

Few question this achievement. What is questioned, however, is the financial cost society is willing to pay for this benefit: More than the public housing program, which apparently isolates income groups? More than private rental programs, which avoid these questions of income mix and do not house low-income households?

Social benefits are enormously difficult to quantify. If a government looks at success solely in terms of financial benefits attained, the kind of benefits that accompany co-ops will not be recognized because costs and benefits cannot be easily assigned. Is there an objective that lies beyond achieving housing that is simply affordable, and would it include achieving some form of reasonable social integration? If so, the case for co-op housing would be exceptionally powerful. (A full and complimentary description of life in co-ops is found in Cooper and Rodman 1992.) Co-op supporters handle the question of costs and subsidies this way: Owners are permitted to sell their house and make a profit from it, ensuring that what was once affordable housing becomes very expensive. Thus, while the benefit to the owner seems to accrue just to an individual family, the cost of ownership housing to society is very high. The profit secured is not taxed, yet can amount to several thousand dollars for every year of ownership.

For instance, the average cost of a house in Victoria in 1986 was $120,000, and by 1992 it had more than doubled to $250,000 (British Columbia 1992, p. 12). In Metro Toronto the average price in 1980 was $40,000, and by 1989 it was $275,000, an eightfold increase. The benefit to the owner of an average house during those periods in those cities was about $20,000 per year. If this gain had been taxed at a 75 per cent rate like other capital gains, the government would have netted $15,000 in taxes each year from each homeowner. The tax expenditure, or tax not collected because of the exemption, represented a considerable gift to every family that owned a house.

Co-op residents, by contrast, receive no such benefit. They are the beneficiaries of an annual subsidy, perhaps in the order of $6,000 a year for the first ten or fifteen years of the co-op, but that subsidy is not given at the cost of making the housing unit more expensive for the next family moving in. Thus, it may be argued, the cost to the taxpayer of the co-op unit is less than the cost of an ownership unit, and the next resident of the unit is not required to pay an extra sum because of this cost.

This argument raises contentious issues — particularly revolving around the long-held belief in the benefits of home ownership. Co-op supporters can well argue that this belief needs to be examined: in a country where two-thirds of all households are owners, it is unconscionable that so many Canadians are in core housing need. More non-profit co-ops where housing is not seen as a commodity on which profit can be made, they argue, may well begin to resolve the affordability problem at a reasonable public cost, which might be less than current costs.

Criticizing the non-profit program

The problem of income mix: One criticism that has gained much support is that benefits of the program go not just to low-income households, but to moderate- and, in some cases, high-income households. These critics say that financial contributions to housing should be better targeted to those with low incomes.

In the early years of the non-profit program, there were no income requirements, although considerably more than half those benefiting from the program had incomes below the median. After the 1979 amendments, at least one-quarter of the households benefiting had low incomes (that is, in the bottom two income quintiles). After the 1986 changes, the percentage of those with low incomes increased further.

If the objective is to achieve a degree of income mix, then some households with more than low income are bound to receive benefits. Journalist David Lewis Stein wondered why people "who are incensed by a few well-off co-op residents feel no similar anger against large corporations, whose tax breaks are scandalous ripoffs," and concluded: "it is because big corporations create wealth. They provide jobs. They are taking more than their fair share, but they are at least giving something back. The high-income co-op member and the welfare cheat are just taking" (Stein 1990).

One response to the criticism of a possible undeserved benefit is to require annual income testing of tenants, and eviction of those with an income above a predetermined level. But what tenant will want to live with this condition, this insecurity and uncertainty, where eviction can occur if the tenant is successful at work? Such tenants would seek to live in situations where income testing is not on the agenda, where the significant issue is whether the tenant can meet the rent and respect neighbours.

An added difficulty is determining the income limit to be imposed. Should the program state that households with incomes in the first three quintiles will be mixed, but that high incomes in the fourth or fifth quintile will not be included in the mix? What is the rationale about limiting certain incomes? Is the issue the number of residents with higher incomes? Most people would probably agree that a majority of units should be available to households with incomes below the median. But after that, what is acceptable? Is it acceptable if 10 per cent of tenants have incomes in the fifth quintile, but not acceptable if that number is 15? How many is too many?

Furthermore, how would income limits be enforced? By a kind of welfare police? Would this enforcement be cost-effective (Miron 1993, p. 363-64)?

One problem is that little is known about higher income households in non-profit and co-op housing. Do these households have lower or middle incomes when they move in and then become better off, or do they have high incomes right from the start? If they achieve high-income status while they live in a non-profit unit, how does this occur? And why do they continue to live there, when presumably there are many other choices they could make? While we know that about half of co-op members have low incomes and receive a rent-geared-to-income supplement, we do not know how many high-income households live in non-profits and co-ops. These questions require answers to help frame the debate a bit more precisely.

The alternative is to simply cancel the goal of income mix, and concentrate the program on tenants with low income — somewhat like an improved public housing program. This is a viable approach, but it has a substantial limitation: programs directed only to those with low income have little voter support. Universal programs — programs that provide benefits to everyone, including those with higher incomes who don't deserve the benefits — have a much greater political popularity, and benefits going to those with higher incomes can be captured by governments through various taxation schemes (McQuaig 1993, Chapter 2). Programs limited to lower income households have limited political popularity. The best example of this consequence is what happened to the non-profit program once it was directed by the federal government to only those with low income: it was quickly cancelled.

184 Houses and Homes

Thus the argument against non-profits based on income mix has a very definite edge to it: income mix implies benefits to those with higher incomes. Limitations on those benefits limit the income mix that will occur.

What is surprising, given the tensions surrounding this issue, is the lack of useful academic commentary about the merits or shortcomings of an income mix strategy. The effect of income mix could be assessed using a number of different factors: crime, education, community services, resident satisfaction, friendship — to name a few. But there appear to be only four rather small and inconclusive studies about income mix: two studies by students, one in Ontario, one in Vancouver; one study for a provincial government; and one study in Australia (Saldov 1981; Hough 1981; Sarkissen and Heine 1978; and Siu-Che Ng 1984). The one statement that sums this material up comes from the Australian study: "From the literature a number of ideas and hypotheses about mix emerge. In general, answers do not" (Sarkissen and Heine 1978, p. 96). One is thrust back onto generalities about what makes good cities and good neighbourhoods, one of the matters discussed in Chapter 4. Choice in housing seems important, and arbitrary rules about which income groups may live in an area — whether rich or poor — negate that choice.

Granted, many quarrel with diversity and attempt to keep "different" people out of their neighbourhood (as noted in Chapter 4). But few would argue that this reaction is a virtue, and most would say that this kind of discrimination does not lead to healthy cities. In principle it is difficult to quarrel with the idea that diversity is preferable to homogeneity — perhaps even if the former has a cost.

Tenant/resident selection: The other side of the income mix question is how residents and tenants with low incomes will be selected for non-profit projects. The key question seems to be: Should there be one large door that provides access to all social housing, or should there be many smaller doors providing access to particular social housing organizations? The former provides one comprehensive waiting list, which will make it easy to assess the extent of housing need as expressed by the number of applicants. The latter will provide a number of different waiting lists, some of which will involve overlap as applicants get themselves onto several waiting lists. Different approaches have different advocates. (These arguments are fleshed out in some detail in Sewell 1988.)

Some government officials believe that a single tenant selection system for all social housing should be put in place. Thus, in any municipality, there would be one list of low-income applicants, and when a rent-geared-to-income vacancy occurs in any public or social housing project, the household at the top of the list for the size of unit in question should be offered it. The waiting list would in all likelihood be based on a point system that assesses housing need (as occurs for public housing), so that those with the highest need, such as a family living in a hostel, would be at the top of the list and receive housing first.

Co-ops argue that housing need is an important issue, but not the only issue in resident selection. Co-ops want residents who will be actively involved, and who can demonstrate an ability to get along with others. These factors, they believe, must be taken into account when interviewing applicants. Co-ops often suggest that they do not wish to take just the household at the top of a needs list: they want to choose among low-income applicants to ensure that the applicant chosen will be compatible with the co-op concept. Co-ops argue that they are not simply providing housing, but they are also building a supportive community.

Many non-profits agree with the co-op arguments, although since the landlord–tenant relationship is more pronounced in non-profits, they are not quite as firm about commitment to the non-profit community. However, many non-profits appeal to special needs, and want to ensure recognition of these needs in tenant selection, just as they wish to ensure a reasonable balance of different kinds of tenants. Few non-profits wish to be overburdened with tenants who have very high social needs. As well, many non-profits want to give recognition to applicants living in the vicinity of the project, so that the non-profit can have strong roots in a particular neighbourhood.

Two further arguments have been advanced against choosing tenants only on the basis of need. First, this method of selection would result in all new tenants coming from extremely stressful situations — they are moving in not so much because this happens to be a place they would like to be part of, but because the place they are now living is intolerable. There are real questions to be asked about whether this method of tenant selection does anything to create strong communities, which, as noted in Chapter 3, are an important aspect of successful housing arrangements.

Second, if tenants are selected only on the basis of need, then only the neediest will be housed: length of time on the waiting list will mean nothing. Applicants expressing an interest to live in a particular project will have no chance of seeing that interest fulfilled unless they can somehow make their housing need more severe. Some have suggested that a good selection system would mix need and time of application: to provide some balance between need and interest, at least half the tenants should be selected according to when they applied.

In most of Canada tenant selection is not a burning question, since so few social housing vacancies occur. But in Ontario, where social housing is still being constructed in 1994, it is a matter of some significance, and for the last several years the Ministry of Housing has been attempting, over the vociferous objections of the co-ops and non-profits, to establish a single waiting list based mainly on need.

The cost comparison argument: Various arguments have been made about the cost of the non-profit program in comparison with that of other programs. The 1983 CMHC *Evaluation* attempted several such comparisons — particularly between non-profit programs and private rental programs — but they are not persuasive.

The difficulty in making comparisons should not be overestimated. First, there is the question of determining the actual cost of the public subsidy, either through dollars or tax expenditures, a problem already noted in both Chapters 1 and 2. This problem exists for both public and private units, and often is more severe for private units because of tax expenditures, whose value is rarely known.

Second, there is the difficulty of differentiating between the nature of the subsidies involved. The non-profit program involves two different subsidies. One subsidy brings the economic rent down to the market rent — referred to as the "supply" or "bridge" subsidy. The other subsidy helps some tenants with low income meet the market rent — the "income assistance" subsidy. Unfortunately, these subsidies are not clearly differentiated by the federal or provincial governments, making it very difficult to talk intelligently about what subsidies are actually involved.

Third, what value is to be assigned to a social benefit like income mix? If it is a real social good, what is it worth? Answering this question might also provide a dollar figure for the value of the social improvement that occurs when no households live in poverty.

Fourth, what value is to be assigned a non-profit outcome? The expectation with non-profit units is that they will never enter the market, that their value (and ensuing rents) will never be increased because of what someone wants to pay for them. What is the value of this benefit? Should one assume it will be small, because at the end of the thirty-five-year mortgage the structure will be in such disrepair that it is virtually without value? Or is that unnecessarily pessimistic?

These are difficult questions, and they have not been addressed in a thorough enough manner to permit definite answers. One can rely on intuition, and say that the non-profit status must be worth something; that the social integration that appears to accompany the co-op program is worth something. But how much? One comparison made by the Co-operative Housing Federation of Canada in 1990 has some interest (CHFC 1990b, pp. 13-14). A 75-unit high-rise non-profit co-op in downtown Toronto built in 1985 (Hazelburn Co-op on Jarvis Street south of Dundas Street) was compared with a 476-unit private apartment tower in downtown Toronto completed the same year (Horizon on Bay, on Bay Street just north of Dundas Street), developed privately with assistance under the Canada Rental Supply Plan. Excluding rent-geared-to-income subsidies, the co-op received $5,134 per unit less in assistance over the first five years. That comparison ascribes no value to the larger percentage of lower and moderate-income households housed in the co-op than in the private rental building, assuming the usual comparison holds favouring the non-profit's appeal to low-income residents. At the same time, the comparison does not cover the life of either project. The CRSP subsidies continue for just fifteen years, while subsidies to the co-op will continue for a longer period, depending on various factors, including the possibility that subsidies will decrease.

Without better information, it is difficult to decide the cost argument. Intuition favours the non-profit side, on the ground that it eats up fewer public dollars than other programs that supply housing for low-income households in a manner that mixes them with others. Some evidence supports this, but better studies are needed.

The cost of construction and management: Some complain that social housing units cost more to construct than units created by private investors, and cost more to manage. This argument has been most forcefully made in the 1992 Report of the Provincial Auditor in Ontario.

The Auditor's report analyzed 241 projects containing 15,621 units approved in 1990 and 1991. (For data referred to here, see Ontario Auditor 1992, p. 125ff.) The previous year, 1989, had been the peak for real estate prices and construction costs, both of which fell rapidly throughout the following three years. For instance, an 800-square-foot two-bedroom unit that cost $156,000 to build in 1989 could be built for $106,000 two years later. The report found that this reduction in price was not reflected in the social housing projects analyzed. In Central Ontario, where the new house price index (excluding luxury condominiums) fell 16 per cent from 1990 to 1991, the cost of non-profit projects increased 9.5 per cent. In Southern Ontario, a general 6.0 per cent decrease was set against a 3.5 per cent increase in non-profit project price.

Various kinds of administrative malpractices were cited: not enough competition in the selection of sites; inadequate consideration of site remediation costs; appraisals that were too high. Further, it was claimed that the Maximum Unit Prices were used as target prices rather than an upper limit, and if MUPs had been adjusted downwards, then construction bids would have come in at lower amounts. Non-profit providers claimed in response that they had simply been caught in a time-lag, where commitments made in 1988 and 1989 didn't get fulfilled until a few years later when the price committed to seemed unreasonably high.

An analysis was also made of monthly operating costs in the Toronto area. The report found that "the average controllable [operating] cost of the 45 non-profit projects was $210 per unit per month, 102 per cent higher than for Toronto private rental accommodation of $104" (p. 135).

The point is made strongly that private landlords do a better job controlling labour, administrative, and material costs than do non-profits. Because of subsidy arrangements, there may not be the incentives in place for non-profits to control operating costs as strongly as the private sector. Unfortunately this comparison does not include amounts for tax expenditures available to the private landlord but not available to the non-profit landlord. Nor does it reflect the replacement reserve factored into the non-profit rent — whereas private landlords are not required to maintain such reserves, and their tenants will be expected to fund capital improvements to the building out of increased rents. If both matters had been taken into account, the difference in rents might have been negligible. The cost of government programs of any kind has been a contentious matter for many decades, and criticism of the non-profit housing field is not unexpected. Various administrative arrangements have been made to control costs, including MUPs to control overall costs; the use of skilled development consultants to work with non-profit providers; requirements for several bids to be obtained for construction; and a host of approvals, which some providers claim do more to drive up costs than contain them.

Similar concerns were expressed about the public housing program in the 1960s, leading to the proposal-call approach, where developers were asked to propose projects at a fixed cost, and the housing authority chose those that seemed to be the best financial deals. This system made financial sense, but it resulted, as Dennis and Fish documented, in second-class sites being proposed, and in construction details not meeting expectations.

It must be recognized that construction and administration costs have a habit of getting out of hand, whether what is being done is a simple home renovation (as any homeowner will attest) or a large project. Administrative procedures must be continually reviewed to ensure their effectiveness. On this point, social housing can't be singled out for faults greater or different than those of other building projects.

Conclusion

Since they were introduced in 1973, non-profit housing programs have spawned more than 200,000 units of housing that have permitted low-income households to live as neighbours of middle-income residents. These programs have created socially successful communities, although they have been subject to criticism around questions of cost and income mix. The creation of non-profit housing companies by many municipalities shows the extent to which non-profit housing has been popular with the public in ways that were not possible with public housing. Further, there seems to be strong evidence that co-ops provide supportive communities for a diverse range of people. As the non-profit programs were wound down in the early 1990s, providers looked for innovative ways to build affordable housing without relying on government subsidies.

Chapter 10

Rent Controls

Of all housing issues, perhaps rent regulation and control provokes the most public debate and disagreement. Like most other important issues, this one is complicated and fraught with questions often answered by ideological opinion rather than by clear, objective information. Debate about rent controls takes place on a level of principle that rarely descends to the real world; people don't like to be specific enough about the kind of rent controls they are advocating or opposing to present a cogent, realistic argument. This chapter attempts to review various aspects of controls, providing available information and setting out the major issues in contention.

A brief history of rent controls

Rent controls or regulations (the terms are used synonymously here) were first introduced by governments in the Western world, including the Canadian federal government, during the First World War. They were used as one form of price control seen as appropriate for coping with the national emergency, and were gradually withdrawn after the war. They were then reimposed during the Second World War. After 1945 they were retained in New York City, Hong Kong, Britain, many European cities, and other places where problems with rental housing seemed severe. (The best source for the history of controls is Adams et al. 1986, pp. 9-117.)

Controls were mandated by the Canadian Wartime Prices and Trade Board in 1941 to control maximum rents. They were widened the next year to include charges for room and board, and then to provide security of tenure; in 1943, they were extended to commercial properties. After the war ended, controls were gradually withdrawn. In 1950 the federal government asked the provinces to assume responsibility for rent control, and in 1951 all federal rent regulation ended.

A number of provincial governments assumed control over rents, as the federal government had asked: Alberta, from 1950 to 1955; British Columbia, from 1951 to 1955, when municipalities were given rent control authority; Manitoba, from 1951 to the early 1960s; Saskatchewan, starting in 1950 (after which controls became ineffective); Ontario, from 1951 to 1954. In 1951 New Brunswick and Prince Edward Island gave municipalities the authority to control rents, although none assumed it. In 1951 Nova Scotia followed the same route as New Brunswick, and large communities such as Halifax, Yarmouth and Sydney tried controls with little success. Quebec imposed controls in 1951, and in 1962 passed legislation allowing municipalities to elect to withdraw from controls, but that was followed by an amendment the next year specifically applying controls to certain municipalities. Controls were in effect in Newfoundland in 1949 when it joined Canada, and they remained so until the 1970s.

Prodded by the inflation issue of the early 1970s, in 1975 Prime Minister Pierre Trudeau imposed wage and price controls, following similar action in United States and other countries. Since the British North America Act made landlord–tenant relations a provincial responsibility except in times of national emergency (as during the wars), the federal government could only ask that provinces enact their own controls. The federal government indicated its preference for a cost pass-through system where certain rent increases were permitted and others were allowed if justified, rather than the arbitrary rent freezes of wartime. Apart from Quebec, which had maintained controls since 1951, and British Columbia, which had imposed controls the previous year, all provinces enacted controls by the end of 1975 or early 1976.

In most cases these controls were seen as temporary. They were abandoned in Alberta in 1980; in British Columbia in 1984; in Manitoba in 1980 (but new controls were introduced in 1982); and in New Brunswick in 1979 (where new controls were introduced in 1983). Controls remained for much longer periods in Prince Edward Island, Nova Scotia, Ontario, Saskatchewan and Quebec, although the nature of those control changed considerably over time.

Types of rent control
There are three different kinds of rent controls. Each approach results in different outcomes; defining the kind of control under consideration is a crucial first step in analyzing costs and benefits.

Basic control: The most straightforward kind of control is that which outlines a simple formula to determine what rent increase is permitted. This includes rent freezes (as imposed during the First and Second World Wars in many countries, including Canada) and rent roll-backs (as imposed in Santa Monica, California, in 1979); set percentage increases (as imposed in New York in the late 1940s for several decades); and set dollar-figure increases. The main issue in this type of control is establishing the base rent onto which any increase is to be added.

The merit of this system is that it is easily understood by landlords and tenants alike. The main criticism is that no matter when basic controls are imposed, there are bound to be similar properties where rents differ (rents for similar properties differ for a host of well-understood reasons, including the extent to which the landlord knows the tenant); thus the return on similar properties will be different simply because of differences in base rents at the moment controls are imposed. As controls continue, these differences will become aggravated, penalizing the landlord who had set a lower rent and rewarding the landlord who had set a higher rent.

Cost pass-through control: A second form of rent control allows the landlord a basic increase, and permits a further increase under certain conditions. This system has been the most widely used in Canada and in the Western world.

The "certain conditions" under which rents can be increased above a basic amount vary according to government decree. One condition is actual or anticipated expenditure: if the landlord can prove higher costs than set out by government guideline (whether for operating or capital expenditures), then an increased rent can be imposed in order to permit the added expenditure to be passed through to the tenant.

A second condition might be profit, or return on investment. This condition would permit a landlord to increase rent above the basic increase if the landlord can show that his profit or return on investment is less than what government considers reasonable.

A third condition might be market conditions: if the landlord can show that his rents are lower than general rents for comparable units, then an added increase could be made.

As can be imagined, the issues raised in cost pass-through systems often revolve around proof: proof of unusual expenditures actually incurred; proof of real investments on which a return is due, or proof of low profits; proof of real market comparisons. Governments must establish well-staffed commissions to review evidence submitted and make decisions on landlord applications and tenant objections. The hearing and decision-making process takes time, and imposes costs on all parties. The issues are often very complicated and fraught with detail, so there is little certainty about the rents finally set, and little understanding of why increases are what they are. While the cost pass-through system makes sense on paper and seems equitable, it is extremely difficult to administer in an understandable fashion.

Negotiated controls: A third form of controls might be called negotiated, or consensual controls. Under these controls, landlords and tenants are encouraged and expected to reach their own settlement of an acceptable rent; where they are unable to do so, either landlord or tenant may apply to a mediator or third party to help resolve the dispute. This is the form of control in place in Quebec, where the administrative body, the Régie de logement, which can be appealed to in case of dispute, may establish whatever rent it deems equitable in the circumstances.

This control might be seen as just a way of dealing with very unusual situations, such as a stiff increase being imposed on a long-term tenant unwilling to move, since it imposes little more than the general control that flows from the working of the rental market itself. It does not limit the amount of rent which might be charged, or the increase which might occur.

Complicating factors

The three systems of controls become complicated in real-life situations by the manner in which they are applied. Since the controls interfere with what otherwise is a vibrant and complicated market system, all manner of variation arises in the arrangements that are made. Hoping to change that system with one piece of legislation is unrealistic. A whole régime of actions must be taken, and they cause considerable complication. The following factors are important for successful implementation of controls.

Defining the units affected: Many jurisdictions have restricted the application of controls to certain kinds of rental units. For instance, in order not to discourage new rental construction, rental units built after a set date (such as the date of introduction of rent control legislation) have been exempted. Or, to indicate that controls are intended to protect those with lower incomes, some jurisdictions apply controls only to units renting below a certain amount, or to units below a certain size. For administrative purposes, and to avoid the political problem of enraging small landlords, controls sometimes apply only to buildings with six or more units.

Some jurisdictions (Ontario is a good example) begin by limiting the applicability of controls — such as to units built before 1980, or to rents below $750 per month. But after political pressure is applied the exemptions are lifted, incurring the wrath of those who built new units on the understanding that they would not be caught by controls.

The effect of permitting exemptions is to entrench variations in a rental system that has little uniformity. Inequities and disparities grow greater the longer the exemptions and controls are in place.

The need for secondary controls: A second area of complications comes from the need to control side effects. Legislation must be put in place to ensure that controls are effective, and that various parties do not find ways to get around them. There are many kinds of legislation that accompany rent controls to make them effective.

For example, rent controls will have no effect if tenants do not have some right to stay in their unit and press their case against a landlord who is attempting to impose an unauthorized rent increase. They must be given security of tenure so that they cannot be evicted simply for exercising their rights. Security of tenure legislation often prevents eviction unless tenants have committed a criminal offence, act in a manner that interferes with other tenants, or do not pay rent regularly, or unless the landlord or the landlord's family wishes to move into the tenant's unit. Security of tenure provisions must be accompanied by ready rights of access by the landlord and tenant to the court system.

Another difficulty with controls, as already noted, lies in determining the base upon which acceptable rent increases are calculated. The longer controls remain in effect, the more important it is that this base figure be known so that interested parties know what to base their calculations on in any specific instance. Further, new tenants moving into a unit will often want to know what the former tenant was charged, in order to determine if the rent they are being charged is within the limit set by the controls. A rent registry is the best way of collecting and making available this information. The registry must have the power to require that this information be provided, it must be able to record and exhibit the rent for all units, and it must be accessible at reasonable times to interested parties.

Set-up costs for rent registries are expensive, given the number of rental units involved in any jurisdiction and the need to amend records as rents are changed on an annual basis.

A third problem is "key money." Some rental units will be very desirable, and some households will be willing to pay more than the allowable rent to occupy those units. Even assuming that all landlords are adequately supervised, allowing someone other than the landlord — whether the building superintendent or a tenant who is subletting — to accept payment of a sum above the allowable rent would breach the intention of rent control. (This is called somewhat euphemistically "key money," since it is said to relate not to the cost of renting the unit, but to getting a key to it.) Thus, legislation must be passed to set up some policing mechanism to prevent key money being paid or accepted. An administrative arm must be then established to ensure that parties are discovered and prosecuted.

One way of slipping out of rent controls is by taking the unit off the rental market. This is most easily done by converting the rental building into a set of condominium units, each unit with its owner who can propose to move into his "home" after evicting the tenant. Often existing tenants are offered discounts to purchase the unit they occupy, and by so doing landlords attract considerable support in the building for the conversion. Most cities where rent controls have been in effect have seen a spate of such conversion applications, which are interpreted as a direct threat to the supply of rental housing. Legislation is usually passed to prevent such conversions.

Another response of landlords to rent controls is demolition of the rental units themselves. This occurs particularly where units are rented at the low end of the market and where substantial repairs may be required, or where a market for more expensive rental units or other uses is envisaged. The threat of demolition may provide the landlord with negotiating room. Often legislation is passed to take away this threat as well as the possibility of the threat becoming a reality.

A related method of escaping from controls is to evict the tenant for proposed renovations, effect renovation or change of some sort, and then re-rent the unit at a new sum. Obviously, this kind of renovation can deny tenants security, can change lower rent units into higher rent units, and can generally lead to abuse. Accordingly, effective rent control must also include controls on how and when landlords can undertake renovations.

Security of tenure and controlled rent are of little help to a tenant who must put up with conditions of poor repair. Accordingly, controlled rental units must meet clear standards of repair, and there must be mechanisms for regular inspections (in cases of complaint), orders requiring remedial action, and where action is not taken by the landlord, appropriate prosecution. These functions are often carried out by municipal building officials; but in any case, the setting and enforcement of housing standards must accompany residential rent controls.

Administration: A third complicating factor is the need for a body to oversee rent controls and the legislation required to support them. The body must be capable of receiving and investigating complaints; holding hearings to provide approvals required, particularly in the cost pass-through system; taking effective action to ensure laws are adhered to; and so forth.

This body is often called a Rent Review Commission (as in British Columbia and Nova Scotia) or some close variation thereof, but some jurisdictions have personalized the function into the Office of the Rentalsman (as in Saskatchewan, New Brunswick and Prince Edward Island). The Commission or Office is responsible for administering rent control legislation, including such matters as ensuring that tenants are properly notified of rent increase applications, permitting the filing of information and its review by all parties, arranging hearings and providing notification of decisions.

In Ontario, the cost of administering rent controls was $32.9 million for the fiscal year ended March 31, 1992. Since there are about 1.2 million rental units in Ontario, the direct cost of administering the rent control system in 1992 was about $27.00 per unit.

Arguments for rent control

There are certain standard arguments that advocates raise in defence of controls. They argue that controls prevent rent gouging and exorbitant profits; maintain or increase the amount of affordable housing available to low-income tenants; maintain a mix of housing in neighbourhoods; give tenants security of tenure; stabilize rents in time of economic or social instability; and deal with problems and imperfections in rental housing markets. (These arguments are set out and discussed in detail in Stanbury 1986.)

Rent gouging: Controls were introduced in many provinces in 1975 because of allegations of rent gouging by landlords as inflationary pressures resulted in large rent increases, or as landlords took advantage of a market opportunity to replace lower paying with higher paying tenants. It was a term often heard from the mouths of politicians as they opted for controls.

A less emotive approach to this subject might be to talk about "excessive" rent increases, or "excessive" profits: gouging implies wilful harm, as in gouging out an eye. But the intention is the same: to stop something that is seen to be too much, or too big.

Allegations of gouging often occur when tenants feel trapped by an inflationary, speculative or limited market, or when the rental market has broken down and doesn't work in the beneficent way markets are "supposed to" work (Hulchanski 1984). The charge implies unfairness, or a landlord achieving a windfall or exorbitant profit. It signals the battle of a powerless person (a tenant) against a big capitalist (the landlord).

But whether "gouging" occurs is a matter of individual judgement, which cannot otherwise be categorized. A 15 per cent rent increase may be considered gouging if done in isolation, but a 15 per cent rent increase authorized by a rent review commission under a cost pass-through system of controls might be considered reasonable. For several years in the early 1980s, for instance, the Residential Tenancy Commission in Ontario permitted increases in excess of 50 per cent in 2 per cent of the cases that came before it (Thom 1987, Vol. 2, p. 19). Was the Commission mandating gouging?

Any type of rent control is capable of preventing a landlord from raising the rent of a single tenant unreasonably, and to that extent controls may be called effective in preventing gouging, provided that gouging is defined as an increase which in the circumstances is unreasonably high.

Affordability: As noted in Chapter 2, the issue of affordability is a complicated one. However, comments are in order on the extent to which rent controls maintain affordable rents for tenants with lower incomes.

Extensive studies have been done on the cost pass-through system in place in Ontario, and while the details of Ontario's system are specific to that province, the conclusions drawn can probably be applied in a general fashion to any variety of cost pass-through systems (Thom 1987, Vol. 2, pp. 22ff.). The conclusion of these studies is that most of the financial benefits of controls go to higher income tenant households, not to lower income households. The following chart indicates percentage of tenant households by income, compared to percentage of benefits from controls:

Table 10.1			
Benefits of rent control to tenants occupying rent-controlled units in Ontario, by income group, 1981			
Household income in Ontario, 1981	*under $15,000*	*over $ 15,000*	*over $20,000*
Percentage of all tenant households	44	56	38.6
Percentage of $ benefits from rent controls to tenant households	16.5	83.5	60.0
(In 1981, average household income in Ontario was $17,600.) Source: Thom 1987, Vol. 2, p. 23.			

As those reviewing the material note:

> The bulk of the gross and net pecuniary benefits go to tenant households which have incomes well above the poor to moderate level and which have no affordability problems. This fact helps to explain why controls are established in the first place and why they persist. The bulk of the saving in the form of lower-than-market rents go to the majority of households that are *not* poor. (Stanbury and Vertinsky 1985, pp. 6-113f. Emphasis in original)

Why is it that lower income households don't share in the benefits of controls as much as higher income households? One reason might be that higher income tenants live in more expensive units. A 5 per cent control on a unit renting for $800 a month allows a rent increase of only $40, when the landlord might really want to increase rents by 10 per cent or $80, giving the household a benefit of $40 a month through controls; whereas a tenant in a $600 unit will receive only a $30 benefit in the same situation.

Another reason might be the access to professional services available to higher income tenants: accountancy skills to review submissions prepared by the landlord; legal skills for negotiating or arguing before appropriate tribunals; organizing skills in creating and maintaining a strong tenants' group that can deal with the landlord on an equal footing; and the financial wherewithal to maintain a sustained and lengthy dispute with the landlord, should that come to pass. These characteristics make government regulations powerful tools in the hands of higher income tenants. The unstated assumption is that low-income tenants have little political influence — an assumption difficult to quarrel with in any jurisdiction. As usual, those with the skills and influence are the ones who secure most of the rewards.

For these reasons, tenants who face the most significant affordability problems are least likely to find that rent controls help resolve those problems. As one landlord organization argued: "Middle and upper class tenants have been saving, investing and taking holidays at the expense of their landlords (some of whom have incomes well below their tenants), at the expense of the taxpayers (who are footing the bill for both controls and new non-profit and co-op units), and at the expense of those tenants who really need help" (FRPO 1989, p. 5).

The Thom Commission concludes: "Rent regulation is not an appropriate way of dealing with the affordability problem of tenant households ... The only effective approach to resolving affordability problems is to commit the necessary public funds to provide budgetary programs which assist the low-income households" (Thom 1987, Vol. 2, p. 189).

Other factors add to the difficulty those with the lowest incomes have in achieving significant protection through rent controls. When vacancies occur in rent-controlled units, landlords will usually rent to tenants who will offer them the least amount of trouble and expense. Often income is used as a judge of these matters, with landlords being more likely to rent to higher income tenants. In addition, lower income tenants are less likely to have access to legal resources if they are treated badly, and more likely simply to move on rather than press their rights. Thus landlords of lower rent units are more able to illegally increase rents beyond the level authorized by controls, in order to respond to demand (Fallis and Murray 1990, p. 54).

For all these reasons, the argument that rent controls help address the affordability problem of lower income tenants must be approached with great caution.

None of these arguments should be taken to imply that tenants generally do not benefit from controls. As a group, tenants do benefit in quite tangible ways. In Ontario in 1986, after pass-through controls had been in effect for eleven years, it was estimated that rents were 20 per cent lower than they would have been without controls. If rents had been increased at the same rate at which building operating costs increased, they would have been 33 per cent higher (Thom 1987, Vol. 2, pp. 14-16). In the first seven years of controls, the loss of income to landlords — a sum that was transferred to tenants in the form of lower rents — was estimated to be between $260 million and $375 million, or about $31 per month per rental unit in Ontario (p. 16). While many of these benefits flowed to tenants with higher incomes, other tenants at least did not find that their situation deteriorated.

Maintaining housing mix: Since the publication in 1961 of Jane Jacobs's book *Death and Life of Great American Cities*, many planners have argued that a neighbourhood containing a mix of household sizes and incomes is preferable to the more homogeneous groups found in new suburban subdivisions.

A closely related argument is that existing downtown neighbourhoods are valuable resources, and rather than being threatened with demolition for parking lots, urban renewal, office buildings or expressways, they should be protected and stabilized. One necessary tool for stabilization, it is often argued, is rent control, since after a decision has made to protect the area from demolition, neighbourhood property values and rents will increase and existing tenants will be forced out.

Controls, then, may be a part of the strategy needed to promote neighbourhood stability and mix. Other elements could involve demolition and renovation controls, two matters which often follow the imposition of rent controls. Certainly, these controls could help "freeze" individual situations and offer some tenants a level of security, at least in the short term.

It is more questionable whether rent controls ensure neighbourhood housing mix over the longer term. As already noted in the discussion on controls and the problem of affordability, controls seem to offer little to the lower income tenants whose residency in a neighbourhood one would wish to protect. Other methods, such as non-profit housing, might be more appropriate for achieving mix and stability.

Security of tenure: Most jurisdictions in Canada have long had legislation protecting tenants from random evictions at the whim of landlords. Rent controls provide one more level of security from random eviction.

Some question the amount of extra security rent controls themselves actually provide, particularly since authorized rent increases can be quite high. For several years in the early 1980s in Ontario, landlords of roughly half of all buildings were authorized by the Residential Tenancy Commission to increase rents in excess of 16 per cent a year; about one-quarter of all buildings were authorized to increase rents in excess of 10 per cent a year (Thom 1987, Vol. 2, p. 19).

Controls can do nothing to help the tenant meet the rent. Reductions in household income are not met through reductions in rent, since rents are not tied to household income. Any security that exists comes from knowing that a large increase is not going to be imposed precipitously, without warning, but will be subject to a lengthy approval process.

Many also argue that the best security for a tenant is a marketplace that offers large numbers of vacant units for rent, so that the competition among landlords for tenants keeps rents down — although the moving and dislocation costs of continually seeking an inexpensive unit can often be equal to the rent increase the tenant is trying to avoid. Security of tenure would be meaningless without effective rent regulation.

It is clear that lower income households are more secure with controls than without them, even if that security is not all they might wish.

Stabilizing rents: The market for rental units is somewhat different than that for other kinds of goods. Most purchases can be made by reviewing what is available, then making a decision. If the price is more than the purchaser can afford, or the quality is not what is expected, a purchase need not be concluded. But with rental housing the decision is made immensely more difficult and costly, since if a new unit isn't found, the tenant will have to meet the terms and conditions applying to the existing residence. And if the new rent of the existing residence is unsatisfactory, the tenant will have to pay the economic and emotional cost of moving. Even the market for purchases that involve a considerable part of the household income, such as a car, does not compare in these matters.

Further, it has often been noted that the time taken to increase rental supply is considerable — two, three or more years to buy the land, get through the planning process, and then complete construction. Some investors will be able to plan ahead and read the market several years in advance, but some will not. Where a local change suddenly increases demand (such as a large new employment opportunity, or an infusion of new investment, as occurred in Vancouver in the late 1980s and early 1990s), there can be real pressure on rents.

Rent controls can help provide stability in these situations where rent is changing rapidly because of market conditions. The Thom Commission notes: "Anything done to limit rent increases under tight market conditions will have the effect of increasing the prevailing rent level at other times. This is unavoidable if the industry is to earn an adequate long-run return" (Thom 1987, Vol. 2, pp. 154-55). However, prices that go up often also come down, and it is unfair to say that rents only rise. Once the recession of the early 1990s hit central Canada, the increases in rents and real estate prices of the boom years of the late 1980s were rolled back considerably. Rent controls in Ontario helped provide some stability during that period.

Imperfections in the rental market: This objective might also be stated as using rent controls to improve economic efficiency (Stanbury 1986, Chapter 4).

From 1950 until the mid-1970s, rent controls were not generally in effect in Canada. Nevertheless, rents decreased in relation to other costs during that period. For instance, the Consumer Price Index quadrupled from 1950 to 1981 in Canada, whereas rents increased only two and one half times (Thom 1987, Vol. 2, p. 156). If we judge on the basis of this evidence alone, it would be unreasonable to conclude that there are significant long-term rental market imperfections that need addressing.

But this statement leaves unanswered two questions. First, who decides what "the long term" is? Economist John Maynard Keynes said, "In the long run we are all dead." While some will note that there is little evidence to suggest controls are useful in creating a more efficient economy in the long term and that the market might work well on its own over the long term, others will present good reasons why intervention is useful and needed now.

Second, although the market might work well in general over the long term, it may work to the disadvantage of specific groups, particularly those with low income, in the short *or* long term. As noted in Chapter 2, low-income Canadians have not been well served by the housing market throughout the second half of this century. It is because low-income households are not well served by the housing market that programs such as rent controls are proposed.

Arguments against rent controls
The standard arguments of those who oppose rent controls are that they have a negative effect on new construction and vacancy rates, reduce the capital value of rental properties, reduce government revenue, and have other negative impacts.

Effect on new construction and vacancy rates: For some, a reduction in new construction follows rent controls as surely as night follows day (Downs 1988). Lawrence Smith provides data to show that after controls were introduced in Ontario, total rental starts fell noticeably, even though ownership condominium starts remained strong (Smith 1991, p. 324).

Smith believes that the imposition of rent controls in 1975 explains the drop in unassisted rental starts — a loss that was not made up for by the infusion of program money into assisted rental starts.

Others, much more wary in their interpretation of these statistics, believe that it is simplistic to blame the change in starts on the

	Table 10.2		
	Ontario Housing Starts, selected years		
	Total singles, semis & duplex starts	*Total rental starts*	*Unassisted rental starts*
1969	35,484	39,897	27,543
1972	46,169	46,134	39,097
1975	42,212	10,394	3,775
1978	36,556	21,105	6,935
1981	29,973	14,366	n/a
1984	33,726	9,413	2,455
1987	67,560	15,688	7,370

Note: "Unassisted" refers to starts that were not in the non-profit or non-profit co-op sector.
Source: Smith 1991, p. 325.

imposition of controls. Some note that starts fell precipitously in 1975 before controls were imposed in Ontario, and suggest that there may have been overbuilding of rental units in the early 1970s. Further, other factors explain the change: new household formation declined by 25 per cent after 1976; interest rates more than doubled after 1979; and real income growth began to slow considerably after 1975 (Thom 1987, Vol. 2, p. 29). Others argue that it was a simple cost problem: rents necessary to cover costs and provide a reasonable return on equity were "well above the rents prevailing for similar units in the existing stock — even those in the uncontrolled rental stock" (Clayton 1984, p. 16).

It seems that the available data are open to several different interpretations. To conclude that the imposition of controls is bound to lead to a decrease in new rental starts is probably unfounded — although for obvious reasons no one has suggested that the imposition of controls will lead to more rental starts. One group modestly states, "Rent controls do not increase supply" (FRPO 1989, p. 6) — but of course they were never intended to do that.

Parallel to the argument about negative impacts on new construction is the notion that controls trigger a decrease in rental vacancy rates. Using Metro Toronto as the example, Smith estimates the natural vacancy rate in Metro to have been 5 per cent during the 1960s, slipping to 3.9 per cent until 1974. Controls were imposed in 1975 and vacancy rates plunged, generally staying below 1.0 per cent for 15 years (Smith 1991, p. 330). It should be noted that with the depressed economy of the early 1990s in Ontario, vacancy rates in many cities including Toronto increased considerably, in some cases above 2 per cent, even though controls remained in place.

In contrast, in Calgary and Edmonton vacancy rates had risen to more than 10 per cent in the mid-1980s (after controls had been removed in 1980); in Winnipeg to 5 per cent in 1980 when controls were lifted, then below 1 per cent after controls were reimposed in 1982. In most American cities, where controls were generally not in place, vacancy rates were rarely below 4 per cent, and often more than 7 per cent (Thom 1987, Vol. 2, pp. 349-50).

Some argue that the fall in vacancies is a result of some tenants feeling they have such a good deal, they don't move when we might expect them to; others present the more far-fetched scenario of an owner selling to move into a rent-controlled unit. Others counter with the suggestion that controls allow tenants to save enough money to make a down payment on a house — so the real effect of controls may be to increase home ownership (Thom 1987, Vol. 2, p. 34). Smith takes this argument one step further, suggesting that controls "have a spill-over effect on the home ownership housing market" and push those prices upwards (Smith 1991, p. 319).

The argument that controls reduce vacancy rates has the same strengths and weaknesses as the argument that controls reduce the amount of new rental starts.

Reduced capital value of rental properties: There seems general agreement that, operating under rent controls, landlords spend less on repair and maintenance, and on conserving structural elements of buildings (Thom 1987, Vol. 2, p. 39). While there is little empirical evidence to support this general conclusion (Thom 1987, Vol. 2, Appendix G), given the imputed financial transfer from landlords to tenants already noted, it seems reasonable in principle.

A building that is not well maintained will obviously fall in value. Further, Smith argues that "rent controls significantly depress capital values because they depress the current and expected future rental stream and/or increase the appropriate discount rate by increasing the risk associated with an expected real income stream" (Smith 1991, p. 312). The amount by which the capital value of the rental property is reduced is likely to depend on the exact details of the controls in force, and the general state of the economy at the times when controls are in place.

However, there are examples in Ontario, where controls have been in place for almost twenty years, that disprove this general principle. In 1982, Cadillac Fairview Development Corporation decided to sell off its large holding of residential buildings — almost 20,000 rental units. It sought the best offer it could get, and finally sold to companies affiliated with Greymac Mortgage, at an average price of about $30,000 a unit. The transaction was subject to much attention (many tenants were worried about what would happen next), and ultimately charges for fraud were laid against the principals of Greymac because of mortgage irregularities. Many of the properties purchased by Greymac were then offered for sale by government liquidators. In 1989, after a public bidding process, twenty-year old apartment buildings in the vicinity of Yonge and College Streets in downtown Toronto were purchased for $70,000 per unit, or more than twice as much as they had been purchased for seven years earlier.

Can one generalize on the Greymac experience? Are there reasons other than controls that have as significant an impact on the capital value of rental properties?

Reduced government revenue: It has already been noted that rent controls impose an administrative cost. What is less often acknowledged is that controls decrease tax revenue. Landlord revenue is reduced, resulting in a loss of income tax that is not made up by the increased taxes from savings available to tenants. Capital values of the rental property might be reduced (although, as noted, the evidence for this is not certain), resulting in the possibility of lower property tax and capital gains tax.

Forgone tax revenues in Ontario because of rent controls were estimated in 1984 to be between $160 million and $236 million, broken down as follows:

Table 10.3		
Forgone tax revenue, Ontario, 1984 ($ millions)		
	Lower limit $	*Upper limit $*
Income tax	$51.9	101.9
Property tax	70.0	80.0
Capital gains tax	36.0	50.4
Provincial capital gains	2.3	3.8
Totals	160.2	236.1
Source: Thom 1987, Vol. 2, p. 44.		

It should be noted that the property tax revenue estimate assumes that controls have adversely affected new construction, so that figure includes lost revenue from units not built. The provincial capital gains estimate reflects the decrease in corporation capital tax base that is due to the reduction in sale prices.

These figures should be treated with some care, particularly since there is evidence that capital values do not decrease as expected because of controls. Further, most decisions of government can be criticized as in some way forgoing tax revenue of some kind.

Other impacts: Since rent controls are accompanied by an administrative system that can quickly become complicated and congested, some argue that the ensuing delays cause the government to lose credibility in the eyes of those involved (particularly landlords). Tenants face uncertainty until their cases are heard, and then often must face a large retroactive payment covering approved increases for several years in the past. Some say controls result in an increase in illegal units, such as basement apartments, which operate outside not only rent control legislation but also zoning and building bylaws — although this might more be a function of the shortage of rental accommodation than of controls themselves (Smith 1991, pp. 337-38).

Abandoning controls

The Thom Commission came to the following conclusion about the cost pass-through controls in place in Ontario:

> The traditional focus of rent regulation, which is to set rents by reference to costs on an individual building basis, is not acceptable either as a practical means of maintaining a healthy investment environment or a means of achieving a balance of fairness between landlords and tenants. An alternative approach to determining a fair market rent is needed. It should have two steps. The first should be to determine the fair market rent level for the market as a whole based on the industry's long-run return on investment. The second step should be to make provision for similar rents being charged for similar units, so that the rents for individual units generally would be in line with the overall fair market rent level. (Thom 1987, Vol. 2, pp. 64-65)

The Thom report's recommendations for a fair market rent system were not adopted by the Ontario government. In some jurisdictions, provincial governments found occasion to end controls without major political damage, but in others controls remain in place for reasons which seem questionable, given the above discussion. Can controls be ended easily?

In Canada, about one-third of all households live in rental accommodation. In Atlantic Canada the proportion of renters is somewhat lower, it is slightly higher in British Columbia, and in Quebec there are almost as many renter households as owner households (Hulchanski 1988, pp. 6-8). In cities, the proportion of tenants is higher, and in many cities tenants count for more than half the population. Given that the number of landlords is much smaller, in the eyes of a government tenants as a group look to be in a position to exercise powerful influence if controls were proposed to be abandoned. Accordingly, abandoning controls is not always easy.

There are a number of different ways in which controls can be abandoned. Some governments do it all at once, in a blanket move. Sometimes one level of government abandons controls, giving another level the option of picking them up — as the federal government did at the end of the Second World War with local governments. Some change one form of control for something softer or more consensual, as Quebec did in the 1960s.

There are also more gradual approaches: allowing controls to lapse on any vacant unit; allowing controls to lapse once rents have exceeded a set amount; allowing controls to lapse once vacancy rates have reached a set level in an area; and so forth (Arnott 1981).

The method chosen will obviously relate to the perception of problems by the government making the decisions, and to the projected political ramifications. The largest political problem will usually come from tenants who have been protected and now fear that landlords will raise rents substantially in a very brief time. It was for this reason that Thom recommended that the move to a system of fair market rent controls be implemented over a number of years, with rents being allowed to rise slowly and gradually from the controlled to the market level. At the same time, protection would remain in place for tenants claiming to be unfairly treated. Once the fair market system in is place, Thom recommends a continuing review mechanism to which tenants and landlords can have access.

There are two significant questions raised in abandoning controls. First, what mechanism will be put in place to ensure that tenants have real security? If tenants do not have security from unreasonable rent increases, they have no reasonable security at all. Thom suggests a continuing review mechanism to help tenants.

Second, what programs will be in place to ensure that tenants with lower incomes are able to live in good housing that they can afford? This question lies at the root of all housing policy. If this question can be reasonably addressed, then the case for controls is significantly weakened.

Conclusions

It is difficult to make insightful arguments about the merits or demerits of rent controls in general: specifics are needed about the kinds of controls under discussion and the general problems being experienced in the housing market. While an absence of regulation might be the most desirable situation of all, one cannot always assume that the housing market acts fairly to those seeking an affordable place to live or provides them with adequate security. It is on these bases that controls are best justified. At the same time, removing controls is difficult, and is most easily done while providing other forms of security to tenants (such as high vacancy rates) and implementing programs to provide tenants with more housing opportunities.

Chapter 11

Homelessness

In the seedier parts of Canadian downtowns one was always able to find a small group of men called "winos," or "the homeless." Their numbers were small, and most Canadians expected a few shelters and churches to look after their needs. The Salvation Army usually ran a hostel that provided a bed for the night, and then made sure the men were on the street by 7 a.m., waiting at designated corners for offers of labouring jobs.

Society certainly had its misunderstandings about this handful of men. Most did not have alcohol problems, as many believed — indeed, fewer than one-third had addictions of any kind. Ten years earlier in their lives most of these men would not have been categorized as "losers;" indeed, ten years earlier they would have been judged as doing perfectly well — but in the intervening time they ran into personal misfortune such as a lost job, a broken marriage or a mental breakdown, and they were never able to pull their lives back together. Society saw them as people who had done themselves in through personal choices.

How innocent and wrong-headed such a picture seems in the mid-1990s. Today, homelessness is a major phenomenon in all North American cities, and few voice the easy answers heard a decade or two ago. Jonathan Kozol (1988) shows just how appalling and desperate the situation can get in his book *Rachel and Her Children, Homeless Families in America*, describing New York City in the mid-1980s.

Homelessness in Canada

There are few places in the downtowns of Canadian cities where signs of homelessness are not evident: people sleeping over air vents, in bus shelters or in empty storefronts; men, women and youths begging wherever people pass by; frequent encounters with individuals who don't seem to be in full possession of their mental faculties; women offering sexual services on many street corners.

The change has been clear, and it has been sudden. Homelessness, like food banks, became a noticeable public issue in the late 1970s and early 1980s. In 1981, there was one food bank in Canada — in Alberta — and there were a few, almost invisible, homeless people. In 1991, there were 292 food banks across the country, and there were many quite visible homeless (Oderkirk 1992, p. 7).

Getting an accurate figure on the number of homeless in Canada is very difficult. Who is considered homeless? How can one count them?

There are several broad categories of people who might be considered homeless. Two that are widely agreed on are people without shelter — that is, living outside in the elements; and people who use emergency shelters as a permanent form of accommodation. Some also consider people paying more than half their income in rent as fitting in the category of "homeless" (Ontario 1988, p. 38).

The first category includes a wide range of living arrangements: empty buildings; cars; shacks under expressways; parks, when the weather is not too inclement; and so forth. It is difficult to know how many there are who fit in this category. On any summer night in Toronto one can count several hundred people sleeping in a handful of downtown parks — a count the author did in the late 1980s. During most winters in every large Canadian city several people are found frozen to death after trying to sleep in abandoned automobiles or garages. Accounting for all these lost urban souls is very difficult.

Systematic attempts have been made to determine the number using emergency shelters. The Canadian Council on Social Development undertook a study of all shelters in Canada on January 22, 1987 (McLaughlin 1987). The study showed that there were 472 shelters across Canada, with a nightly capacity of 13,797. Among the 283 shelters that provided data for the survey, occupancy was 77 per cent (although in Ontario, occupancy was 101.5 per cent). If the 77 per cent figure held for the shelters that did not report, one can assume that about 10,000 persons stayed in shelters that night.

The report found that in 1986, 260,000 individuals spent at least one night in a shelter, with an average stay of 19.4 days. It is reasonable to assume that some individuals stayed in more than one shelter during the year; on that basis the study estimated the number of different people using the 283 shelters which reported for the study at 130,000. These figures have been thought to be low, given the way the survey was done (Fallis and Murray 1990, pp. 20-21).

Who are the people who use shelters? No one really knows, and few wish to generalize. A Toronto study found that 30 per cent of hostel users are under the age of twenty-five (Ontario 1988, p. 36). Perhaps two-thirds of hostel users are single men; a separate group of shelters for battered women is occupied by women and children. Some women who use shelters aren't homeless in the way some people are who have no prospects of a permanent place to live: they are fleeing an abusive relationship and need emergency shelter while arranging a new place to live.

The third group that might be considered homeless are those who pay more than half their income as rent, or live in overcrowded, substandard housing. Generally, about 14 per cent of renters in large cities in Canada are in this position (Ontario 1988, p. 38). The reason for including this group is that they are households at serious risk, living in situations that are certainly unstable, perhaps doubling up with others in arrangements that might collapse at any moment. The inclusion of this group among the "homeless" may be debatable, but it is important to recognize that after leaving the relative stability of a household able to meet rent on a regular basis, homelessness is a matter of degree. As Fallis and Murray conclude:

> We have no firm data on the numbers of homeless, or the numbers of people along the continuum of housing problems. We do not know exactly how many people are without a roof over their heads, how many are in residential hotels or doubled up with friends, how many are basically without a fixed address, or how many are at risk of falling back into one of these positions in the continuum. (Fallis and Murray 1990, p. 264)

Several factors are generally agreed on as the causes of the recent increase in people without permanent living accommodation. First is gentrification, the purchase and renovation of houses in older parts of Canadian cities by the middle class. Gentrification led to a substantial loss of housing that had been available to those who are now homeless.

The 1971 census found that 206,000 people in Ontario, for instance, lived as roomers or boarders in private dwellings. In 1981, that figure was 112,000 (Bairstow 1986, p. 8). Thus, the amount of rooming and boarding accommodation — traditionally the least expensive for single individuals — had been cut in half in a ten-year period. This trend continued during the 1980s as the real estate sector boomed, and it is fair to assume that another 50,000 rooming units was lost by 1991. As noted in Chapter 4, gentrification first affected the least expensive housing, much of which was used as rooming houses. While the 1970s saw non-profit housing built, most was for families or for senior citizens, and very little was made available for low-income singles. It was not until the 1979 amendments that non-profit programs could be used for single-person accommodation.

Second, the 1970s was the era of de-institutionalization. Many believed that psychiatric institutions were not as helpful to the mentally ill as community-based services could be, and as one way of cutting expenditures, governments generally agreed that long-term residents of mental institutions should live in the community on their own. The change was quite astounding:

> Throughout Canada, the number of psychiatric hospitals decreased by one third between 1970 and 1978. The length of stay for affective and psychotic illnesses also decreased by one third. In 1960, 50 per cent of the 75,000 Canadians in mental institutions had been hospitalized for more than seven years; today, nine out of ten patients are hospitalized for less than one month. (Parkdale 1988, p. 39)

It is now known that many of the de-institutionalized were unable to function on their own, and that support services were not put in place before they were shown the street. As one report lamented, "public policy failed to ensure not only that housing was in place in the community, but also that people would have adequate incomes and the necessary support service arrangements to live an independent life" (Ontario 1988, p. 34).

Thus the key reason that so many people were homeless in the 1980s is that the housing they used to live in was taken away from them, and little housing was made available to replace it. The traditional pattern of rooming houses sprouting to meet the demand had been thrown off kilter by the gentrification phenomenon. There is some evidence that the situation was aggravated by roomers' rents rising more quickly than the income available to them — welfare, other government support or minimum wages for short-term work (Ontario 1988, p. 34).

The problems leading to homelessness may be rooted in the very nature of cities, "partly caused by the operation of the urban economy itself and partly caused by liveable cities that stimulate gentrification. Our very urban success and affluence causes problems for the poor" (Fallis and Murray 1990, p. 269).

Responding to homelessness

The traditional response to homelessness has been the hostel. Until the mid-1970s, almost all hostels were for single men. Then, as family violence became more of a public issue, hostels for women and children were formed.

In recent years, some have seen hostels as part of the problem rather than part of the solution, and "a barrier to the provision of real housing."

> Hostels are the most obvious example of social agencies doing the opposite of what they purport to do [citing Ivan Illich as a source]. Rather than decrease homelessness they may actually increase its likelihood ...
>
> Because of their ignorance about the actual poor living arrangements and conditions in most hostels (e.g., dormitory style living, lack of privacy, threat to safety), the general public tends to see hostels as an adequate and appropriate response to homelessness. (Admittedly, they are better than being left to freeze to death in the street.) More appropriate alternatives such as the provision of *real* housing are therefore seen as a less urgent need. The problem has, by most accounts, been dealt with. Those who are homeless now have a "home". (Ward 1989, p. 7)

Jim Ward makes the point that providing a bed in a hostel isn't in any way comparable to providing a person a home to live in. Most hostels require people to leave during the day — some think those who stay in hostels should seek jobs during the day, others say there simply isn't the staff or money to control a hostel full of people during the day — and the dormitory arrangements mean that there is no sense of privacy for anyone. "There is," writes Ward, "no place of one's own that can be called 'home'" (1989, p. 7).

Women's hostels and shelters are better funded than hostels for single men, and they seem to work on different principles. Women's hostels generally try to help women and their children find stability and a permanent place to live: men's hostels generally just provide temporary accommodation. As Ward notes, the feminist movement has helped make this important difference (1989, pp. 11-15).

While few see hostels as any kind of permanent solution, there seems to be some general agreement about the improvements that should be made to hostels on an interim basis. One study concludes that basic standards for a hostel system should include:

- 24 hour access to the residence;
- private, secure lockers for storage;
- an improved staff-to-resident ratio;
- an emphasis on helping people access permanent, affordable housing and the necessary support services. (Bairstow 1986, p. 70)

Few hostels provide these services. The limited political power available to the homeless means that their ability to improve the situation is very restricted. "Homeless people experience a lack of power that is equivalent to their lack of income and their lack of housing" (Toronto 1990, p. 2). Political bodies find that they don't have the money or commitment to make these changes, and the homeless are unable to exert the necessary political pressure to bring them about.

Housing solutions and support services

The approach to homelessness that has gained much support among those who worry about such things centres on the question of powerlessness: one problem can't be solved without addressing the other. Thus, simply offering housing won't be enough; the offer must include support services appropriate to the individual involved.

On its simplest level, these advocates argue that the following kinds of services must be made available:

- Income support — that is, a regular income stream adequate for basic necessities. In many provinces, welfare rules do not allow payment to anyone living in a hostel or shelter, or otherwise without a permanent address. This problem must be confronted.
- Crisis intervention and treatment. Physical problems must be attended to. Health problems among the homeless are, as one can imagine, substantial. Many homeless people have problems

with their feet because of the walking they must do, often in shoes that don't fit. Mental illness is often evident, and must be treated — usually over an extended period of time. Problems of abuse of alcohol or drugs must be addressed.
- Rehabilitation and personal development. This obviously can only take place once the individual is settled and secure.

The Homes First Society, an organization in Toronto devoted to providing long-term housing for street people, has developed programs to address these matters. Unlike the hostel solution, which suggests that providing a place to sleep will help resolve the problem, the Homes First approach is based on a recognition of the damage done by living without a home for any length of time.

> When people have permanent shelter they start thinking of housing as an obtainable goal. When the time-lines are removed, behaviours are not dictated by feelings of failure or pressures around achievement; men and women are free to move at their own pace towards whatever sort of housing suits their needs ... The longer people are on the streets, lacking the structure of a community residence, the longer it takes them to move off the street.
>
> Homes First believes that the family and friendship relationships, sense of place, belonging and community that form around people in stable housing are the primary supportive elements which problem-focused social services can complement, but never replace.
>
> Many people have been so debilitated by being homeless that it would be a lengthy process to learn to live in one place for a period of time. Most housing options do not take into account this learning time. Also, most housing options were not developed with input from these people, and therefore management and design do not acknowledge their needs and ideas. (Greaves 1990, pp. 14-15)

Homes First's first project in the early 1980s was a "highrise rooming house," a nine-storey building in downtown Toronto. Each floor held two apartment units of either four or five bedrooms. Each apartment unit is treated as a separate rooming house, operated by a different social agency. Those offered housing must learn to live with the other roomers in the apartment. Although each apartment unit is subject to

Photo: Charlotte Sykes

StreetCity in Toronto consists of seven houses built inside a factory building, which ensured that the houses did not have to be constructed to be weatherproof, but could be clad in wall-board inside and out. The photo looks down the "street" between two houses. The rafters holding up the roof are visible, as well as the skylight.

the management rules of the agency responsible, it is intended to be long-term housing — that is, it is a permanent place to live until the tenant decides to move out.

Homes First is responsible for a number of other permanent housing projects for the homeless, each including support and empowerment programs. Perhaps its most innovative project is StreetCity. The Society obtained a lease from a factory building purchased by the City of Toronto, and decided to build within the factory six houses. Since the houses were within the factory shell, they didn't need the expense of being secured from the weather, but could be covered in wallboard. The idea was to have the homeless themselves build the houses, using appropriate construction supervision.

In December 1988, forty men moved into the factory to begin construction. At night they slept on mattresses on the floor. By March

Photo: Manitoba Housing Department

Veterans' Manor is built two blocks off Winnipeg's Main Street strip and consists of fifty-six apartments for permanent residency and four units for overnight or emergency shelter. Residents are from single occupancy hotel rooms in the area. The building was opened in February 1990. Financing was made available under the provincial/federal non-profit program, some equity from the sponsoring group, and funds from the Winnipeg Core Area Initiative.

1990, construction was completed, and thirty-seven women and thirty-five men began moving into the six large houses, all separated by interior streets. Writes Greaves:

> The energy of StreetCity is easy to feel as you walk around. The real work of building the community within StreetCity, and of planning the development of permanent housing options for these people, continues. The process is very like the successful transition from squatters' settlements to permanent communities in Third World countries, where diverse groups of people with a common interest in making a decent life for themselves work with governments and community based organizations. Homeless people are the Third World in our First World. When we deal with them as a major resource in solving the problem, it works; when we treat them as the problem, it doesn't. (1990, p. 15)

Apart from support services, the need is for more housing to replace that lost to low-income single people in the past twenty years. Given the amount lost, the number of units needed is substantial. Bairstow suggests 25,000 units a year for ten years, just for Ontario (Bairstow1986, p. 145). These need not always be new units: it is possible to buy existing buildings, such as single-occupancy hotels, as Vancouver and some American cities have found (p. 26).

Under the leadership and prodding of the Downtown Eastside Residents Association, several single-room occupancy hotels have been renovated and converted into permanent housing in Vancouver. Some forty-three units have been created in the renovated Gresham Hotel, and because of revenues from the rent of ground floor retail, on-going subsidies are not required. In the New Continental, 110 residential units have been made available for single people (British Columbia 1992, p. 89). Similar initiatives have been undertaken in the Toronto area under the leadership of the Rupert Hotel coalition.

A British Columbia commission has proposed that the government commit $7.5 million a year for each of three years to undertake homelessness initiatives in partnership with community organizations. This would help where problems of homelessness are now evident in that province — Vancouver, Victoria, Kelowna and Nanaimo (British Columbia 1992, pp. 90-91).

Conclusions

The issue of homelessness is a large one and, like poverty, pushes at the edges of our ability as a society to respond. As one study noted:

> Homeless people are the true "low-income" people in this city. Some of them are "no-income." They make ends meet in a variety of ways, most of which are unsatisfactory to them as human beings and are unsatisfactory to the rest of us in the city. (Toronto 1990, p. 2)

Responding to homelessness is expensive and time-consuming, and goes beyond simply providing housing. Useful initiatives have been undertaken in several large Canadian cities, and they provide the basis for more significant national and local programs, which are clearly needed.

Chapter 12

Toward a Reform Agenda

When we are confronted by big social problems such as housing affordability or homelessness, we tend to conceive of big reforms. But that approach holds little hope for meaningful change. Big social problems are often better understood as an accumulation of smaller problems, and they are often not best addressed by big solutions that imply an all-or-nothing approach. Big solutions assume all the information needed to make a good decision is available, and they ignore the likelihood of unintended consequences. As a result, they are not helpful as starting points.

The American social critic Christopher Jencks puts it well in his discussion of the American underclass:

> If we want to understand what is happening to those at the bottom of American society, we need to examine their problems one at a time, asking how each has changed and what has caused the change. Instead of assuming the problems are all linked to each other, we need to treat their interrelationships as a matter for empirical investigation ...
>
> Changes ... require an immense amount of trial and error ... Instead of looking for ways of improving our institutions, we tend to blame some politicians for every failure and look for a replacement. Politicians therefore become specialists in avoiding blame, not in solving problems. This may be unavoidable in a large, diverse society. But if we cannot manage piecemeal reforms, looking for metasolutions is almost certain to be time wasted so far as the American underclass is concerned. If we want to reduce poverty, joblessness, illiteracy, violence, or despair, we will surely need to change our institutions and attitudes in hundreds of small ways, not in one big way. (Jencks 1992, pp. 202-3)

This chapter adopts that approach and proposes a number of different changes which do not constitute a single package — some can be done without calling on others — but which seem reasonable on their own. Many proposals are based on information that is now available, and might be reconsidered if persuasive, conflicting information became available. In some cases small experiments should be tried to see if the results are as anticipated — although given the length of time it takes for housing programs to become established, it is hard to see any such experiment having a useful life shorter than five or six years.

The difficulty with ideas for reform is the extent to which they are weighed down by political ideology. Ideological freight accompanies all political decisions and has frequently prevented otherwise reasonable people from arriving at a consensus. While it is difficult to be free of ideology, we should do our best to recognize this limitation, and as much as possible we should attempt to prevent ideology from clouding public policy decisions, particularly in the field of housing, where the dollar amounts involved are relatively large and the long-term consequences are astounding. Every attempt should be made by critics, commentators, and politicians to separate ideological issues from the empirical world of what seems to be links between cause and effect.

One big hurdle is determining goals and objectives. The private sector wishes to make a profit, and must do so or suffer grave consequences. The non-profit sector, including co-ops, wishes to create community, which can be successfully defined in myriad ways. What is the goal of government in engaging in housing issues?

Some say cynically that the objective of governments, in spite of all the fine words of the politicians, is control for its own sake. Indeed, many in the profit and non-profit sectors can cite chapter and verse of government housing programs where control overwhelmed any positive accomplishment of a particular program. A failure to be flexible in implementation when flexibility could ensure the spirit of a program would be achieved is a source of major disappointment and complaint for many housing providers. This tendency for government involvement to be accompanied by inflexible control must be recognized as a serious limitation both in what governments can achieve and in what others think they can achieve. One way to deal with this shortcoming is for governments to clearly accept that an important public goal in housing policy is as much as possible to remove barriers and controls standing in the way of the supply of good, affordable housing. As we will see, this is a theme that runs through a number of reform proposals suggested here, at all levels of government.

The larger problem is that very few people continue to hold the belief that governments represent the public interest: many believe governments have interests of their own and are no more likely to give voice to public interests than the private sector, religious institutions, or cultural groups. Finding the "public" interest in the late twentieth century often occurs when a number of different interests (including government) convene to discuss what they all agree on. This truth should also be acknowledged, and the design of programs should be undertaken with this in mind.

Thus, two limitations should be acknowledged at the start of any reform process in housing: governments must recognize the need to reduce barriers to the supply of good, affordable housing, and there should be no assumption that governments are particularly wise in understanding or embodying the public interest.

Principles to guide policy choices

As this book has tried to make clear, there are many policy choices available. Too often, governments have lurched into programs without defining what they were trying to do, or whom they were trying to serve. In retrospect, those decisions can be attacked because they have not met basic principles that should underlie important housing initiatives. Perhaps setting out criteria will help provide a road map for choosing policies to pursue.

The following discussion proposes principles on which new housing policy in Canada should be based.

The most important long-term goal of housing policy should be to create and maintain an adequate supply of housing that is affordable. As a society, we can't afford to create a supply of affordable housing, then sell it off so that its assurance of remaining affordable disappears — as happened with the stock of Wartime Housing Inc., discussed in Chapter 8. Public investments in affordable housing — whether that housing is owned privately, or by some government or agency, or by the non-profit and co-operative sector — should attempt to ensure that housing will not become unaffordable over time. Rather, a stock of affordable housing should be created and policies put in place to ensure that it expands. Thus, one principle should be:

1. The objective of housing policies and programs in Canada should be to create and maintain an expanding stock of housing that is affordable on a long-term basis for Canadian households.

All Canadians deserve to be housed well at a cost that is affordable to them. The whole community suffers when people are poorly housed or where one sector of the community is isolated or hived off from others.

But what is the meaning of "affordable"? As noted in Chapter 2, this word has had different definitions over the years. At one point housing was affordable if it ate up no more than 20 per cent of gross family income, then 25 per cent, and currently 30 per cent. These changes in meaning have always taken place at a bureaucratic level, rather than being subject to a wide-ranging public debate and political decision.

It is impossible to craft comprehensive housing policies without addressing what is meant by "affordability." Many homeowners pay less than 20 per cent of their income for housing; many tenants pay more than 30 per cent. But of course every situation is different: some owners are quite willing to pay half of their income into housing costs, recognizing the investment they are making; a single person might well be able to afford paying 35 per cent of income for housing, whereas a household with a child might find that entirely out of the question.

To a large extent the definition of affordability is something whose greatest impact is on renters, not owners, and it is reasonable that the definition refer directly to non-owners. A reasonable definition — one that has historical precedent and is something of a compromise — is that housing is affordable if it takes no more than 25 per cent of the gross income of a non-owner household. Some might argue that this percentage is still too high, and that it represents a very low standard of living (low standards of living are ones where necessities swallow a great deal of household income; high standards of living are those where there is a large amount of discretionary spending), but in fact it represents a scaling down of current measures. As well, it is easily understood, and can become a useful benchmark in assessing how well Canadians are being housed and what the goal of housing policies should be.

With this in mind, the second principle should read:

2. All Canadians deserve to be housed well at a cost that is affordable to them, and for non-owner households an affordable cost is one that consumes no more than 25 per cent of gross income.

Many Canadians currently live in housing that consumes more than 25 per cent of gross income. Approximately 1.5 million households experience this problem.

Housing doesn't exist in the abstract. In most cases it is part of a community, a group of other houses. Housing located in a community that has deteriorated, is isolated from or bereft of services, or that has become ghettoized to consist of one kind of income group — one thinks of some large public housing projects discussed in Chapter 8 — can hardly provide the kind of social experience Canadian families should expect. Accordingly, a third principle should read:

3. Neighbourhoods should be designed or modified to be supportive and diverse.

For many decades, the validity of government programs was assessed by the amount of public funds involved. But governments no longer have the financial resources to throw money at problems, and that change may well provide the opportunity to implement more useful programs. Some programs don't require funding, but rather policy changes that governments might find more painful to support than allocating money.

Many good solutions will draw on private monies and talents to accomplish public objectives. Since the private sector can't afford to provide housing below cost, however, nothing but public subsidies will ensure that low-income households find affordable housing.

There are many housing suppliers: large companies and small ones; for-profit and non-profit companies; co-operatives; individuals; community, religious and social groups; municipal governments and their agencies; provincial and federal governments and their agencies. Sometimes suppliers take on untraditional roles to good effect; sometimes different interests will combine to fill new niches. These changes should be accommodated. Different interests will show creative leadership at different times; it should not be assumed that leadership will come from government. Trying to enforce a distinction between the public and private sectors is not always helpful.

Combining ideas about limitations on public funding and the need to allow all actors in the housing milieu to play useful roles results in a fourth principle:

4. The skills and talents of all sectors and suppliers should be called upon to help address housing problems.

As described in Chapter 4, it is only recently that the desirability of the sprawling city is being widely questioned, but new evidence seems very persuasive: cities are more efficient and provide a healthier and more diverse social environment, and they are closer to becoming environmentally sustainable if they are more compact. Proper design and material use can also result in impressive savings in energy and water use, a good example of how making extra capital investments reduces operating costs and negative environmental impacts. Accordingly:

5. The creation of new housing should largely take place within existing urban envelopes through infill schemes, in building forms compatible with what has already been built, and in ways that conserve energy and water. Where greenfields development does occur, it should be done in a compact manner.

Few will quarrel with these five principles, but they are not without their loose ends. They do not make any assumptions about how housing will be provided for those with lower incomes, nor what kind of housing it will be, primarily because those are issues of implementation. They do not assume that housing for low-income households will always be supplied in rental accommodation; ownership housing might have more substantial benefits. The key, as always, is to be clear about direction, and let the details about how to get there be worked out along the way.

One larger question is whether the housing market can be made to work better in a more self-regulating way. Many people seem to assume that low-income Canadians will be well housed only if governments pump more money into programs to house them. Are there ways in which the housing market can be made to work so that the needs of low-income Canadians are met without so much new money continually being poured in?

One part of this problem is that some of those involved in housing are continually taking money out of the housing market in the form of increased prices, in the process making existing housing more expensive for everyone. For example, the capital gain on the sale of a private home goes directly into the owner's pocket, and as that takes place with many properties, the cost of housing generally rises for everyone, making the needs of low-income households all the more severe. If the market can be changed to modify that leakage into private pockets, or if it can help capture some of that increase, housing problems might become much more easily solved. It seems better to discourage the surpluses generated from the housing market from flowing into private pockets than to constantly feed the market with more public funds. Programs directed at this objective would make the housing market more of a closed self-regulating system, and it might then work better in almost everyone's interests.

This leads to a sixth principle:

6. As much as possible, the housing market should be made self-enclosed, so instead of surpluses constantly leaking out into private pockets and new public funds constantly being injected, surpluses in the housing market are captured and re-invested to help meet housing needs.

The reforms put forward in this chapter are based on the preceding six principles. These principles should be the basis for housing policy reform in Canada.

Barriers

Governments, following cultural trends and political pressures, have put in place a number of barriers to the creation of good, affordable housing in supportive and diverse communities. A review of these barriers raises serious questions as to whether they achieve useful results. Many could be removed with positive results. The following are the more significant barriers.

Development standards: Most municipalities have technical standards that new housing and subdivisions must meet. Many of these standards are "gold-plated," creating extra and unnecessary costs, which raise the price of housing. Some examples are excessive dedications for road right-of-ways; excessively wide road pavements; boulevards; too many catchbasins and sewage manholes; expensive and unsatisfactory methods of dealing with storm water; excessive land dedications for parkland. These kinds of development standards should be carefully reviewed (Ontario completed a review in late 1993; see Ontario 1993) and changed accordingly.

A related set of standards are found in provincial building codes. These specify construction standards, purportedly to ensure safety for inhabitants but often spilling over into other areas. While standards dealing with safety should be maintained, those dealing with convenience or unreasonably high safety standards should be reviewed and changed. Thus, a standard that requires electrical plugs to be located every three feet in kitchens might be relaxed to every five feet, and only apply in certain parts of the kitchen. A standard requiring airtight houses also requires the provision of air circulation systems, at considerable cost, and perhaps airtightness should be reconsidered. A standard that requires two stairways for fire exit in small buildings might be replaced by the European system of one stairway and "safe" areas, which seems to be at least as safe and permits a much more economical building form for the kinds of smaller structures proposed for Main Streets. Canada should be aware that other countries that have good housing use much different and less costly standards; we might follow suit.

These kinds of barriers may appear insignificant, and on first glance can be justified by various professionals. Nevertheless, they add up to considerable extra costs, and in many cases they can be solidly challenged as not being the best way to achieve a stated objective. Governments should convene committees of diverse interests — builders, architects, engineers, housing providers, fire safety officials and so forth — to review development and building code standards.

Zoning: One recent municipal trend has been a considerable tightening of permissable uses and building forms, so that virtually no change is permitted in neighbourhoods without forcing an applicant to run the gauntlet of a lengthy, risky and costly rezoning process. In many cases, zoning makes difficult or impossible the very changes that help keep a neighbourhood vibrant and healthy — small changes that strengthen family housing, local schools and shops, by ensuring there are opportunities for new households to move into the neighbourhood. The creation of second units and Main Streets buildings, both discussed later in this chapter, are two examples of healthy changes generally prohibited by current zoning provisions in most Canadian municipalities.

Municipalities should attempt to loosen zoning in existing neighbourhoods to encourage small-scale change. It should be recognized that for cultural reasons this change will not always be easy, but local councillors should provide leadership to help provoke needed changes in this area.

Contaminated sites: If new housing is to be built within existing urban envelopes, it will probably be located on land that once served a different use. As the economy has changed since mid-century, industry has disappeared altogether or has left the city for the suburbs, and thus much of the developable land in existing cities is old industrial land. Many fear that this land is contaminated and must be cleared in advance of purchase or redevelopment: the fear of possible environmental liability has discouraged possible mortgage lenders and purchasers alike.

Unfortunately, there are few helpful standards a developer can turn to in order to determine what steps must be taken to clean up an industrial site. Most standards are developed on an ad hoc, site-by-site basis, and often they are impossibly high: they try to protect humans against the smallest of risks, not recognizing that such barriers to intensification encourage the development of more suburban land, which probably causes worse contamination (of air and water) and numerous auto accidents that result in injury and death.

What is needed is a reasonable set of guidelines for dealing with contaminated sites. These guidelines should define no more than reasonable risks and should point the way to economical ways of resolving problems. They should be developed by provincial governments since they have the appropriate expertise to address issues of contamination in conjunction with municipalities, local environmental groups, builders, developers and others.

Lot levies: The municipal lot levy on a new home is often about 10 per cent of the purchase price — from $10,000 to $30,000, depending on the municipality (British Columbia 1992). Although this amount is paid in the first instance by the developer, it is passed directly on to the purchaser. Thus a 10 per cent reduction in the cost of a new home in many municipalities could be achieved by eliminating lot levies.

However, lot levies cover the cost of municipal services many new owners expect: schools, community centres, libraries, an effective sewage treatment system and so forth. Could these be funded in different ways that do not have such an impact on the purchase price?

One suggestion is to return to the way these services used to be provided and funded by the municipality, often through local improvement taxes where the designated beneficiary properties paid this cost in taxes over the life of the debenture necessary to fund these capital facilities. There are several merits to returning to this approach. First, while many services such as water and sewage are mandatory, owners could vote on whether they want discretionary services — and they might decide to have lower taxes rather than a service such as a community centre, which they may see as not necessary at the time. Second, the cost of borrowing by the municipality may be less than for the developer. Third, the cost can be paid for over ten or twenty years rather than up front in a lump sum, which would usually be easier for a purchaser to afford.

Another suggestion is to reapportion the cost of these services across the whole community as proposed in British Columbia, rather than simply sticking the new members of the community with them (British Columbia 1992). One benefit of this approach is that it gets the existing community involved in questions about its own growth, and how and where it might best occur.

There are clear alternatives to the barriers caused by high lot levies, and they should be explored by municipalities.

Landlord and tenant laws: Many landlords complain of the significant length of time it takes to evict a tenant who refuses to pay rent or causes disruption to other tenants. Landlords have found that it can cost thousands of dollars and five or six months (of lost rent) to evict a tenant who decides to use all available legal recourses to fight eviction.

This is a barrier to the creation of new rental housing. If an owner senses there will be a great struggle to evict a tenant for good reason, why go to the trouble of creating and renting a second unit?

Tenants' rights must be protected so that decisions about eviction do not occur except after a fair hearing where the tenant's case can be presented. But there is no reason why this process should be lengthy: an expeditious hearing and decision should be anticipated by all parties, and the courts should ensure that this occurs. In cases where there is default in rent payment, or where tenant behaviour is causing a disruption to other occupants, parties should expect that a case be heard and a decision rendered within forty days of application, and any decision speedily enforced.

Landlord and tenant matters are a provincial responsibility, and provinces should vary existing procedures to ensure that these expectations are met.

Rent controls: Many landlords and developers claim that rent controls inhibit the construction of new housing, but as noted in Chapter 9, there is considerable uncertainty about this conclusion.

When controls were removed in various provinces, there was no rush to build rental housing, either because the condominium option provided a quicker return, or because newly constructed housing was so expensive that the rents needed were beyond what the market could bear. Examples in some American cities, particularly the fast-growing sun-belt cities, show that rental housing can be built on a competitive basis if costs are kept low by not requiring anything but surface parking; using inexpensive construction techniques, such as frame construction (not masonry) in two- or three-storey structures, set on cement slabs rather than an excavated basement; and requiring no interior hallways or stairways — all of which allows speedy construction. These conditions are rarely obtainable in Canadian urban areas, whether because of climatic conditions or municipal standards to create a compact urban form, and thus these kinds of savings are rarely achievable regardless of whether rent controls are in place. Thus the debate about the effect of rent controls on large-scale rental projects is almost academic, since construction costs are so high that rents will exceed what the market will bear.

The merit of rent controls is that they provide real security of tenure. If there are no controls, the tenant can be evicted by the landlord's simply demanding a steep increase in rent, and this can occur whether or not there is a high vacancy rate in rental units. The problem with removing controls in those provinces where they exist is finding some alternative way of giving the tenant security, and until this problem can be addressed, there seems no alternative but to keep controls of some kind. As noted in Chapter 9, an alternative to pass-through controls such as those found in Ontario is the consensual model of controls as used in Quebec. The former gives tenants security in rent increases; the latter provides more flexibility, depending on the negotiating skills of the parties and the decision of the provincial body in cases of dispute. The Thom model of a fair market rent system is yet another approach which could be tried.

In view of the need to provide tenants with real security of tenure, it is not proposed that controls be removed where they now exist.

Housing supply

There are about 10 million housing units in Canada, and about 200,000 units are added each year. Is this rate of addition appropriate to meet housing needs?

As discussed in Chapter 2, a host of factors must be taken into account to establish the demand for new units, and still more information is required to determine the number of units needed to ensure that they are affordable. But as a generalization for discussion purposes, it seems that a new supply of about 200,000 units a year should be adequate to meet demand. In all likelihood, the private sector will be able to supply many of these new units.

However, as already noted, few of these new units will be provided in large-scale rental buildings. Most new units provided by the private sector will be fee or condominium ownership units, whose price is often beyond the means of the bottom two income quintiles. One problem that must be addressed in housing supply is how non-ownership housing will be made available, given the market problems facing the private sector in its supply.

How many units a year should be provided to meet affordability requirements? Currently, more than one and a half million Canadian families have an affordability problem as defined in the principles set out earlier in the chapter. Assuming all other factors remain the same, the problem of housing affordability could be fully addressed within ten years if 150,000 affordable units were made available each year. This need not be new housing, but could be achieved by making subsidies of various kinds available to existing units, as well as to new units.

However, 150,000 affordable units each year for ten years is far beyond the number of affordable units supplied in any of the past twenty years, and can be considered an unreachable target. A more realistic target, achievable although still high, is the creation of an additional 50,000 units of affordable housing a year. This number of affordable units was achieved in the fiscal year 1987–88.

It seems reasonable to assume that while the private sector will be able to provide some less expensive units (particularly in second units), most units within the reach of those with affordability problems will require special government subsidy and intervention. Building new units in the hope that an increase in units will result on its own in lower cost units (the trickle-down theory) will not address questions of affordability. Thus, while constraints on the supply of inexpensive housing should be removed, this in itself will not resolve affordability issues, which are not just related to questions of supply, but also of distribution. Proposals to meet these issues are outlined in the remainder of the chapter.

Often the supply of new housing gets all the attention in discussions about housing supply; however, housing supply policies must also address existing units, which are 98 per cent of the supply, since if they can't be protected there will be serious problems. Further, these existing units are often more amenable to programs speaking to issues of affordability. Thus the discussion will begin with existing housing.

Existing housing

The most substantial problems regarding existing housing are found in apartments in high-rise buildings. This form of housing constitutes a significant percentage of total housing units in large cities — in some city centres, as already noted, almost one-third of all housing. The current condition of these high-rise structures leaves much room for worry, and unless immediate action is taken, the long-term future of this housing is in doubt.

The cost of repairing a high-rise building constructed in the early 1970s is almost $15,000 per unit. This could be funded with rent increases of about 10 per cent a year, but that kind of increase is politically impossible to sell, and many landlords fear it would result in many units remaining vacant. For these reasons, it is wishful thinking to expect these repairs to be made in the normal course of events. But the problem cannot be left to fester: some solution must be found. This kind of rehabilitation work is a fine way to create employment, particularly in the construction trades, and job creation money might be better spent here than on new roads and other public infrastructure.

One possibility is for governments to make grants to landlords to help cover repair costs. Grants could be made subject to a number of conditions: that public funds be matched by funds contributed by the landlord; that rents be subject to control for a certain period of time; and so forth. It is questionable whether this approach will fulfil the first principle set out earlier, namely to expand the stock of affordable housing in the long term.

A second possibility is for programs to be established encouraging non-profit and non-profit co-operative groups to purchase high-rise buildings and make needed repairs, with appropriate loan guarantees from government. As noted in Chapter 3, some argue this could be affordable to tenants using a graduated payment mortgage instrument with only a government loan guarantee, to ensure that lenders will participate. Others argue that if the scheme was that easy, it would be proposed by the private sector, which has shown no interest in it. In all likelihood some public monies will be needed to ensure that rents are within market rates, and to give the non-profit company or co-op enough flexibility to meet unforseen needs. Using non-profits and co-ops ensures there is no leakage of dollars invested in housing.

A third approach is to immediately begin requiring, by law, that landlords of buildings of more than three storeys (or whatever size is agreed on) establish reserve funds. These funds could be under public control; if under private control they must be monitored in an effective manner. Funds placed in a replacement reserve should be made tax deductible. It is unclear exactly what percentage of revenue should be required to be contributed to reserve funds; non-profit companies and co-ops are currently required to maintain reserve funds, putting in 3–5 per cent of revenue annually. This amount may be adequate to fund large repairs such as a boiler replacement or a new roof, but not ongoing ensuite repairs, such as replacement refrigerators or kitchen cupboards. The details of this approach will probably vary from place to place, but they must be addressed.

Landlords and others might suggest other innovative ways of ensuring that high-rise buildings remain for the long term in a state of good repair. All proposals should be looked at carefully to find schemes that work and that meet the six basic housing principles outlined above.

In any case, effective programs must be put in place immediately to ensure the repair of high-rise apartment buildings.

New housing

New housing can be built in a number of forms and in a number of locations, with or without the use of public funds. In keeping with the basic principles set out above, the first three suggestions for creating new housing would all be put into effect within the existing urban fabric. All provide housing that is generally less expensive to

Old housing with new life: this nineteenth century home in Ottawa's Sandy Hill neighbourhood has been renovated into three large units.

Photo: City of Ottawa Housing Department

the consumer than what has been provided in the last few decades, although this housing will probably not be affordable to those in the bottom two quintiles without government aid. Because of their small scale, these suggestions do not require large, integrated development companies for success (although those companies may certainly decide to participate); they all can be accomplished with the involvement of small entrepreneurs.

The five suggestions are not advanced to be limiting in any way, but to provide a focus on the kind of housing that should be encouraged.

Second units: The least expensive new housing to create is housing that is carved out of something that already exists. The prime example of such housing is second units or basement apartments. Homeowners should be permitted to make a second unit without restriction, provided basic safety conditions and housing standards are met. Provinces should move to prevent municipalities from restricting such units, perhaps in the same manner as the province of Ontario, which has introduced legislation to this effect. Provinces should also set building code standards for second units so that they are not second-rate units, and so that municipalities do not try to prevent them by requiring them to meet unnecessarily high standards.

The merit of second units is that no public costs are involved in their creation, since homeowners who hope they can rent the space will pay for them. Most second units are fully contained within an existing house, so the cost of their creation does not involve new exterior walls or connections, but simply interior change that can be accomplished for probably no more cost than the revenue generated by the first year's or two years' rent. A second advantage is that many second units are rented at prices that are at the low end of the market, and so are available to some households with lower incomes.

A close cousin to the second unit is the granny flat, the unit over the garage or off a back lane or, if the house was constructed in the nineteenth century, in the coach house. This kind of intensification should also be encouraged, although since new structures might be involved, some zoning controls might be applied to ensure appropriate additions.

Three questions may be raised about the effect of second units. First, if there are no restrictions on second units apart from reasonable building standards, how many will be created? The answer seems to be that perhaps a small percentage of all homeowners in cities will decide to create a second unit, although across the country that can amount to a substantial number. If there are 5 million houses in Canadian cities and a second unit is created in 1 per cent of these houses, that amounts to 50,000 new units.

In the end, second-unit legislation is permissive, and compels no positive action. Whether these units are provided at all will depend on local markets. A few neighbourhoods may experience a noticeable change because of their location — such as those adjacent to universities, where student demand for housing is high — although the effect of permitting second units in these situations may be to regularize existing illegal units and bring them up to standard. It is hard to give credence to the argument that introducing reasonable standards will somehow lead landlords to close down existing second units.

Second, what effect will second units have on municipal sewage systems, which often are close to capacity? At most, they might add 3–4 per cent to the sewage load. However, if municipalities decide to require water conservation devices such as low-flow toilets for new and second units, the new load will be marginal. Perhaps some

Photos: City of Vancouver Planning Department

Fairview Slopes in Vancouver is Canada's best example of attractive high-density low-rise housing. At fifty-five to eighty units per acre, the density of these projects is comparable to, or higher than, that of most suburban high-rise residential buildings, yet it is accomplished within a thirty-five-foot height limit. In both cases this housing was built and is owned by the private sector.

limitations may be required for the creation of second units in homes on septic systems, but the only restriction on second units in homes on a central sewage treatment system should be reduced water consumption, with its added environmental benefits.

Third, what effect will second units have on parking? Not all occupants of second units will own cars, particularly since studies suggest they generally have lower incomes, but some undoubtedly will. Communities with on-street overnight parking have usually found that the additional cars generated by second units are hardly noticeable, and can be accommodated in a system of on-street permit parking, with interested car-owners renting garages and spaces privately as they wish. Communities where on-street overnight parking is not permitted seem to experience more problems, since driveways and garages are often already overrun with cars. The easiest solution seems to be to permit on-street parking, which makes good use of large paved areas that otherwise serve no purpose during the night. The addition of more residents to the neighbourhood will improve the prospects for good transit service and the economical viability of corner stores — two devices that help create a living environment where a private automobile is not quite so necessary.

Main Streets: Intensification usually refers to new buildings erected within the existing urban fabric, such as replacing an old factory building with a row of new houses. The Main Streets program refers to intensification on main arterial streets through the building of four- and five-storey structures, perhaps with a commercial establishment on the grade level, with apartments above.

Main Streets housing was a popular form of housing in Canadian cities before the Second World War, but with the rise of the shopping mall and the decline of the retail strip few recent examples can be found. It seems to be a good way to introduce small numbers of new residential units into a neighbourhood in a manner that respects and even strengthens existing forms and uses. Main Street projects were once seen as a good way of investing money for retirement, and their renewed popularity may re-establish this kind of investment.

The amount of new housing that may be created through a Main Streets approach depends on factors such as zoning, parking and the rental market. Zoning controls must be calibrated so that it is not difficult to receive approval for such projects. Experience teaches that the cost of waiting for a rezoning will in almost every case make a small Main Streets project uneconomical: thus, municipalities must establish the desired size and use of structures to be permitted so such projects can be built as-of-right, without requiring approvals. Further, if excessive parking requirements are established by the municipality, the developer will be unable to meet them on site (given that so many sites are small, accommodating only eight or ten small apartments), or the cost of putting parking underground will make the project uneconomical. Municipalities should specify reduced parking standards, such as requiring no parking spaces for the first ten units on a site. Few Main Streets projects will be built if the market for rental residential units, or perhaps commercial space, is soft.

There are two larger questions about Main Streets housing that remain unanswered. First, do people have a prejudice against living on a main street, above a shop? Do people think it is too noisy? that there is not enough open space? If this prejudice exists, can it be countered by examples of good design and proximity to services? These are conjectures raised by sceptics, and answers will emerge only as Main Streets housing gets built and experience is gained.

Second, is development on main streets economically viable? The fear here is since units can only be created by new construction, working in tight sites, on a small scale, construction costs will be high. Further, sites might be expensive on a unit basis, and there may not be any ready market for the commercial space created at grade. Perhaps these factors present difficult choices for developers, who may initially show some reluctance to building on main streets. Again, time will tell.

Municipalities have grown used to the idea that new development should happen only on raw land, and that change should never happen in existing areas. Changing these habitual ways of thinking will be important for all who play a role in new housing supply.

Provincial governments may take an active role here too, as suggested for second units. Many local councillors adhere to the view that stable residential neighbourhoods should face no kind of change, even if that change strengthens structures and networks that are already there, or restores those that were there in the past. Few local councillors seem pleased with the idea that a development, even a small-scale development, can be built without their personal approval. Provincial legislation enabling Main Streets development may be helpful.

Photo: Avi Friedman

Infill housing will surely become much more common as cities look for easy ways to increase densities without large-scale demolition. This example shows how GROW-home-style houses have been fitted nicely into a street in Montreal.

Less expensive housing: One useful approach is to allow the construction of less expensive housing. The fourteen-foot wide GROW home designed in Montreal is a good example of what has been done and should be repeated: building a strong shell with a modest width, then leaving interior finishes to the owners to complete when funds are available. In cities other than Montreal developers have found other ways of building inexpensive free-hold houses: quadroplexes (where four houses are all built in the same structure), semi's and town-houses.

The assumption of the GROW home is that interior detailing, which can often be completed by the buyer, can add as much as one-third to construction costs; if it is not done the builder can offer the house at a very attractive price. Some builders speak disparagingly about this saving, since they have found that buyers are more interested in buying (and paying more for) a finished house than for an unfinished one. They also argue that it costs money to leave a house "unfinished," since materials that would otherwise be covered must be applied with care if they are to be exposed. But the builders can be left to argue among themselves: there seems no reason why various degrees of interior finish should not be pursued.

Assuming the cost of construction is $60 a square foot, then a thousand-square-foot house could be constructed for about $60,000, and with the price of a building lot, could be ready for marketing at close to $100,000. (Lot levies then get added on, as do marketing fees.) There is every reason to believe that in large cities where the average price of a new home is twice that amount, these kinds of homes would sell if built, allowing many who now can't afford to buy homes to do so.

However, at the time of writing, most municipalities in Canada shun the construction of inexpensive homes such as those with a fifteen- or sixteen-foot frontage, and require lengthy (and often unsuccessful) planning procedures. Municipalities have laid down a host of rules about lot size and set-backs (on the strange assumption that they should be attracting only expensive houses with large tax bills), as though the function of the municipality was to ensure that everyone lived in expensive housing. Many municipalities only permit inexpensive townhouses in a condominium form — forcing these owners to pay for their own garbage collection, street-cleaning, snow-ploughing and street-lighting — making it very obvious they are unwanted, second-class citizens.

Perhaps municipalities should be required by provincial legislation to permit the construction of less expensive houses such as the GROW home, although there's no reason why inexpensive houses shouldn't come in twenty-foot widths as well as fourteen-foot widths. Certainly, there may be some locales where such houses don't quite fit in, but they should be permitted in most parts of the city. They could be built as infill housing or as part of a new subdivision.

The irony of the situation should not be missed: imagine needing legislation to permit a less costly item to enter the marketplace — that's apparently what's needed when it comes to ownership housing.

Redesigning public housing: Many of the problems of large public housing projects have to do with design. These areas of cities should be "regularized" — that is, redesigned so that they are laced with public streets, front doors face onto those streets, and uncontrolled open space is made into controlled front and back yards.

Better yet, plans should be developed to do this in a way that makes more intensive use of the publicly owned land on which projects sit. The three examples of public housing redesign considered in Chapter 8 showed that on average an extra 200 units could be built into each large project. Across the country, redesign of larger projects could result in a gain of more than 50,000 units on project land.

Redesign not only addresses the serious shortfalls of large projects; it also provides an opportunity to add more units and to review management options. As projects are redesigned to become buildings on streets, consideration should be given to transferring buildings to non-profits and co-ops, and to including different forms of tenure, including the possibility of ownership of new units.

New communities: While it is most desirable that new housing be created in areas that are already developed, this will not occur in all cases, and the creation of new communities will continue to be a reality. How should these new communities be shaped?

Chapter 4 has provided a background suggesting that new communities should be compact; contain a mix of uses in a fine enough grain to ensure the likelihood of pleasant and frequent pedestrian activity; and include a variety of types of accommodation, with a variety of price ranges, most buildings being four storeys or less. The characteristics of the sprawling suburb should be avoided. GROW home–type housing should be included. Provincial planning policies may be required to ensure that this new form is achieved in green-fields development.

Financial reforms

Not all the needed changes can be accomplished by design and planning changes: financial reforms are critical in ensuring that the basic housing principles are met, and that all Canadians are well housed at a cost they can afford. The following proposals outline some important directions that should be pursued.

CMHC Direct Lending: CMHC is able to borrow money at less expensive rates than a co-op or a non-profit because of the amount borrowed, and because it is a government agency. Thus, loans secured directly from CMHC rather than from a bank will provide for less expensive housing. This practice is called direct lending.

CMHC abandoned direct lending in 1978, but announced that it would again become available in summer 1993, estimating a saving of about $100 million over five years (*Report on Business,* July 22, 1993, p. B3). One wonders at the amount of extra costs paid by residents of non-profit and co-op projects between 1978 and 1993 because CMHC had cancelled direct lending. Direct lending should remain a standard approach of CMHC.

Mortgage instruments: As noted in several places in this book, innovative mortgage instruments are very helpful in achieving needed change. There is no reason to assume that the most familiar instrument, the equal payment mortgage, is appropriate for all situations. The non-profit co-operative sector has developed as an alternative the interest linked mortgage (ILM). Since mortgagors do not have to build a safety factor into the ILM contract to cover what future interest rates might be, rates are less expensive. The efficiency of the ILM is that there is no inflation risk.

Another alternative has already been mentioned: the graduated payment mortgage (GPM). Its drawback is that it depends on the expectation of inflation, and if there is no inflation, difficulties loom.

A recent innovation is the shared equity or shared appreciation mortgage. This arrangement is of particular interest to social housing providers (discussed in Chapter 9) that are attracting some equity from residents in return for restrictions on return when the residents wish to sell. These shared equity arrangements are in their infancy in Canada, but are used successfully in other parts of the world in periods of rising expectations. As non-profit and co-op funding from governments grows more scarce, more of these experiments will surely be undertaken.

Nothing prevents parties from arranging their own innovative mortgage terms. However, lenders can be expected to be reluctant to enter into innovative terms when traditional terms meet their financial needs. It may be necessary for governments to provide guarantees to lenders to make innovative arrangements work as the federal government began to do in 1953 in guaranteeing mortgages for new house purchases.

Capital Cost Allowance: The owners of residential rental buildings are permitted to treat depreciation at a rate of 5 per cent of value as a capital cost allowance, even though projects usually appreciate in value. This fictional arrangement costs the government hundreds of millions a year in lost revenue; as discussed in Chapter 7, there is disagreement about the exact amount. For our purposes, it is assumed that CCA costs $200 million a year in lost revenue, a sum that is very much on the conservative side of estimates.

As already noted, this tax expenditure is not directed at low-income tenant households, but is applicable to all residential rental property. It appears to have no positive impact on the creation of new units, and its continued existence during the past decade has done nothing to alleviate the sharp decline in rental units across the country. There seems no reason to assume that ending CCA will have a negative impact on either new rental starts or on rent paid by tenants, although landlords can be expected to oppose losing this write-off. This tax expenditure is of no benefit in meeting the basic principles on housing set out at the beginning of this chapter, and its beneficiaries seem to be the owners of rental property, most of whom are found within the top two income quintiles.

Accordingly, there is no value in continuing this tax expenditure, and it should be cancelled. Cancelling CCA should ensure that federal government income increases about $200 million a year.

Capital gains tax: The profit made on the sale of a personal residence is exempt from capital gains tax, whereas other capital gains are taxed at a rate of 75 per cent. (Formerly the capital gains tax rate was 50 per cent, then it was changed to 66 per cent in the late 1980s, then to 75 per cent in the early 1990s.) The revenue forgone by this tax expenditure is debatable, but a federal task force estimated it to be $1.5 billion per year in the mid-1980s when the rate was 50 per cent. Further, a lifetime tax exemption of capital gains totalling $100,000 is available for all Canadian residents, and many gains on the sale of personal residences would probably fall within this exemption.

As house prices rise, owners who sell realize large gains. For the owner who is selling to purchase a new home in the same locale, those gains amount to little, since the new home the owner wishes to purchase in the same locale has also increased in value. Rises in house prices help those who through knowledge or chance can take advantage of a price rise in one place that is not occurring in another. Thus, selling a house in Toronto for $500,000 in 1989 when prices were at a peak and then buying a comparable house in Western Canada for $200,000 gave a household a real gain. At the same time, someone trying to move from Calgary to Vancouver in 1992 found the difference in house prices a real impediment, and indeed companies have found that high house prices made it difficult to recruit staff from other parts of the country. Price increases are of great benefit to those who speculate in houses, as many higher income individuals in the late 1980s did when the federal government gave tax exemptions (which ended in 1992) to certain large capital gains.

Taxing capital gains on houses may moderate the swings in house prices. Capturing some of this increase will help make the housing market more self-contained, since it will put brakes on the tendency for housing to become more expensive when it is put on the market. It will help stop profit from leaking into private pockets.

Most people seem to treat home ownership not so much as a way to make money when selling one house and buying another than as a means to gain security while amassing the family's largest investment. For these owners, a tax on some of the gain made on sale will not be seen as a threat to ownership. Further, a tax on some of this gain will be paid mostly by households with incomes in the top three quintiles, since by and large they are the households that own houses.

Accordingly, the capital gains tax exemption on the sale of personal residences and the lifetime $100,000 exemption should be ended. As noted, there are three benefits to these reforms: since 75 per cent of the increase in sale price will be taxed away, as with other capital gains the rise in the price of ownership housing will be moderated; a revenue source will be available to fund more housing programs; for most owners, the tax will not be seen as an imposition since the main purpose for owning has more to do with creating an asset and a home than with achieving a capital gain. Ending this tax expenditure fits well with the six principles outlined earlier in the chapter.

Some will argue that if capital gains are to be taxed, then payments made to buy the housing should be deductible from income, as is the practice in the United Kingdom and the United States. As argued in Chapter 5, this change should not occur. Housing is different than other capital assets in that it is used and enjoyed (lived in, to be frank) while it is being purchased, and the mortgage payments are in the form of rent for that use. To permit this rent to be deducted from income makes no more sense than permitting tenants to deduct from income the rent they pay.

There are various ways in which the exemption could be reduced and ended. One could exempt gains under a certain amount (say $25,000) or impose a sliding tax rate that increased according to the difference in buying and selling prices, although these proposals lose the simplicity of treating capital gains on a personal residence the same as other capital gains for tax purposes. As well, mechanisms will have to be built in to give recognition to capital improvements to the building.

Some may object to the fact that ending these exemptions, perhaps good in itself, will provide governments with yet more money that they might spend poorly. One method of avoiding this possibility is to ensure that when the exemptions are ended the revenues generated be dedicated to housing purposes so they are not available as general revenue. In any case, the primary reason for ending the exemptions is to stop leakage in the housing system, not to create new sources of revenue. From a housing point of view, things would work best if housing prices did not rise and if no capital gains resulted.

Expenditure commitments

The federal government spends slightly less than $2 billion annually on housing-related matters (not including tax expenditures). This is about $70 per capita, by most accounts a modest sum. It does not seem unreasonable to suggest this sum should be increased to at least $100 per capita in order ensure that the housing needs of the 1.5 million families with affordability problems are addressed. While the cost of this increase could be met (or more than met) by changes in tax expenditure proposed above, the increase can be justified whether or not there are offsetting revenues: the change is important to those in society who are the least well off. Further, money spent ensuring households are well housed is probably offset by savings in other social expenditures, although it is hard to allocate these savings directly or show a direct correlation of cause and effect.

The amounts spent on housing by provincial governments vary widely. Political priorities differ, and some provinces spend most when cost-sharing programs are available with the federal government. Municipalities spend little, although cities that have a strong tax base are likely to spend more on housing (usually through supporting a housing policy and non-profit delivery administration) than cities with a weak tax base. It makes sense that these expenditures vary, since one city's problems are rarely those of another. The shortcoming of a national housing program is that it assumes that all cities and provinces face the same problems at the same time, which of course they don't. The best approach at the federal level is clearly one that allows flexibility.

Provinces should have a goal of spending at least $10 per capita on housing problems. In recent years Ontario has been spending more than $50 per capita (and this should not be reduced), but

Ontario seems quite unusual in its commitment to housing compared to other jurisdictions. Ten dollars per capita across the country would provide another $250 million, and would allow provincial governments to support and target federal programs appropriate to local needs.

It is easy to suggest that even more should be allocated to housing problems; however, all governments are facing financial constraints. As well, the real difficulty might not be the amounts needed, but agreeing on the best ways of spending the money.

The most significant housing problems in Canada are those faced by low-income households, and it makes sense to devote considerable funds and policy tools to this problem. Suggestions have been made for urban design and zoning policies to create new kinds of desirable housing for Canadians with differing incomes; but the spending of housing dollars should generally be directed to serving the needs of low-income households.

How can this be done so that the most benefit is achieved for each dollar spent and so the program has political muscle? As already noted in Chapter 9 and as described in Linda McQuaig's *The Wealthy Banker's Wife* (McQuaig 1993), programs designed to appeal only to those with lower incomes quickly lose voter support and are cancelled. Thus good housing programs for households with lower incomes should be designed to have universal application and, in accordance with the six housing principles stated earlier in the chapter, should create diverse and supportive communities.

There is no single program that responds to all situations. Programs are effective (both cost effective and effective in delivering results) in some situations but not in others. Some programs will have unintended results, and for that reason may have to be abandoned. The key is keeping the general principles in mind, and acting accordingly.

No suggestions are made here about how much money should be spent on which program, or about how cost-sharing should work to ensure that programs are reasonably funded. Traditionally, for good reasons discussed in Chapter 1, the federal government has led the way with money, and there seems no reason for that to change. Provincial governments should also contribute, and should develop their own programs to respond to problems as they see them. Municipal governments can play an important role in planning and land-use regulation, although their funds derived from user fees, property taxes and provincial transfers are much more limited than those of senior governments. All governments must be involved. Housing problems will not be solved by the actions of one government alone.

The following programs seem appropriate recipients of public funds:

Rent supplement: The rent supplement program provides for contracts to be entered into where government guarantees the negotiated rent, requires the tenant to pay rent geared to income (currently 30 per cent), and reimburses the landlord the difference between the rent paid by the tenant and the negotiated rent. In British Columbia, administrative arrangements call for the tenant to pay the full rent, with the government reimbursing the tenant directly.

These arrangements may not be effective in markets where vacancy rates are low, since offering these agreements will provide landlords with another opportunity to raise rents, thus aggravating the rental situation. There is some thought that the key might not be so much the vacancy rate, which is difficult to estimate fairly, but the turnover rate, and that if the turnover rate is more than 10 per cent, then rents may not be affected by rent supplement agreements.

But where vacancy rates are not low or where the turnover rate is satisfactory, using these agreements may be a cost-effective way to ensure that low-income households are well housed at an affordable rent. Agreements should be secured for no less than five years, and preferably ten or more, to give households security.

These arrangements should be available to households paying more than 25 per cent of income in rent, which in most cases will be households in the bottom two quintiles.

Non-profit housing and co-op providers are prime candidates for such agreements, and most now hold agreements covering about one-half of their units. (When, because of higher vacancy rates in the rental markets, non-profits and co-ops experience vacancies, rent supplement agreements should be extended to these vacant units as quickly as possible.) Agreements with one landlord covering one or two units can cause undue paper work, but if the administrative arrangements can be worked out — perhaps through local housing organizations willing to administer them — these agreements would be an excellent way to support second units in houses, or new Main Streets housing. For those who still believe that the concentration of low-income households itself is a problem, rent supplement agreements help disperse families with different incomes throughout the community.

The shelter allowance is often considered similar to rent supplement, but in that arrangement the subsidy attaches to the tenant, who negotiates the rent with the landlord. Many in the development industry have been urging adoption of a national shelter allowance program, estimated to cost $765 million annually, that would provide 70 per cent of families in core need with an extra $115 per month (Clayton 1993a). The program has been criticized as being more of a method of income support, since it does nothing to ensure more housing supply; more particularly, it is said to contain cost estimates that are much too low. It also would have the effect of taking money from the creation of housing that is affordable in the long term (Hulchanski 1993a).

In any case, rent supplement programs — or shelter allowances, if they are decided on — should never be funded at the expense of programs to provide affordable housing in the long term. To prevent leakage of profits, they should be attached to non-profit and co-operative housing, and should be available to the private owners only as a stop-gap measure or to create supply (for example, to encourage second units). The benefits should clearly flow to the tenants, with careful regard that the program is not causing rent inflation.

How many units should the federal government consider funding through such a program? At a cost of $340 per month or $4,000 per year for one unit (the Clayton estimate of $115 per month seems unrealistically low), the cost of agreements on 50,000 units would be $200 million per year. But the figure settled on would depend on programs pursued at the same time to increase affordable supply and on commitments already made.

There is an added problem with these agreements: they don't provide housing for low-income families in the long run. Housing is provided for low-income families only so long as such agreements are in place, and experience has shown that when vacancy rates fall, private landlords tend to allow agreements to lapse, or to renew only at very high prices. (This does not happen in non-profit or non-profit co-operative developments, given their mandates to house low-income households.)

Thus, rent supplements alone will never produce a comprehensive, long-lasting approach to housing low-income households. Unless combined with other programs, they constitute a short-term, stop-gap approach, which should be used appropriately.

Non-profit and non-profit co-operative housing: Non-profit approaches, whether of the rental or co-operative kind, appear to have been at least as cost effective as private rental housing, and maybe more, and generally have been more available to low-income households, as documented in Chapter 9.

Some argue that large private companies are able to bring expertise and entrepreneurial ability to the construction of new housing (with attendant cost savings), particularly since, unlike non-profits, they do not have to rely on government officials for approvals at each step of the way. However, no one has figured out how the non-profit program can proceed without some bureaucratic overlay of approvals and still meet public objectives. There is a propensity for government to overregulate and control, as noted earlier in this chapter, and the non-profit sector (particularly in Ontario) feels quite worn out by these bureaucratic twists and turns.

The advantage of the non-profit approach is that it provides housing in the long term for low-income households. Further, a strong case can be made that housing co-operatives and many non-profits create strong communities that are very effective in providing supportive links between different kinds of people.

The perceived drawback to the non-profit program is the long-term subsidy involved, even if arrangements are made to borrow on the private market with appropriate government guarantees. This complaint is voiced by some even though in the long term these subsidies are no greater (and probably less) than those previously available to private sector housing. The index linked mortgage has been shown to reduce these costs, and should be used much more widely for housing programs. What is clear is that sizable amounts of non-ownership housing will not be created without government subsidy of some kind, and that non-ownership housing for low-income households will require further public subsidies.

But the question is raised: Are there other viable options for creating more non-profit and co-op housing than the programs in place for the past twenty years?

One interesting possibility not yet widely discussed is using the difference between the book and market value of non-profit and co-op projects as an asset to be borrowed against to raise funds to create more non-profit and co-op housing. It would be another example of attempting to stop the "leakage" in the housing market and making the market more self-contained.

Non-profits and co-ops have mortgage arrangements that call for costs to be fully paid down at the end of the thirty-five-year mortgage term. Legislation prohibits the non-profit or co-op from selling the project and allowing members to pocket the profits, which seems only reasonable; but nothing prohibits members, once the capital is paid, from simply reducing rents by more than half to rates sufficient just to cover operating costs. If this were to occur, (and the opportunity will be there for some projects early in the next century) then non-profit residents or co-op members would be pocketing the surplus, rather than returning it to the housing market system.

It would be far better to see non-profits and co-ops take this extra capital and use it for funding new housing. The extra capital is best expressed as the difference between book and market value, and could be realized by taking out a mortgage against the project for that amount, and providing the cash to a community-based land trust. The land trust would then use this capital to acquire existing units and convert them to non-profits or co-ops, or buy land and build new units. In this way, the surplus generated through these social housing programs can be ploughed back into more community-based housing rather than being pocketed privately.

The federal government could play a significant role in this process. It could establish the basis on which this generation of capital and its transfer can occur, although provincial legislation may also be required, given that this is a matter of property and civil rights under the constitution. Further, it could encourage this process by matching grants or other kinds of subsidies.

There are very positive benefits to such arrangements. Non-profits and co-ops would have a real incentive to control costs, since surpluses generated could go toward new housing, rather than being returned to various governments as now called for by existing social housing agreements. New social housing would not require 100 per cent government funding or guarantees — the very provisions that lead governments to impose rules and regulations that hobble non-profit and co-op creativity. Only partial government support would be needed, so social housing providers could be more imaginative in seeking diverse funding arrangements. In fact, creating capital out of existing assets gives them a degree of freedom they have always wanted but have never had. They would then be able to compete and co-operate with the private sector in the provision of housing and the creation of supportive and diverse communities.

In short, this kind of change presents an opportunity to build on the strong base of social housing created in Canada in the past twenty years. Housing associations in the United Kingdom have used these kinds of opportunities for many years to create an independence for themselves and manoeuvreing room when trying to secure the needed public subsidies. Governments in Canada should now show their support for these new directions.

It is difficult to know how many units the non-profit and co-op sectors would be able to spawn each year. One factor would be the amount of capital that might be generated from existing projects; another the extent of government subsidies; a third the income mix pursued in the new projects (which might be a continuation of the 50 per cent low-income ratio generally in place); a fourth the arrangements that could be worked out with private lenders; a fifth the arrangements with future residents for shared equity. Further, special care will have to be taken to ensure that non-profits and co-ops do not strip away so much of their assets that they are unable to fund necessary capital repairs: buildings do become worn out, and capital replacement costs are large.

Since there are now close to 500,000 social and public housing units in Canada, it may not be unreasonable to suggest an initial target of 5,000 units a year funded in this manner. Federal government support should be by way of grants related to the capital generated by the non-profits or co-ops and available to the land trust. Initially the grant could be two or three times the capital available, although various kinds of experiments should be tried. Funding should be either for new units or, since the object is to create affordable units and not particularly to add to housing stock, the purchase of existing units. Once there is some experience with the program, the federal grant should be reassessed and made on a matching basis. A target of 20,000 units a year is desirable, but that may be much too optimistic.

It will be important to ensure that non-profits and co-ops are able to build projects that house not only low-income households, but others as well, as they have traditionally done. Innovative approaches will be required to work out the details, blending funding arrangements from public and private sources, as well as appropriate levels of rent supplement support.

While this program proposes an imaginative new direction in which the social housing sector can become an actor on its own, not so tightly tied to government programs, it is admittedly modest in scope: it meets a very small proportion of the need for affordable housing. However, it seems unreasonable to suggest starting an untried program except at a modest scale to ensure that it is effective. Modest programs are nothing to be ashamed of at this time, provided they are congruent with the housing principles outlined earlier in the chapter. Successful small experiments should be expanded into larger programs.

At the same time, some aspects of the non-profit and co-op programs must continue. The non-profit program provides needed thrust for housing for special needs groups, and funding for at least 1,000 units should be allocated to these groups every year. Funding must continue and must expand for rural and native housing, matters that have not been dealt with at length in this book. And there seems no reason not to continue traditional non-profit and co-operative programs at a reasonable level — say 15,000 to 20,000 units a year — until the new initiatives are proven one way or another.

Ownership opportunities: There seems no good reason to assume that rental housing is all that low-income households can expect, or that rental housing will become their ghetto. Instead, opportunities for ownership housing for low-income households should be explored. But the mistakes of the past should not be repeated.

The key lesson to be learned from the discussion in Chapter 6 is that successful ownership programs for lower income households must be targeted carefully; the programs must not assume that the income of these households will rise quickly to meet increased mortgage commitments. Instead, experiments should be tried with programs that reach the top end of the second quintile income grouping — that is, the least poor of the target group. Those programs might involve capital grants — since capital grants reduce monthly payments — along with tough resale provisions; because of their low incomes, these families have problems with high monthly payments. Further, the programs should permit the purchase of used housing as well as inexpensive new housing.

It has been suggested that helping lower income families buy housing might be one of the most inexpensive ways of making housing affordable to them — an assumption that might well be tested. Success should be measured in the standard ways: do the programs meet the housing principles outlined earlier?

Housing for the homeless: The homeless require more than housing: they also require personal support and community development. This is an added cost burden and requires designs that do not always provide entirely separate units, as is currently done. Some homeless seem better suited to rooming and shared accommodation, some to individual apartments.

Shared accommodation can be provided in traditional rooming houses — houses where rooms are rented and kitchens and bathrooms are shared — run by private individuals (under appropriate licensing) or not-for-profit organizations. It can also be provided in new or renovated structures, of which the high-rise rooming house or StreetCity, discussed in Chapter 11, are but two examples. In Vancouver, arrangements are being made to lease blocks of rooms over taverns or in single-room occupancy hotels.

The important point is that funds are needed to supply support services and community development initiatives as well as physical accommodation if the homeless are to again become functioning members of society.

The number of units that should be supplied is in the order of 15,000 a year, which would address 10 per cent of the problem annually, as well as it can be measured. Given the need for shared accommodation and small apartments, this would translate into the equivalent of about 3,000 houses in cities across the country — not a particularly large number. Also required are support funds of perhaps $3,000 per person per year for several years. The total cost of this commitment, at $250,000 a house (including rather modest costs for renovations), is $750 million plus a further $75 million in support costs annually. Since $750 million represents outright purchase, this cost does not accumulate from year to year; the support costs will be on-going. These costs might well be shared with provincial governments.

With these objectives in place, Canada should be able to address and resolve the homelessness problem in ten years.

Other concerns

This agenda has not included firm numbers on programs or expenditures. From one point of view, it would be easy to estimate the exact revenues available to the government, and how those revenues should be spent on each of the program initiatives suggested here. But that approach is simplistic. There are few firm answers in addressing housing problems, and it is better to be clear about intentions and how those intentions might be fulfilled. The programs and policies suggested here look promising, but only experimentation will prove whether they fulfil their promise. If they do not work as expected, other experiments should be tried.

Further, this agenda has not covered all problems. It does not include proposals to deal with what seems to be a growing oligopoly on suburban land, mainly because the agenda assumes that development will occur mostly within developed areas of cities rather than on the fringes. Others who consider this problem a serious one should look for actions to end the undue influence of these few large players in land development.

This agenda does not respond to the growing interest in equity-based seniors' housing, or to proposals for co-housing (a form of shared control) and other co-operative schemes, mentioned in Chapter 9. It is assumed the proponents of these schemes will fully develop their own proposals for implementation and they can be considered at that time. They might well fit within the initiatives suggested around land trusts.

Conclusions

There is no single, simple answer to the substantial housing problems faced by many Canadians, but there are a number of different approaches that seem likely to help resolve those problems. A loosening of planning and zoning controls will do much to allow less expensive housing to be built, and there would probably be a sizable market for it if this occurred. However, to ensure that housing is available for households with low incomes, there is no choice but to devote public funds to this purpose. A number of policy options seem viable, but they require reasonable experimentation to ensure that they meet basic housing principles, and that they use taxpayers' dollars efficiently.

Appendix

This appendix describes information provided in Tables 6.3 and 6.4 concerning the Tower, Kellythorne, Cherrystone, and Sandy Hook areas. Each area is designated by the name of a street central to the subdivision in question. Tower and Sandy Hook are located in Scarborough; Kellythorne and Cherrystone in North York. When first put on the market, each subdivision was "the next one out" at the developed edge of the Toronto urban area; that is, each abutted the urban area rather than being separated from it by undeveloped land.

The *sale price* in Table 6.3 is an average of prices as determined from Affidavits of Land Transfer Tax attached to deeds in the appropriate registry offices. Except in the case of Sandy Hook, prices for houses are at this amount (in Tower prices on any given street are all the same) or very close to the figures shown, varying above and below this amount by one or two thousand dollars, presumably because of custom finishes. In Sandy Hook, the average given is for 10 metre lots, where houses are one-and-a-half to two storeys. Sale data were arrived at by reviewing deeds for a dozen purchases in each community.

Average sale price in Table 6.3 is the average sale price in Metro Toronto. Figures are from the Real Estate Board of Metro Toronto for the years 1953, 1963, 1971, and 1981. The board's figures for 1953 and 1963 include all properties sold — both residential and non-residential — since those are the only data the board has. On the advice of board staff, these figures have been discounted respectively by $424 (1953) and $517 (1963) to arrive at estimated average price of residential properties sold in those years. Figures for 1971 and 1981 are for residential properties only.

Average family income in Tables 6.3 and 6.4 is from Statistics Canada Census Data for the Census Metropolitan Toronto area for the years 1961, 1971, and 1981. Median family income for 1971 was $10,626; for 1981, $27,775; median family income is not available for 1961; neither median nor average family income is available for 1951. Estimated average family income for 1951 is $5,400.

Down payments in Table 6.4 vary depending on family circumstance, so the figures used here are arrived at after reviewing sale data. In Tower and Kellythorne, few purchasers varied from the amount shown. In Cherrystone, some purchasers paid $15,000 in cash, and there are several instances of purchasers taking out a second mortgage to come up with a down payment of $10,000. In Sandy Hook, some purchasers paid entirely by cash, some made down payments as low as $25,000, and some paid more than $40,000. The $40,000 figure is a median estimate of down payments made. Sale data were arrived at after reviewing deeds for a dozen purchases in each community.

References

Adams, Eric B., Pearl Ing, Janet Ortved, and Mary Jane Park. 1986. *Government Intervention in Housing Markets: An Overview.* Study 29 for Commission of Inquiry into Rental Tenancies (Thom Commission).

Alexander, Christopher, Sara Ishikawa, Murray Silverstein, et al. 1977. *A Pattern Language.* New York: Oxford University Press.

Allester, David. 1993. "Delinking Development Rights and Economic Development." *City Magazine* (Spring).

Anderson, Arthur, and Co. 1984. *Federal and Provincial Government Expenditures to Assist and Promote Rental Housing in Canada for 1976–82.* Prepared for Canadian Home Builders' Association. (Cited in Chant 1986.)

Arnott, Richard. 1981. *Rent Control and Options for Decontrol in Ontario.* Toronto: Ontario Economic Council.

Bacher, John. 1993. *Keeping to the Marketplace: The Evolution of Canadian Housing Policy.* Montreal and Kingston: McGill-Queen's University Press.

Bairstow, Dale. 1986. *A Place to Call Home. Housing Solutions for Low-Income Singles in Ontario.* Report of the Ontario Task Force on Roomers, Boarders and Lodgers (Chair: Dale Bairstow), for Ontario Ministry of Housing.

Banting, Keith G. 1990. "Social Housing in a Divided State." In *Housing the Homeless and Poor,* eds. George Fallis and Alex Murray. Toronto: University of Toronto Press.

Barnhorst, Richard, and Laura C. Johnson, eds. 1991. *The State of the Child in Ontario.* Prepared for the Child, Youth, and Family Policy Research Centre. Toronto: Oxford University Press.

Berridge Lewinberg Greenberg Ltd. 1991. *Guidelines for the Reurbanisation of Metropolitan Toronto.* Prepared for the Municipality of Metropolitan Toronto. (Draft.) December.

Blumenfeld, Hans. 1991. "Mismatch between Size of Households and of Dwelling Units." In *The Canadian City,* ed. Kent Gerecke. Montreal: Black Rose Books.

Bossons, John. 1993. "Regulation and the Cost of Housing." In Miron 1993, pp. 110-35.

Bourne, L.S. 1993. "The Changing Settlement Environment of Housing." In Miron 1993, pp. 271-88.

British Columbia. 1992. "New Directions in Affordability." Report of the Provincial Commission on Housing Options, Ministry of Municipal Affairs, Recreation and Housing. Victoria. December.

Canada. 1986. Task Force on Program Review. *Housing Programs in Search of Balance.* Ottawa: Supply and Services Canada.

Canada's Future. 1991. *Shaping Canada's Future Together, Proposals.* Ottawa: Ministry of Supply and Services Canada.

Canadian Housing Statistics. (Various years). Ottawa: CMHC.

Carter, Tom, and Ann McAfee. 1990. "The Municipal Role in Housing the Homeless and Poor." In Fallis and Murray 1990.

Carver, Humphrey. 1947. *A National Housing Policy for Canada.* Prepared for the Canadian Welfare Council.

————. 1948. *Houses for Canadians: A Study of Housing Problems in the Toronto Area.* Toronto: University of Toronto Press.

————. 1975. *Compassionate Landscape.* Toronto: University of Toronto Press.

Chant, John. 1986. *Overview of Alternative Rental Housing Policies.* Study 19 for Commission of Inquiry into Rental Tenancies (Thom Commission).

CHFC. 1990a. *Communique.* Ottawa: Co-operative Housing Federation of Canada. March.

————. 1990b. *Response to the CMHC Consultation Paper on Co-operative Housing.* Ottawa: Co-operative Housing Federation of Canada. November.

————. 1991. "Presentation to the Special Joint Committee on a Renewed Canada." Ottawa: Co-operative Housing Federation of Canada. December.

Citizens Committee. 1932. *Report of the Citizens Committee on Housing in Halifax, Nova Scotia.* (Cited in *Report of the Lieutenant-Governor's Committee on Housing Conditions in Toronto.* 1934. Toronto: Hunter-Rose [Chair: Herbert A. Bruce].)

Clayton, Frank A. 1993. "Time to Seriously Consider Shelter Allowances." *Canadian Housing.* 10, no. 2 (Fall), pp. 18-19.

Clayton Research Associates Ltd. 1984. *Rent Regulation and Rental Market Problems.* Prepared for Commission of Inquiry into Rental Tenancies (Thom Commission).

Clayton Research Associates Ltd. 1987. *Medium and Long Term Projections of Housing Requirements in Canada.* Prepared for Canada Mortgage and Housing Corporation. December.

————. 1991. "The Changing Financial Environment: What It Is Doing to the Housing Industry." Prepared for Canadian Home Builders Association, with financial assistance from CMHC.

————. 1992. "Housing Markets and the First-Time Buyer." A presentation to the RE/MAX Quarterly Forum, November 12.

————. 1992a. "Clayton Housing Report." Toronto. August.

————. 1993a. "Clayton Housing Report." Toronto. June.

CMHC. 1979. *Report on CMHC.* Task Force on CMHC. (Chair: Donald J. Mathews.) Ottawa. October.

————. 1983. *Sec. 56.1 Non-profit and Co-operative Housing Program Evaluation.* Ottawa: CMHC. November.

————. 1985. *Consultation Paper on Housing.* Ottawa: CMHC. January.

————. 1990a. *Evaluation of the Public Housing Program.* Ottawa: CMHC. April.

————. 1990b. *Evaluation of the Federal Co-operative Housing Programs.* Ottawa: CMHC.

CMHC/HUD. 1981. *Housing Affordability Problems and Housing Need in Canada and the United States. A Comparative Study.* Ottawa: CMHC and the U.S. Department of Housing and Urban Development. February.

Coleman, Alice. 1985. *Utopia on Trial: Vision and Reality in Planned Housing.* London: Hilary Shipman.

Commission on Planning. 1993. *New Planning for Ontario.* Commission on Planning and Development Reform. Toronto: Ontario Ministry of Municipal Affairs.

Cooper, Matthew, and Margaret Rodman. 1992. *New Neighbours: A Case Study of Co-operative Housing in Toronto.* Toronto: University of Toronto Press.

CUCS. 1983. *Shelter Allowances and Canadian Housing Policy: A Review and Evaluation.* Research paper 148, Centre for Urban and Community Studies, University of Toronto.

CUI. 1993. *The Intensification Report.* Toronto: The Canadian Urban Institute. May.

Cullingworth, J.B. 1979. *Essays on Housing Policy, the British Scene.* London: Allen and Unwin.

Dennis, Michael, and Susan Fish. 1972. *Programs in Search of a Policy.* Toronto: James Lewis and Samuel.

Derkowski, Andrzej. 1972. *Residential Land Development in Ontario.* Prepared for Urban Development Institute of Ontario. November.

Dineen, Janice. 1974. *The Trouble with Co-ops*. Toronto: Green Tree Publishing.

Don Community. 1990. "Downtown-to-Don Community Association." (Flyer.) Toronto. November.

Dowler, Robert G. 1983. *Housing Related Tax Expenditures: An Overview and Evaluation*. In co-operation with the Co-operative Housing Foundation of Canada, Centre for Urban and Community Studies, University of Toronto. February.

Downs, Anthony. 1988. *Residential Rent Controls: An Evaluation*. Washington, D.C.: The Urban Land Institute.

Engeland, John. 1990-91. "Canadian Renters in Core Need." *Canadian Housing* 7, no. 4, pp. 7-11.

Fallis, George. 1980. *Housing Programs and Income Distribution in Ontario*. Toronto: Ontario Economic Council.

———. 1985. *Housing Economics*. Toronto: Butterworths.

———. 1993. "The Suppliers of Housing." In Miron 1993, pp. 76-93.

Fallis, George, and Alex Murray, eds. 1990. *Housing the Homeless and Poor*. Toronto: University of Toronto Press.

Ferguson, Jock. 1988. "Behind the Boom: The Story of York Region." An eight-part series in *The Globe and Mail*, October 26 to November 3.

Foot, David. 1986. *Housing in Ontario: A Demographic Perspective*. Study 20 for Commission of Inquiry into Rental Tenancies (Thom Commission).

Fowler, Edmund P. 1992. *Building Cities That Work*. Montreal and Kingston: McGill-Queen's University Press.

Fraser, Graham. 1972. *Fighting Back*. Toronto: Hakkert.

Friedman, Avi, and Vince Cammalleri. 1992. "Evaluation of Affordable Housing Projects Based on the Grow Home Concept." Montreal: McGill University School of Architecture. April.

FRPO. 1989. "Annual Report 1989." Fair Rental Policy Organization. Toronto.

Gau, G.P. 1982. "Impact of the ARP and MURB Programs on the Vancouver Housing Market." Prepared for CMHC. (Cited in Dowler 1983, p. 52.)

Greaves, Liz. 1990. "Homes First and Street City." In *Housing — A Right*. The Power Plant, Toronto. June. Published as an insert to *NOW* magazine.

Greenspan, David. 1978. *Down to Earth.* Federal/Provincial Task Force on the Supply and Price of Serviced Residential Land. (Chair: David Greenspan.) Ottawa. April.

Hannley, Lynn. 1993. "Substandard Housing." In Miron 1993, pp. 203-19.

HDRC. 1990a. *Preparing for the "Nimby" syndrome.* Housing Development Resource Centre. Toronto. September.

————. 1990b. *The Municipal Approval Process for Small Nonprofit Housing Projects.* Housing Development Resource Centre. Toronto. August.

Hellyer, Paul. 1969. *Task Force on Housing and Urban Development.* Ottawa.

Hodge, Gerald. 1986. *Planning Canadian Communities.* Toronto: Methuen.

Hough, George. 1981. "Tenant Receptiveness: Family and Senior Citizen Mixing in Public Housing." Prepared for the Ontario Ministry of Housing.

Howenstine, E. Jay. 1983. "Converting Public Housing to Individual and Co-operative Ownership: Lessons from Foreign Experience." Prepared for Department of Housing and Urban Development, Washington, D.C. August.

Hulchanski, J. David. 1984. *Market Imperfections and the Role of Rent Regulations in the Residential Rental Market.* Study 6 for Commission of Inquiry into Rental Tenancies (Thom Commission).

————. 1985. "Private Rent Supplement Programs: The Canadian and American Experience." Presented to the City of Vancouver Planning Commission. October.

————. 1988. *Canada's Housing and Housing Policy: An Introduction.* School of Community and Regional Planning, University of British Columbia. Vancouver.

————. 1990. "Canadian Government Housing Expenditures: A Ten Year Review." *Canadian Housing* 7, no. 1 (Spring), p. 19ff.

————. 1992. "Property Rights No, Housing Rights Yes." *Policy Options* (October), pp. 21-23.

————. 1993a. "Here We Go Again: The Latest Lobby." *Canadian Housing* 10, no. 2 (Fall), pp. 20-22.

————. 1993b. "New Forms of Owning and Renting." In Miron 1993, pp. 64-75.

————. 1993c. "And Housing for All: Opening the Doors to Inclusive Community Planning." *Plan Canada* (May), pp. 19-23.

Huxtable, Ada Louise. 1984. *The Tall Building Artistically Reconsidered*. Berkeley and Los Angeles: University of California Press. Revised, 1992.

Jacobs, Jane. 1961. *Death and Life of Great American Cities*. New York and Toronto: Random House.

Jencks, Christopher. 1992. *Rethinking Social Policy*. Cambridge: Harvard University Press.

Johnson, Laura C., Barbara Muirhead, and Deborah Hierlihy. 1993. "The Physical Environment as a Determinant of the Health and Well-Being of Children and Youth: A Review of the Literature." Prepared for the Premier's Council on Health, Well-Being and Social Justice, Province of Ontario. February.

Kjellberg, Judith, ed. 1984. *Shelter Allowances, Rents, and Social Housing*. Toronto: Centre for Urban and Community Studies, University of Toronto.

Kozol, Jonathan. 1988. *Rachel and Her Children, Homeless Families in America*. New York: Crown Publishers.

Krumholz, Norman, and John Forester, 1990. *Making Equity Planning Work*. Philadelphia: Temple University Press.

Kunstler, James Howard. 1993. *The Geography of Nowhere*. New York: Simon and Schuster.

Ley, David. 1991. "Gentrification: A Ten Year Overview." In *The Canadian City,* ed. Kent Gerecke. Montreal: Black Rose Books.

Lorimer, James. 1978. *The Developers*. Toronto: James Lorimer and Company.

Lynch, Kevin. 1984. *Good City Form*. Cambridge: MIT Press.

Marks, Denton. 1986. *Housing Affordability and Rent Regulation*. Study 8 for Commission of Inquiry into Rental Tenancies (Thom Commission).

Markusen, James. R., and David T. Scheffman. 1977. *Speculation and Monopoly in Urban Development*. Toronto: Ontario Economic Council, University of Toronto Press.

McAfee, Ann. 1983. "Who Lives in Non-Market Housing." City of Vancouver Planning Department.

McKellar, James. 1993. "Building Technology and the Production Process." In Miron 1993, pp. 136-54.

McLaughlin, Mary Ann. 1987. *Homelessness in Canada: The Report of the National Enquiry*. Ottawa: Canadian Council on Social Development.

McQuaig, Linda. 1993. *The Wealthy Banker's Wife*. Toronto: Penguin Books.

Miron, John R. 1988. *Housing in Postwar Canada: Demographic Change, Household Formation, and Housing Demand.* Montreal and Kingston: McGill-Queens University Press.

————, ed. 1993. *House, Home and Community: Progress in Housing Canadians, 1945–1986.* Montreal and Kingston: McGill-Queen's University Press.

————. 1993a. "On Progress in Housing Canadians." In Miron 1993, pp. 7-21.

————. 1993b. "Demographic and Economic Factors in Housing Demand." In Miron 1993, pp. 22-40.

MMA. 1992. *Apartments in Houses: Some Facts and Figures.* Toronto: Ontario Ministry of Municipal Affairs, and Ministry of Housing. October.

Moore, Peter W. 1979. "Zoning and Planning: The Toronto Experience, 1904–70." In *The Usable Urban Past,* ed. Alan Artibise and Gilbert A. Stelter. Toronto: Macmillan of Canada.

Munro, Andrew C. 1987. "Small and Large Developers Under Regulation." Queen's University, Kingston.

Murray, James A. 1962. "The Architecture of Housing." Canadian Housing Design Council. (Lecture.)

Murray, James A., and Henry Fleiss. 1970. *Family Housing, A Study of Horizontal Multiple Housing Techniques.* Canadian Housing Design Council.

National Council of Welfare. 1990. *Pension Reform.* Ottawa: NCW.

Newman, Oscar. 1972. *Defensible Space.* New York: MacMillan.

————. 1981. *Community of Interest.* Garden City, N.Y.: Anchor Books.

Newman, Peter W.G., and Jeffrey R. Kenworthy. 1989. *Cities and Automobile Dependence: A Sourcebook.* Aldershot: Gower International.

North York. 1993. "New Housing Policy Proposed for North York." North York Planning Department. Summer.

OAHA. 1964. *Good Housing for Canadians.* Arnprior, Ont.: Ontario Association of Housing Authorities.

Oderkirk, Jillian. 1992. "Food Banks." In *Canadian Social Trends.* Ottawa: Statistics Canada. Spring.

OHBA. n.d. *Housing: Restoring the Dream.* Ontario Home Builders' Association. Toronto.

Ontario. 1985. "Municipal Non-profit Housing, A Review of the 1984 Portfolio." Ontario Ministry of Municipal Affairs and Housing.

————. 1988. *More Than Just a Roof.* Final Report of the Ministry's Advisory Committee on the International Year of Shelter for the Homeless, Ontario Ministry of Housing. Toronto.

————. 1993. "Making Choices: Guidelines for Alternative Development Standards in Ontario." Ministry of Housing and Ministry of Municipal Affairs. Draft report, October. Toronto.

Ontario Auditor. 1992. *1992 Annual Report.* Office of the Provincial Auditor, Government of Ontario. Toronto.

Osborne, David and Ted Gaebler. 1993. *Reinventing Government.* New York: Plume Books.

Parkdale Community Legal Services. 1988. "Homelessness and the Right to Shelter. A View from Parkdale." *Journal of Law and Social Policy* 4.

Patterson, Jeffrey. 1993. "Housing and Community Development Policies." In Miron 1993, pp. 320-38.

Pevsner, Nikolaus. 1936. *Pioneers of Modern Design.* New York: Penguin Books. Revised 1960, reprinted 1977.

Poapst, James V. 1993. "Financing of Post-war housing." In Miron 1993, pp. 94-109.

Poulin, André. 1991. "Exploratory Study of Three Models of Equity Co-operatives." Prepared for CMHC. April.

Prak, Neils L., and Hugo Priemus, eds. 1985. *Post-war Public Housing in Trouble.* Delft, The Netherlands: Delft University Press.

Regina vs. Bell, 1979, Supreme Court of Canada. 10 OMBR 142, 9 MPLR 103.

Rose, Albert. 1980. *Canadian Housing Policies 1935–1980.* Toronto: Butterworths and Company.

Rose, Barry. 1993. "Ontario New Home Warranty Program." *Municipal World.* (St. Thomas, Ontario). July, p. 26.

Rose, Damaris, and Martin Wexler. 1993. "Post-war Social and Economic Changes and Housing Adequacy." In Miron 1993, pp. 239-56.

Ross, David P. 1980. *The Canadian Fact Book on Income Distribution.* Ottawa: Canadian Council on Social Development.

Rowe, Peter G. 1991. *Making a Middle Landscape.* Cambridge: MIT Press.

Rowe, Peter G. 1993. *Modernity and Housing.* Cambridge: MIT Press.

Rybczynski, Witold. 1986. *Home, A Short History of an Idea.* New York: Viking Penguin.

Saldov, Morris. 1981. "A Review of the Social Integration Effects of Social Mix, with Particular Reference to Housing and the Ontario Rent Supplement Program." Paper prepared for course work with the Faculty of Social Work, University of Toronto.

Sarkissen, Wendy, and Warwick Heine. 1978. *Social Mix: The Bournville Experience*. Bournville Village Trust and South Australia Housing Trust.

Selby, Joan. 1985. "Urban Rental Housing in Canada, 1900–1985." M.A. Thesis, University of British Columbia, School of Community and Regional Planning, p. 210. (Cited in Hulchanski 1988.)

Sewell, John. 1977. "Land and Suburbs." In *Second City Book*, ed. James Lorimer and Evelyn Ross. Toronto: James Lorimer and Company.

———. 1988. *Changing MTHA*, and *Key MTHA Documents*.

———. 1993. *The Shape of the City*. Toronto: University of Toronto Press.

———. 1994. "Suburbs Then and Now" in *The Changing Canadian Metropolis*. Institute of Governmental Studies, Berkeley, California.

Shaffner, R. 1975. "Housing Policy in Canada: Learning from Recent Problems." *HRI Observations* 9 (August). Montreal: C.D. Howe Research Institute, p. 2. (Cited in Rose 1980, p. 11.)

———. 1979. *Housing Needs and Economic Policy: The Mortgage Interest and Property Tax Deduction Proposal*. Montreal: C.D. Howe Research Institute.

Simpson, Ray. 1993. "Residential Intensification: The Wrong Planning Debate." *The Intensification Report*. The Canadian Urban Institute. March.

SITE. 1982. *Highrise of Homes*. New York: Rizzoli International Publications.

Siu-Che Ng, Winnie. 1984. "Social Mix in Urban Neighbourhoods: An Assessment of the Concept and a Review of Social Mix in Vancouver's Neighbourhoods." M.A. Thesis, University of British Columbia.

Skaburskis, A. 1993. "Net Changes in Canada's Post-war Housing Stock." In Miron 1993, pp. 155-72.

Smith, Lawrence. 1977. *Anatomy of a Crisis: Canadian Housing Policy in the 1970's*. Vancouver: The Fraser Institute.

———. 1991. "Rent Control and a Program for Rent Decontrol in Ontario." In *Breaking the Shackles: Deregulating Canadian In-*

dustry, ed. W. Block and George Lermer. Vancouver: The Fraser Institute, pp. 305-44.

Spurr, Peter. 1976. *Land and Urban Development.* Toronto: James Lorimer and Company.

Stanbury, W.T. 1986. *The Normative Bases of Rent Regulation.* Study 15 for Commission of Inquiry into Rental Tenancies (Thom Commission).

Stanbury, W.T., and John D. Todd. 1990. *The Housing Crisis: The Effects of Local Government Regulation.* Prepared for the Laurier Institute. January.

Stanbury, W.T., and I.B. Vertinsky. 1985. *Rent Regulation: Design Characteristics and Effect.* Study 18 for Commission of Inquiry into Rental Tenancies (Thom Commission).

Steele, Marion. 1991. *Conversions, Condominiums and Capital Gains: Changes in the Structure of the Ontario Rental Housing Market.* Research Paper 181, Centre for Urban and Community Studies, University of Toronto. May.

————. 1993. "Incomes, Prices, and Tenure Choice." In Miron 1993, pp. 41-63.

Stein, David Lewis. 1990. "Keeping Wolves out of Co-op Housing." *Canadian Housing* 7, no. 3 (Fall), p. 66.

Streich, Patricia A. 1993. "The Affordability of Housing in Post-war Canada." In Miron 1993, pp. 257-70.

Thom, 1987, Vol. 2. *Report of the Commission of Inquiry into Residential Tenancies.* Vol. 2. (Commissioner: Stuart Thom.) Province of Ontario. April.

TNPRC. 1993. "A Proposal to Purchase, Rehabilitate and Convert." Toronto: Tenants Non-profit Redevelopment Co-operative Inc. October.

Toronto. 1986. "High Rise Apartments: The Issue of Conservation." City of Toronto Planning and Development Department. September.

Toronto. 1990. *Homeless, Not Helpless.* Report of the Homeless Persons Outreach Project, City of Toronto.

————. 1992. "City of Toronto High Rise Apartment Conservation Study." Hemson Consulting Limited, Fraser & Beatty, and Morrison Hershfield Limited, for City of Toronto Housing Department. November.

————. 1993. *City Planning.* City of Toronto Planning and Development Department. July.

UDI. 1993. *President's Comments*. Urban Development Institute, Toronto. July.

UDI Pacific. 1993. "Back to the Future: Re-designing Our Landscapes with Form, Place and Density." Urban Development Institute Pacific Region. Vancouver.

Van Nus, Walter. 1979. "Towards the City Efficient: The Theory and Practise of Zoning, 1919–39." In *The Usable Urban Past*, ed. Alan Artibise and Gilbert Stetler. Toronto: Macmillan, pp. 226-46.

Ward, Jim. 1989. *Organizing for the Homeless*. Ottawa: Canadian Council on Social Development.

Wolfe, Tom. 1981. *From Bauhaus to Our House*. New York: Farrar Strauss Giroux.

Zubowski, L.E. 1989. "The Influence of Industry Organization on the Supply and Price of Residential Land in the City of Mississauga." Queen's University, Kingston.

Acknowledgements

I have been very fortunate in the good advice I have received from a number of people as I wrote this book. I would particularly like to thank Bill Bosworth, Cassie Doyle, Jack de Klerk, Arthur Gelgoot, Mark Guslits, David Hulchanski, Marianne Moershel, Allison Savaria, Rich Tyssen, David White, and Alexandra Wilson. Of course, they will be disappointed to find that in some cases I have exercised an author's prerogative and put forward a position with which they may disagree — happily relieving them of any responsibility for the views put forward here.

A number of people and organizations across the country have kindly helped with illustrations, and I thank them for the time and energy they have expended. Acknowledgements accompany each illustration. Allison Savaria undertook the logistics of gathering the illustrations.

Thanks to Diane Young and Cy Strom for helpful editing.

Index

Abbotsford Co-op, 166
affordability, 1, 17–25, 82, 87,
   98–101, 140, 162, 171, 181–2,
   197–9, 223–4, 231, 234
appraisal surplus profits, 122
assisted housing, 162
Ataritiri, 179

Bain Avenue project, 166
barriers to housing, 226–31
basement apartments. *See* second units
Bauhaus 48
BC Hydro building, 56–7
Blumenfeld, Hans, 1–2
bonus zoning, 179–80
bridge subsidy, 186
brownfields development, 36
Bruce Report, 134
builders, roles 9, 225

Campus Co-op, 166
capital cost allowance (CCA), 118–120,
   242–3
capital gains tax, 93–4, 181, 226,
   243–5
Carver, Humphrey, 1, 14, 18, 27, 53,
   83, 97
Charlottetown agreement, 6
Charter of Rights and Freedoms, 3
climbing crane, 49
CMHC (Canada Mortgage and Housing Corporation), role of, 9
co-housing, 254
Coleman, Alice, 51, 146, 149–51
community-based housing, 162–3
construction industry, 52–3, 114, 225
contaminated sites, 228
conversion
   of office to residential, 55
   of rental housing to condominiums,
   195
co-operatives, 42–3, 58, 163, 173–4,
   180–2, 185
core need, 20–22, 140, 173, 182

cost comparisons, social and private
   housing, 186–9

de–institutionalization, 213
demographic change, 12–14, 28–31
Dennis/Fish report, 136, 164, 171, 189
density, 43–6, 59, 60–1, 65–6, 76, 78,
   150–2, 159
developers, roles, 27, 114, 225
development cost charges (DCCs),
   110, 229
development permit, 69
development standards, 64, 226–7
Don Mills, 40, 53, 98, 101, 103,
   109–10, 112
Downtown Eastside Residents Association, 219

equity co-operatives, 175, 254
equity zoning, 179
evictions, 229–30
expenditures, 7–8, 245–8

Fairview Slopes, 44, 50, 76–7, 151
False Creek, 11, 76, 179, 236
filter-down, 8, 117
flying form, 49
foodbanks, 211
form (of housing), 39–58, 155–6, 158,
   167–8

Garden City, 59
gentrification, 79–81, 213–4
gold-plating (of services), 70
good housing, 47, 58, 184
government limitations, 221–2
greenfields development, 36, 225
Greenspan, David, 97, 103–4, 109,
   112, 114, 116
Greymac, 205–6
Gropius, Walter, 48
GROW home, 41–2, 64, 83, 239–40

Habitat, 44–5, 50